UNIVERSITY OF YORK
BORTHWICK INSTITUTE OF HISTORICAL RESEARCH

A CALENDAR
of the Register of
RICHARD SCROPE
Archbishop of York, 1398-1405

part 1

R. N. Swanson

BORTHWICK TEXTS AND CALENDARS:
RECORDS OF THE NORTHERN PROVINCE 8

FOR HEATHER

FIRST PUBLISHED 1981

© University of York 1981

ISSN 0305 8506

In the interests of economy this volume has been reproduced by
small offset lithography. The charge made is purely to cover
production costs.

CONTENTS

Introduction   i

Abbreviations   x

Calendar of the Register   1

Index   110

INTRODUCTION

THE DRAMATIC death of Archbishop Richard le Scrope, summarily
executed for high treason outside the walls of his archiepiscopal city
on 8 June 1405, brought the northern province of the English church as
close as it was ever to come to having a saint of sufficient nation-wide
posthumous charisma to rival Canterbury's Thomas Becket as well as
locally challenging York's own St William. A member of a family well-
connected in local and national politics, Scrope had gained the archbishopric of York very much as the governmental candidate: the cathedral
chapter had sought the promotion of Walter Skirlaw from Durham as
successor to Robert Waldby, the deceased archbishop. Although the crown
must have acted with considerable despatch in informing Pope Boniface IX
of Waldby's death, which had occurred on 6 January 1398, and of the
choice of Scrope as his successor, it was not until the summer that he
began to exercise his archiepiscopal functions. Not surprisingly, his
first act was to appoint vicars-general, but precisely when the new
diocesan administration replaced that of the dean and chapter sede
vacante is not clear. The vicars-general began issuing documents at
York on 21 June, but the sede vacante register contains one document
dated to 1 July, and the probate register of the pontificate does not
commence until 6 July.[1] During the political crisis of the downfall of
Richard II, Scrope played a central role in the transfer of the crown
and government to Henry IV, but his later quarrels with that monarch led
eventually to revolt, and ultimately to his death.[2] His execution had
a profound influence on relations between Henry IV and the church during
the next few years and left the diocese without an archbishop until the

---

1. For Scrope's appointment to York, see J. Le Neve (ed. B. Jones),
   Fasti ecclesiae anglicanae, VI: Northern province (London, 1963),
   4. For the appointment of vicars-general and their first acts,
   the late date of sede vacante administration and the start of the
   probate register, see B[orthwick] I[nstitute], Reg. 16, f.168;
   Reg. 5A, f.252v; Prob. Reg. 3, f.1.

2. For a summary of Scrope's career, see A.B. Emden, A biographical
   register of the university of Cambridge to 1500 (Cambridge, 1963),
   513-14.

appointment of Henry Bowet in 1407.[3]   Immediately following his death,
Scrope was venerated as a martyr and his tomb became a centre of popular
pilgrimage, but official disapproval (doubtless influenced by the
political aspect which the commemoration of the dead archbishop soon
acquired) prevented his cult from developing further.   Although
remaining popular, the case for his canonisation still being pressed as
late as 1462, Scrope's sainthood was never officially recognized by the
church.[4]

The chief surviving record of Scrope's governance of the see of
York during his seven years' tenure of the archbishopric is a volume of
some 160 folios numbered Reg. 16 in the series of archiepiscopal registers
now deposited at the Borthwick Institute of Historical Research at York.
It contains not only the archbishop's own register (on folios numbered
1-151), but also the register of ordinations (ff.152-167) and the register
of the vicars-general who administered the diocese during the archbishop's
occasional absences (ff.168-180).   The original limp binding for the
register remains, its contemporaneity being attested by a scribble of
four words, amongst which the names 'Bernardus' and 'Clemens' may be made
out.   The original stiffener for the binding also survives, being a
notarial instrument of December 1370 relating to a matter between St
Leonard's Hospital, York, and the priory of St Oswald, Nostell; but the
whole compilation now has a modern binding dating from the 1930s.

The present composition of the register requires some comment, for
it appears that the arrangement has been altered on at least one occasion.
The original medieval foliation applies only to the section of properly
archiepiscopal business (ff.1-151).   Although this numeration is still
used for this first section of the whole register, it has been rendered

3.   R.G. Davies, 'After the execution of Archbishop Scrope: Henry IV,
      the papacy, and the English episcopate, 1405-8', Bulletin of the
      John Rylands Library, 59 (1976-7), 40-74.   For the problem of the
      succession to York after Scrope's death, see also Le Neve
      (ed. Jones), Fasti, 4.

4.   For a survey of this popular veneration of Scrope and the response
      thereto, see J.W. McKenna, 'Popular canonization as political
      propaganda: the cult of Archbishop Scrope', Speculum, 45 (1970),
      611-22 and refs.   Davies seems rather unfairly to seek to
      denigrate the reaction to Scrope's death as a purely local and
      small-scale cult, but this does not seem justified ('After the
      execution', 40-1).

numerically inaccurate by the treatment which the register received some
time towards the end of the sixteenth century.   At that point the
majority of the blank folios were excised, two of them (formerly ff.
69-70) having been used to accommodate an index to the archiepiscopal
section of the register which was composed at this time, and being
transferred to the front of the volume.   The register of the vicars-
general must have been bound with the archbishop's register before this
reorganisation, as the foliation of that continues through (in a post-
medieval hand) from 155, thus leaving a gap for the four blank leaves
now cut out after f.151.   This foliation also ignores the register of
ordinations, which intrudes between the two collections of other business
and which, following the usual practice, was apparently left unfoliated.
Following the modern rebinding, the foliation of the ordination register
and that of the vicars-general has been amended to form a continuous
sequence from f.151.   During the rebinding process, ff.48-9 have been
transposed, while the refoliation ends at f.180, thereby leaving the
final leaf of the register of the vicars-general (formerly f.168) to be
treated as a flyleaf.   Many of the entries throughout the compilation
have marginal notes for identification purposes, but not all of these
are contemporary.

    The present volume, the first of two which will calendar the whole
of Reg. 16, deals with the first 113 folios of the register.   The
archiepiscopal register is subdivided into parts, within each of which
the documents are entered in roughly chronological order.   The folios
here calendared cover the various territorial jurisdictions – the
capitular jurisdictions of the minsters at York, Beverley, Southwell
and Ripon;   the five archdeaconries of York, the East Riding, Cleveland,
Richmond and Nottingham;   and finally the smaller peculiar jurisdictions,
comprising the archbishop's enclaves of Hexham and Hexhamshire within the
diocese of Durham and of Churchdown in Gloucestershire, the enclaves of
the bishop of Durham and of the prior and convent of Durham in
Howdenshire and Allertonshire and the jurisdictions of Snaith and Selby
and the provostship of Beverley.   The second volume of the calendar
will deal with the more thematic sections of the register – diverse
letters (chiefly correspondence relating to Convocation and grants of
subsidies to the king), testamentary business and the relations with the

suffragan bishops - as well as the ordination lists and the register of
the vicars-general, both of which are arranged in purely chronological
order.

Despite its length, the register of Archbishop Scrope is obviously
not a complete record of his activities within the diocese, but even for
those documents which were registered, there are a few signs of
incompleteness and hurried compilation.   A few entries are inserted
under the wrong territorial headings (although this is sometimes noted
in the marginal titles) and there are occasional blank spaces where
complete documents or other notes have been omitted.   There are numerous
signs of scribal error or confusion, most frequently where it is obvious
that the scribe, although intending merely to abstract a document, was
working from a draft or formulary version.   Dating also tends to be
erratic at times: if the itinerary which can be constructed from the
register is to be believed, the archbishop was at Cawood on 12 March
1398/9 [no.119], yet only two days later was safely installed at Charing
Cross, London [no.5].   Finally, the register even lacks a proper title
page, beginning immediately with the section of documents relating to the
capitular jurisdictions.   What seems to have been intended to serve as
the title page is now the first folio of the first gathering dealing with
the archdeaconry of York (see below, p.11).

A characteristic feature of the York registers which arose from
administrative developments within the diocese is the brevity of the
section dealing with the archdeaconry of Richmond.   Long before the
fifteenth century, the archdeacons there had managed to develop their own
quasi-diocesan administration, sufficiently autonomous to have allowed
for the maintenance of independent archidiaconal registers.[5]
Consequently, almost the sole Richmondshire documents contained in
Scrope's register (nos.630-46) are those recording the fulfillment of
commissions from Francis Carboni, cardinal priest of St Susanna and papal
penitentiary, to grant dispensations to clerics or regularise improper
marriages.   Because the register was never meant to be a complete record

---

5.   See D.M. Smith, Guide to the archive collections in the Borthwick
      Institute of Historical Research (Borthwick texts and calendars:
      records of the northern province 1, York, 1973), 87.

of the archbishop's episcopal activities, a number of other documents survive which have escaped registration here. In some instances the reasons for this are obvious enough. A number of documents must have been awaiting attention when Scrope was executed, but were not processed until after his death. One such was a commission, dated at Cawood on 12 May 1405, and addressed to Bishop Repingdon of Lincoln, concerning an exchange of benefices. The certificate for the completion of the commission appears registered in the sede vacante material.[6]

Despite the obvious caveats which have to be borne in mind, Scrope's register still serves as a useful indication of the state of the diocese of York - and, more generally, of the northern province - during the last eighteen months of the reign of Richard II, and the first six years of the reign of Henry IV. Scrope was not an absentee prelate: the register of his vicars-general lists a mere ten absences, the longest of which was barely in excess of three months; almost all of these absences were occasioned by meetings of the king's council, or Parliament. For the rest of the time, the archbishop apparently remained within his see, chiefly resident at his manors of Cawood, Rest, Bishop Burton, Scrooby, and Bishopthorpe. Only rarely are documents dated from other places within the diocese. The length of time spent at each of the various manors in turn was generally in the region of three to four months, which suggests a fairly settled administrative organisation.

Apart from the other diocesan bishops of the province - those of Carlisle and Durham - the archbishop was aided within his own diocese by one (or possibly two) suffragans. William Northbrugge, bishop Pharensis, whom Scrope had known previously at Lichfield, appears to have been the main suffragan;[7] but Oswald, bishop of Whithorn, who had formerly acted within the diocese of York under Thomas Arundel and Robert Waldby, seems to have been retained as suffragan within the archdeaconry of Richmond:

---

6.   B.I., Reg.5A, f.262-v. The certificate is dated 21 May 1405, dealing with an exchange of the vicarage of Batley, Yorks., for the rectory of Raithby in the diocese of Lincoln. The induction mandate was not issued until 12 June (ibid., f.260v).

7.   Among the English, Northbrugge's see was identified as that of the Faroe Islands (E. Perroy, The diplomatic correspondence of Richard II, Camden Society publications, 3rd series, vol.48, 1933, no.50). If a see in partibus is to be substituted, Hvar, otherwise Lesina, now in Yugoslavia, seems to be the only possibility.

his name, however, does not appear in the archbishop's register.[8]   No
record of Northbrugge's independent activities survives, but his
commission in the register (f.149) makes it clear that he was deputed to
perform many of the more mundane episcopal tasks in the administration
of the see.   On the occasions when he is mentioned, his importance
within the governmental machine is obvious.   His most important
function as far as the present calendar is concerned was to assume
responsibility for all ordinations performed during Scrope's tenure of
York, whether the archbishop was in his diocese or not.

The primary purpose of the archbishop's register was to record the
basic details of diocesan administration, and for the section which is
calendared in the present volume, that generally meant entering details
of successions to benefices.   To these can be added the establishment
of chantries and minor reorganisational activities, but the great
majority of the entries relate to institutions, exchanges and inductions.
As far as the exchanges are concerned, in almost every instance the
necessary commission emanated from Scrope himself.   There are, however,
two cases in which the archbishop was the recipient of a commission, and
these are worthy of mention.   For in both cases the document was issued
by the then archbishop of Canterbury - not Thomas Arundel, who held the
see for most of the period, but Roger Walden, who was briefly intruded
during Arundel's exile in 1397-9.   The appearance of these commissions
suggests that Walden, despite the absence of any records of his
administration at Lambeth, may have exercised effective spiritual
jurisdiction over the diocese during the brief period of his pontificate.[9]

---

8.   Yorkshire Archaeological Journal, 25 (1920), 198, no.217.   Oswald
     was an exile, having been nominated to his see by Pope Urban VI.
     As Scotland remained loyal to the antipopes during the Great Schism,
     he never gained possession.

9.   These commissions are calendared below, nos. 340, 479.   The
     argument against Walden's acting in spirituals is given in I.J.
     Churchill, Canterbury administration (London, 1933), vol.1, 570.
     One possibility would be that Walden arranged for the government of
     his see by vicars-general, whose register no longer survives.   The
     commissions to such officers contained in Scrope's register did not
     extend to granting authority for exchanges of benefices, and it is
     quite possible that Walden employed a similar usage.

Apart from the basic information about institutions and exchanges, Scrope's register occasionally contains other documents which throw light on various aspects of the contemporary church. Licences to celebrate private masses and receive a salary, amendments to ordinations of chantries and vicarages, and decrees for the union of benefices, all illustrate the debilitating effect of the continuing economic crisis of the fourteenth century on clerical incomes. The numerous licences for non-residence granted to those wishing to study provide a considerable addition to the available information on university members during the period, and as a whole the register supplements knowledge concerning their postgraduate careers. The value of the register in supplementing other sources also applies to the occasional papal bulls which are recorded here but no longer appear in the surviving registers among the papal archives.[10] Beyond all this, the register also serves to record popular piety and attitudes towards the clergy, in an age when ecclesiastical reform was much discussed by the educated classes throughout Europe. The ordinations of chantries provide a particularly effective mirror of these popular attitudes.

As the register itself is so totally concerned with the routine matters of diocesan administration, it is hardly surprising that the documents it contains make few reference to contemporary political developments. Occasional hints of these events are to be found in the more thematic parts of the register, but overall the upheavals of 1399 and 1405 tend to give an artificially dramatic veneer to the whole of Scrope's episcopate. Although it is not possible to pass judgement on the efficiency or smoothness of his administration of the see from the register alone – since that, obviously enough, records only the smoothly efficient sides of his governance – nevertheless the register does serve as an important survey of the state of the diocese of York at a vital point in the political and ecclesiastical history of England.

---

10. See R.N. Swanson, 'Papal letters among the ecclesiastical archives at York, 1378–1415', <u>Borthwick Institute Bulletin</u>, 1 (1975–8), nos. 14, 17, 20–5, 29–30.

NOTE ON THE CALENDAR

While the entries which follow maintain the order given in the
register, each entry does not necessarily represent an individual event.
Multiple issues of commissions to archdeacons on the same date have been
brought together under the same number; while with institutions the
issue of the induction mandate has been incorporated under the same
number as the institution, unless the whole mandate has been registered
Where related events occurred on different dates, as with the issue of
an induction mandate following an exchange of benefices, whether to treat
the events as separate entries has depended on their treatment in the
register. Where they are run on, they have been entered under the same
number, but where there is some differentiation (at its most arbitrary,
where the record of the second event starts a new line), then they have
been treated separately. Notarial attestations, even if differing in
date from the main entry, have in all cases been considered as part of
the document to which they relate.

Footnotes have been added only in instances where some elucidation
seemed necessary, to correct obvious errors, or to give cross-references
to printed material. The marginal titles in the register have been
ignored in the calendar, unless they have some bearing on the information
in the entries, or on the lay-out of the register. Square brackets have
been used to indicate editorial insertions or comments, and to bring
together variant spellings of surnames occurring within any one document.

Any calendaring necessarily involves excising some of the
information contained in the original document. In the present case,
this applies most obviously to place-names. Since Nottinghamshire and
the Ridings of Yorkshire have already been covered by the publications
of the English Place-Name Society, it seemed unnecessary to record the
spellings of place-names as given in the register. All have been
silently modernised, as far as this is possible. There are a few
instances where a place remains unidentified, and it has been necessary
to retain the original spelling, but only in cases where the version of
the place-name in the register is not recorded in the printed place-name
volumes, or where later changes of name make the retention of an earlier
version more reasonable, has it seemed necessary to note deviations.

Finally, a word must be said about the dating used in the calendar.

This is usually given as it appears in the register, with the alternative years of Old and New Styles for the months of January – March being indicated thus: 1398/9, 1399/1400, etc. Dating by feast days and regnal years has been retained, but with the appropriate conversion to date, month and year being given in square brackets. The use of the Roman calendar in documents emanating from the papal curia has been silently converted to modern usage, but where documents issued in England are dated by that method, the use of kalends, ides, etc. is retained, again with the appropriate conversion in square brackets.

*****

ACKNOWLEDGEMENTS

This is by no means the first attempt to calendar the register of Archbishop Scrope. Some years ago Mr Neville Webb, a former member of the Institute staff, prepared a calendar of the first 106 folios of the register (now BI., Add. MS.144). Although adopting conventions rather different from those employed in the present calendar, and being generally more concise than the present work, this previous calendar has naturally proved of considerable use in preparing this volume. However, my principal acknowledgement must be to Dr David Smith, who has at all stages overseen the preparation of the text, and saved a newcomer to episcopal registers from a multitude of errors. Any which remain, and any inconsistencies which survive in the text, are of course my own responsibility. I should also like to thank my colleagues, Dr W.J. Sheils and Dr Janet Burton, for their frequent assistance with place-names and palaeographical problems. Finally, I must mention Mrs Edna Meadows, who struggled against a constantly-amended typescript to produce the finished version of the text.

ABBREVIATIONS

B.Dec.	bachelor of decrees
B.I.	Borthwick Institute
br.	brother
B.Th.	bachelor of theology
CPL	W.H. Bliss, C. Johnson, and J.A. Twemlow (eds.), Calendar of entries in the papal registers relating to Great Britain and Ireland: Calendar of papal letters. (14 vols., London, 1893-1960).
dioc.	in/of the diocese of ...
esq.	esquire
Ind.	Note that a mandate for induction was issued (usually to the appropriate archdeacon or his Official; in other cases the recipient is named).
I.U.B.	bachelor of both laws
knt.	knight
lic.leg.	licentiate in law
lic.th.	licentiate in theology
LL.B.	bachelor of law
LL.D.	doctor of law
M.	Master
M.A.	master of arts
n.d.	no date
O.P.	order of friars preachers
O.S.A.	order of St Augustine

CAPITULA

1.   Collation of the wardenship of the hospital of St John, Ripon, to Roger Haward, chaplain, in accordance with the constitution <u>Quia contingit</u>, during pleasure. He is not to dispose of the goods of the hospital by will, but must pass them or their equivalent on to his successors intact. Ind: Dean of Ripon. Rest, 19 July 1398.

2.   Mandate to the chapter of Southwell to induct John Layot, clerk, to the prebend of Halloughton, to which he had been presented by King Richard II by reason of the vacancy of the archbishopric. Rest, 11 August 1398. (1)

3.   Admission of M. John Layot to the above prebend. Rest, 11 August 1398. (1)

4.   Collation of the wardenship of the hospital of St John, Ripon, vacant by the resignation of Roger Haward, to Robert Tanfield, clerk. He is not to dispose of the goods of the hospital by will, but must pass them or their equivalent on to his successors intact. Ind: John de Deen, chaplain. Rest, 17 August 1398.

5.   [f.1-1v] Certificate of Henry [Beaufort], bishop of Lincoln, reciting an archiepiscopal commission (dated at his lodgings near Charing Cross, dioc. London, 14 March 1398/9) for an exchange of prebends between William Noion, prebendary of South Cave in York Minster, and M. William [de] Waltham, prebendary of Dunnington in York Minster and of Leighton Manor in Lincoln cathedral. He had received their resignations (that of Noion in the person of John de Popilton, his proctor), and had instituted them to their exchanged prebends in York Minster, to which they had been presented by King Richard II by reason of the vacancy of the archbishopric. Lodgings at the Old Temple, London, 19 March 1398/9. (2)

6.   [f.1v] Ind: Chapter of York, the dean being absent, for Waltham and Noion to their exchanged prebends in York Minster. Archbishop's lodgings near Westminster, 20 March 1398/9.

7.   Mandate to the chapter of Ripon to admit Nicholas de Bubwyth, clerk, to the prebend of Givendale and Skelton, vacant by the death of Thomas Forester, in accordance with letters of Pope Boniface IX. (3) Cawood Castle, 29 April 1399.

---

1.   Letters in the margin indicate that entry 3 should precede no.2.

2.   Noion also acquired the Lincoln prebend of Leighton Manor as a result of this exchange (J. Le Neve, <u>Fasti Ecclesiae Anglicanae</u>, 1300-1541, I: <u>Lincoln Diocese</u> (1962), 84).

3.   Probably those in <u>CPL</u>, v, 102.

8.   Collation of the prebend at the altar of St Stephen in Beverley
        Minster to Robert Wolvenden, priest, clerk of the archbishop's
        household.   Ind: Chapter of Beverley.   Archbishop's lodgings
        near Westminster, 25 September 1399.

9.   [ff.1v-2] Institution of Wolvenden to the above prebend, on
        the presentation of King Henry IV.   Ind: as above.
        Bishopthorpe, 23 November 1399.

10.   [f.2] Collation of a prebend in the chapel of St Mary and the
        Holy Angels, York, vacant by the resignation of John de
        Popilton (1) priest, to John de Popilton, rector of Patrick
        Brompton.   Ind: Official of the court of York or his
        commissary-general.   Palace at York, 15 December 1399.

11.   Collation of the prebend of Langtoft in York Minster to M.
        Stephen Lescrop, junior, clerk, in the person of Robert
        Wolvenden, precentor of Lichfield cathedral, his proctor.
        Ind: Chapter of York.   Bishopthorpe, 28 December 1399.

12.   Collation of the prebend of Beechill with Knaresborough in
        York Minster to M. Stephen Lescrop, junior, clerk, in the
        person of Robert Wolvenden, precentor of Lichfield cathedral,
        his proctor.   Ind: as above.   Bishopthorpe, [blank] 1399.

13.   [f.2-2v] Certificate of William de Cawode, lic. leg., canon
        of Southwell, reciting an archiepiscopal commission (dated at
        Bishopthorpe, 15 January 1399/1400) to inquire into the vacancy
        and patronage of the chantry at the altar of St John the
        Evangelist in Ripon Minster, to which the chapter of Ripon had
        presented Henry Polles, priest.   After examining certain
        vicars and chaplains, the register of Ripon Minster containing
        the ordination of the chantry, and letters of institution and
        induction from Archbishop Alexander [Neville] to Richard
        Asmunderby, the last chaplain, he had found that the chapter
        held the patronage, and had presented Asmunderby, who had died·
        on 9 January last.   Having found Polles suitable, he had caused
        him to be instituted and inducted to the chantry on 18 January.
        Sealed with the seal of the chapter of Ripon, in addition to
        his own 'quia sigillum meum pluribus est incognitum'.   Ripon,
        19 February 1399/1400.

14.   [f.2v] Commission to the prior of Canterbury and John Wetton,
        master of the college of Maidstone, dioc. Canterbury, to receive
        the resignation by M. John Botlesham of his prebend of
        Osbaldwick in York Minster, and to institute and induct thereto
        M. Robert de Hallom, I.U.B.   Bishop Burton, 16 March 1399/1400.

---

1.   The Christian name should probably read 'Thomas':   see D.M.
        Smith, A calendar of the register of Robert Waldby, archbishop
        of York, 1397, (Borthwick Texts and Calendars: Records of the
        Northern Province, 2, 1974), 36.

15. Collation of the prebend of Bole in York Minster to M. Richard Conyngeston, LL.D., archbishop's chancellor. Ind: Chapter of York. Bishop Burton, 13 May 1400.

16. Collation of the prebend of Barnby in York Minster to Thomas de Hilton, priest, clerk of the archbishop's household. Ind: as above. Bishop Burton, 13 May 1400.

17. [f.3] Collation of the archdeaconry of Richmond, vacant by the death of M. Thomas de Dalby, to M. Stephen Lescrop, junior, in the person of Robert Wolvenden, precentor of Lichfield cathedral, his proctor. Ind: as above. Bishop Burton, 19 May 1400.

18. Collation of the prebend of Tockerington in York Minster to Robert Wolvenden, clerk of the archbishop's household. Ind: as above. Bishop Burton, 19 May 1400.

19. Collation of a prebend in the chapel of St Mary and the Holy Angels, York, vacant by the death of Nicholas Cave, to Nicholas Tydde, clerk of the archbishop's household. Ind: Receiver-general at York. Cawood Castle, 17 August 1400.

20. Collation of the prebend of Weighton in York Minster, vacant by the death of William de Gunthorp, to John Scarle, priest. Ind: Chapter of York. Cawood Castle, 19 September 1400.

21. Collation of the prebend of Norwell Palishall in Southwell Minster, vacant by the death of William de Gunthorp, to M. Richard Conyngston, LL.D., archbishop's chancellor. Ind: Chapter of Southwell. Cawood Castle, 20 September 1400.

22. Collation of the prebend of Ulleskelf in York Minster, held by John Scarle as security for the prebend of Weighton, to Laurence Allerthorp, priest. Ind: Chapter of York. Cawood Castle, 29 September 1400.

23. Memorandum of the admission of Richard Conyngeston to the prebend of Norwell Palishall in Southwell Minster, to which he had been presented by King Henry IV, in the presence of Robert Wolveden, canon of York, Thomas Parker, canon of Lichfield, and John Welton, notary public. In the archbishop's chancery in the manor of Rest, 9 July 1402. (1)

24. [f.3v] Collation of a prebend in the chapel of St Mary and the Holy Angels, York, vacant by the death of John Deen, to M. Thomas Burstall, priest, clerk of the archbishop's household. Ind: Receiver at York. Cawood Castle, 5 October 1400.

---

1. A marginal line connects this entry with no.21. No.23 is clearly a later addition to the register.

25. Collation of a prebend in the above chapel, vacant by the death of William Gysburn, to Nicholas Tydde, clerk of the archbishop's household. Ind: Receiver-general at York. Scrooby, 20 October 1400.

26. Collation of a prebend in the above chapel, lately held by Nicholas Tydde as security for another benefice therein, to John Newark, clerk of the archbishop's household. Ind: as above. Scrooby, 20 October 1400.

27. Collation of the prebend of Langtoft in York Minster to John Elvet, priest, in the person of M. Richard Conyngston, canon of York, his proctor. Ind: Chapter of York. Scrooby, 4 January 1400/1.

28. Collation of the prebend of South Newbald in York Minster, lately held by John Elvet as security for the prebend of Langtoft, to Robert Wolvenden, priest, clerk of the archbishop's household. Ind: as above. Scrooby, 4 January 1400/1.

29. Collation of the prebend of Driffield in York Minster, vacant by the death of M. Richard Ronhall, to M. Stephen Lescrop, junior, clerk, in the person of William Toppeclyff, clerk, his proctor. Ind: as above. Bishop Burton, 4 March 1400/1.

30. [f.4] Collation of the prebend of South Newbald in York Minster, lately held by Robert Wolveden as security for the prebend of Beechill with Knaresborough, to Thomas Longley, priest, in the person of John de Radclyff, clerk, dioc. Lichfield, his proctor. Ind: as above. Bishop Burton, 4 March 1400/1.

31. Collation of the prebend of Beechill with Knaresborough in York Minster, lately held by M. Stephen Lescrop, junior, as security for the prebend of Driffield, to Robert Wolveden, priest, clerk of the archbishop's household, in the person of John de Lepyngton, clerk, his proctor. Ind: as above. Bishop Burton, 4 March 1400/1.

32. Collation of the prebend of Beckingham in Southwell Minster, vacant by the death of M. Richard Rownale, to John Martyn, clerk of the archbishop's household. Ind: Chapter of Southwell. Bishop Burton, 4 March 1400/1.

33. Collation of the prebend of Bilton in York Minster, vacant by the death of John Carppe, to M. Thomas Burstall, clerk of the archbishop's household. Ind: Chapter of York. Bishop Burton, 16 March 1400/1.

34. Collation of the prebend of Tockerington in York Minster to M. Robert de Oxton, LL.B. Ind: as above. Bishop Burton, [blank] March 1400/1.

35. [f.4v] Collation of the vicarage of the archbishop's prebend [at the altar of St Leonard] in Beverley Minster, vacant by the death of Robert Louthorp, to John Bradeley, priest, one of the archbishop's household. Ind: Chapter of Beverley. Bishop Burton, 16 May 1401.

36. Collation of a prebend in the chapel of St Mary and the Holy Angels, York, vacant by the resignation of M. Thomas Burstall, to Walter Patteswyk, priest, clerk of the archbishop's household. Ind: Receiver-general at York. Bishop Burton, 26 May 1401.

37. Collation of the prebend of Studley in Ripon Minster to M. Stephen Lescrop, junior, clerk, in the person of Robert Wolvenden, canon of York, his proctor. Ind: Chapter of Ripon. Bishopthorpe, 18 October 1401. (1)

38. Collation of the prebend of North Newbald in York Minster, to Geoffrey Lescrop, clerk of the archbishop's household. Ind: Chapter of York. Bishopthorpe, 22 November 1401.

39. [ff.4v-5] Procuration by the chapter of York (the deanery being vacant), appointing M. Richard de Conyngston, LL.D., M. Robert Wolveden, and M. Thomas Burstall, canons of York, to inform the archbishop of the election of Thomas Longley (2), canon of York, as dean, and to seek confirmation of the election from the archbishop, his commissary or commissaries. Chapter House, York, 5 January 1401/2.

40. [f.5-5v] Certificate of Robert de Asshburn, rector of St Peter the Little, York, and commissary general of the Official of the court of York, recording his fulfilment of an archiepiscopal commission received on 10 January 1401/2, (recited in full and dated at Bishopthorpe, 9 January 1401/2) to cite all opponents of the election of Thomas Longley as dean of York to attend at Scrooby on 20 January 1401/2. The citation had been published in the choir of York Minster during the celebration of divine service, in the presence of M. John de Neuton, LL.D., treasurer of York and Official of the court of York, and other advocates, proctors, and notaries of the court, officials of the Minster, and other clergy and laity. York, 10 January 1401/2.

---

1. The mandate for admission, in fact dated at Bishopthorpe, 16 November 1401, is printed in Memorials of the Church of SS. Peter and Wilfrid, Ripon, iv, (Surtees Society 115, 1908), 153.

2. Consistently 'Longley' in nos. 40-45, but generally named 'Langley'. See also no.30.

41.   [ff.5v-6] Notarial instrument, recording that Thomas Longley, canon of York, keeper of the King's privy seal, dean-elect of York, had named M. Thomas Weston, M. Richard Holme, and M. Robert Wolveden, canons of York, with William Brynkelowe, canon of Lichfield, as his proctors to receive confirmation of his election as dean of York, and induction from the archbishop or his commissary or commissaries.   In the presence of John Wysebech, rector of Newton Longville, dioc. Lincoln, and Thomas Holden, literatus, dioc. York.   Attested by John Rippeley, clerk, dioc. York, notary public.   Longley's room within the royal manor of Eltham, dioc. Rochester, 27 December 1401.

42.   [f.6] Confirmation of the election of Thomas Longley as dean of York, and release to him of the spiritualities and temporalities of the deanery.   n.d.

43.   Publication of the above confirmation and release, following examination of the election on 20 January 1401/2, in the chapel of the manor of Scrooby.   Scrooby, 20 January 1401/2.

44.   Mandate to the chapter of York to install Thomas Longley as dean.   Scrooby, 20 January 1401/2.

45.   [f.6-6v] Notarial instrument, recording that M. William Brynklow, priest, canon of Lichfield, took the oath of obedience to the archbishop as proctor of Thomas Longley [Longle], priest, dean of York, in the presence of M. Richard Conyngston, LL.D., archbishop's chancellor, Robert Wolvenden, canon of York, M. John Harwod, advocate of the court of York, M. John Staynton, proctor of that court, and M. John de Welton and M. William Topcliff, notaries public.   Chapel of the manor of Scrooby, 20 January 1401/2. (1)

46.   [f.6v] Collation of the prebend of Norwell (Tertia Pars) in Southwell Minster, lately held by M. John Bryd, to M. Thomas Burstall, priest, clerk of the archbishop's household.   Ind: Chapter of Southwell.   Archbishop's lodgings near Westminster, 12 October 1402.

47.   Collation of the prebend of Weighton in York Minster, vacant by the death of John Scarle, to M. Richard Conyngston, LL.D., archbishop's chancellor.   Ind: Chapter of York.   Scrooby, 26 April 1403.

48.   [f.7] Collation of the prebend of Bole in York Minster to Simon Gaunstede, priest, in the person of Nicholas Wymbissh, his proctor.   Ind: as above.   Scrooby, 4 May 1403.

---

1.   This document is followed by a space in the register.   The opening words of another document – which, as far as they can be recovered, were identical with the opening words of no.46 – have been scratched out.

49.   Collation of the prebend of North Newbald in York Minster to
      M. Richard Courtney.   Ind: as above.   Archbishop's lodgings
      near Westminster, 1 June 1403.

50.   [f.7-7v] Ordination of a perpetual vicarage at Mirfield, the
      church having been appropriated to the prioress and nuns of
      Kirklees.   The vicars are to be presented to the archbishop
      for institution.   The priory is to have the tithes of sheaves,
      hay and coppice-wood, and the rectory house.   The vicar is to
      have the offerings, profits, small tithes, altarage, personal
      tithes, and other obventions.   The prioress and convent are to
      provide a house for the vicar, and are to bear all burdens,
      ordinary and extraordinary.   In the case of tenths granted to
      the King, the vicar is to pay 6s. 8d.   The vicar and his
      successors are also to bear all other charges for the adminis-
      tration, and for the cure of souls.   Cawood Castle, 4 August
      1403.

51.   [f.7v] Certificate of Richard Derham, lic.th., dean of the
      royal free chapel of St Martin le Grand, London, reciting an
      archiepiscopal commission (dated at Scrooby, 9 July 1403) for
      an exchange of prebends between Thomas Wardrober [Warderober],
      prebendary of Fauconeres in the said chapel, and Thomas Feriby,
      prebendary of Apesthorpe in York Minster.   He had received
      their resignations and had instituted Wardrober to Apesthorpe,
      in the person of John Welles, his proctor.   Sealed with his
      sigillum commissariatus.   London, 19 July 1403.

      Ind: Chapter of York; for Wardrober to Apesthorpe.   Cawood,
      26 July 1403.

52.   [f.8] Certificate of the dean of Ripon, reciting an
      archiepiscopal commission (dated at Cawood Castle, 7 August
      1403) to inquire into the vacancy and patronage of the chantry
      at the altar of St John the Evangelist in Ripon Minster, to
      which the chapter of Ripon had presented Robert Kendale, priest.
      An inquisition had been held in Ripon Minster, attended by John
      Bondegate, Robert Dorem, and John Ely, vicars of the collegiate
      church, with other vicars and chaplains of the neighbourhood.
      They had confirmed that the chapter held the patronage, and had
      presented Henry Pollys, the last chaplain, who had held the
      chantry as security for a mediety of the parish church of
      Linton in Craven, and had resigned.   Kendale having been found
      suitable, the dean had caused him to be instituted and inducted
      to the chantry.   Ripon, 14 August 1403.

53.   [f.8-8v] Certificate of the chapter of York, the dean being
      absent, reciting an archiepiscopal commission (dated at Cawood
      Castle, 13 October 1403) for an exchange of benefices between
      Alan Cochon, vicar of Aldbrough, and Robert [de] Bardesay,
      vicar of Paull.   They had received Bardesay's resignation,
      and had instituted Cochon to Paull, on the presentation of the
      abbot and convent of Kirkstall.   Chapter House, York,
      16 October 1403.

[f.8v] Ind: Official of the archdeacon of the East Riding, for Cochon to Paull. Scrooby, 19 October 1403.

54. Memorandum that King Henry IV made an offering of gold worth 6s. 8d. during the celebration of mass by the archbishop at the high altar. York Minster, 10 August 1403.(1)

55. [f.9] Ordination of a perpetual vicarage at Misterton, the church having been appropriated to the dean and chapter of York for the fabric and lights of the Minster. Thomas Algerkyrk, priest, had been instituted as vicar, the archbishop reserving the power to make an ordination for the vicarage. Following an inquisition, the ordination is now made. The vicars are to be presented by the dean and chapter of York (or the chapter alone, if the dean is absent) to the archbishop for institution, or to the custodian of the spiritualities if the see is vacant. The vicars shall receive £10 a year from the dean and chapter, payable at the feasts of Christmas, Easter, the Translation of St Thomas the Martyr, and Michaelmas, by the custodian of the fabric of the Minster. The vicars are to inhabit the house and croft belonging to the church, inhabited by John de Schefeld, and are to maintain it at their own expense. The vicars are to ensure the cure of souls, but all other expenses, ordinary and extraordinary, are to be met by the dean and chapter. If any payment to the vicars is overdue by twelve days, it must be doubled. If delayed for a further twelve days, the fruits of the benefice may be sequestrated until satisfaction is made. The dean and chapter are to distribute the annual sum of 6s. 8d. to the poor of Misterton, which is to be delivered by the custodian of the fabric of the Minster. Scrooby, 1 April 1403. (2)

56. [f.9v] Collation of the archdeaconry of Richmond, vacant by the resignation of Nicholas de Bubwith in exchange for the prebend of Driffield in York Minster, to M. Stephen Lescrop, junior. Ind: Chapter of York. York Minster, 18 March 1401/2.

57. Certificate of the chapter of York, the dean being absent, reciting an archiepiscopal commission (dated at Cawood Castle, 8 September 1404) for an exchange of benefices between Roger de Malton, vicar of the prebendal church of Weighton, and Robert de Bagby, rector of Full Sutton. They had received Bagby's resignation, and had instituted Malton to Full Sutton on the presentation of Agnes de Alta Ripa [Dautry] of Full Sutton. Chapter House, York, 3 October 1404.

---

1. Printed in J. Raine (ed.), The Fabric Rolls of York Minster, with an appendix of illustrative documents (Surtees Society, 35, 1859), 191-2, and in J. Raine (ed.), The Historians of the Church of York and its archbishops (3 vols., Rolls Series, 1879-94), iii, 287. In both the event is incorrectly dated to 19 August.
2. For earlier documents relating to this appropriation, see Raine, Fabric Rolls, 187-90.

Ind: Official of the archdeacon of York, for Malton to Full Sutton. 28 October 1404.

58.   [ff.9v-10] Certificate of William de Storteford, canon and Official of London, and custodian of the spiritualities of the bishopric of London during its vacancy, reciting an archiepiscopal commission (dated at Cawood Castle, 17 January 1404/5) for an exchange of prebends between Henry Merston, prebendary of Oxgate in St Paul's cathedral, London, and rector of Cottingham, dioc. Lincoln, and John Martyn, prebendary of Beckingham in Southwell Minster. He had received Martyn's resignation, and had instituted Merston to Beckingham. London, 6 February 1404/5.

59.   [f.10] Ind: Chapter of Southwell, for Merston to Beckingham. 20 February 1404/5.

60.   [f.10-10v] Certificate of the chapter of York, the dean being absent, reciting an archiepiscopal commission (dated at Cawood Castle, 18 January 1404/5) for an exchange of benefices between Henry Thorlethorp [Thorlathorp], parson of the chantry founded at the altar of St John the Evangelist in York Minster, and William [de] Patryngton, parson of the chantry founded at the altar of the Holy Innocents in the same church. They had received Thorlethorp's resignation, and had instituted and inducted Patryngton to the chantry, on the archbishop's collation. Chapter House, York, 20 January 1404/5.

61.   [f.10v] Certificate of Thomas Weston, lic.leg., canon of York, concerning the vacancy and patronage of the church of Kirkby in Cleveland. London, 23 February 1404/5. (1)

62.   [ff.10v-11] Certificate of Philip [Repingdon], bishop of Lincoln, reciting an archiepiscopal commission (dated at Cawood Castle, 15 March 1404/5) for an exchange of prebends between Thomas Parker, prebendary of a prebend in the chapel of St Mary and the Holy Angels, York, and Thomas Hilton [Hylton], prebendary of Carlton cum Thurleby in Lincoln cathedral. He had received Parker's resignation, and had collated his prebend to Hilton, in the person of John de Welton, clerk, his proctor. Lodgings at London, 31 March 1405. (2)

63.   [f.11] Collation of a prebend in the chapel of St Mary and the Holy Angels, York, vacant by the resignation of Thomas Hilton, priest, to Walter Patteswyk, priest, clerk of the archbishop's household. Ind: Receiver-general at York. Cawood Castle, 7 April 1405.

---

1.   Marginal note that this entry should be ignored, being repeated under the archdeaconry of Cleveland: see below, no.336.

2.   The dating clause erroneously gives the year as the eighth of Repingdon's consecration.

64. Collation of the prebend at the altar of St Peter in Beverley Minster, vacant by the death of Richard de Chesterfeld, to M. Richard Conyngeston, LL.D., in the presence of Robert Wolvenden, canon of York, and Thomas Parcour, canon of Lichfield. Ind: Chapter of Beverley. Chapel of Cawood Castle, 17 January 1404/5.

65. Collation of the prebend of Laughten en le Morthen in York Minster, vacant by the death of Robert Faryndon, to M. Richard Conyngeston, LL.D. Ind: Chapter of York. Cawood Castle, 21 February 1404/5.

66. Memorandum of the further collation of the above prebend to Conyngston. Ind: as above. 24 March 1404/5. (1)

67. [f.11v] Certificate of John [Burghill], bishop of Coventry and Lichfield, reciting an archiepiscopal commission (dated at Cawood Castle, 23 April 1405) for an exchange of prebends between M. Richard Conyngeston, LL.D., prebendary of the prebend lately held by John Hall in the collegiate church of St John, Chester, and Nicholas Tydde, prebendary of the prebend lately held by William Gysburn in the chapel of St Mary and the Holy Angels, York. He had received Tydde's resignation, in the person of John Pyry, his proctor, and had collated the prebend to Conyngeston, in the person of M. William Neuport, his proctor. Eccleshall Castle, 2 May 1405.

68. Collation of the prebend of Norwell Overhall in Southwell Minster, vacant by the death of Richard de Chestrefeld, to Robert Wolvenden, priest, clerk of the archbishop's household. Ind: Chapter of Southwell. Cawood Castle, 17 January 1404/5.

69. Collation of the prebend of Weighton in York Minster, lately held by M. Richard Conyngeston, LL.D., as security for the prebend of Laughten en le Morthen, to Thomas Hilton, priest. Ind: Chapter of York. Cawood Castle, 18 March 1404/5.

70. [f.12] Collation of the prebend of Barnby in York Minster, lately held by Thomas Hilton, priest, as security for the prebend of Weighton, to Thomas Haxey, priest. Ind: as above. Cawood Castle, 19 March 1404/5.

71. Collation of the prebend of Oxton and Crophill (Prima Pars) in Southwell Minster, lately held by Robert Wolveden as security for the prebend of Norwell [Overhall] which Richard Chesterfeld lately held, to M. John Ixworth, LL.D. Ind: Chapter of Southwell. Cawood Castle, 19 January 1404/5.

[f.12v: BLANK]

[ff.13-14v: MISSING]

---

1. This repeated collation may reflect a dispute over the succession to the prebend: see J. Le Neve, Fasti Ecclesiae Anglicanae 1300-1541, VI: Northern Province (1963), 65.

72.   Bull of Pope Boniface IX, notifying Richard [le Scrope], late
       bishop of Lichfield and Coventry, of his provision and trans-
       lation to the archbishopric of York, vacant by the death of
       Robert [Waldby].   St Peter's, Rome, 27 February 1397/8.

73.   [f.15v] Commission to John de Neuton, LL.D., treasurer of
       York Minster, appointing him Official of the court of York.
       Rest, 22 July 1398.

74.   [ff.15v-16] Certificate of the chapter of Southwell, reciting
       an archiepiscopal commission (dated at Rest, 13 July 1398) for
       an exchange of benefices between Robert [de] Beswyk, vicar of
       the parish church of the south part of Norwell, and Robert de
       Gaynesburgh, vicar of Maltby.   They had received Beswyk's
       resignation, and had instituted him to Maltby, on the presen-
       tation of the prioress and convent of Arthington.   Chapter
       House, Southwell, 20 July 1398.

75.   [f.16] Mandate to the Official of the archdeacon of York to
       induct Robert de Beswyk to the vicarage of Maltby, following
       the above exchange.   Rest, 25 July 1398.

76.   Appointment of M. John Shcefford, B.Dec., as dean of
       Christianity of York.   Rest, 25 July 1398.

77.   Memorandum of a commission to the above M. John Shefford to
       seek out and receive criminous clerks from the royal justices
       at York, and transfer them to the archbishop's prison. York,
       25 July 1398.

---

1.   This appears to have been the page originally intended to serve
      as the title page of the register.   There is a gap at the top
      of the folio where a title would have fitted, while between
      entries 72 and 73 there is another lengthy gap, which it may
      have been intended to fill by the address clauses of a series
      of notificatory papal bulls addressed to the king, the chapter
      of York, the suffragan bishops of the diocese of York, the
      vassals of the church of York, the clergy of the city and
      diocese of York, and the people of the city and diocese of York,
      informing them of the provision of Scrope to the archbishopric,
      similar to the series contained in the register of Archbishop
      Henry Bowet [B.I., Reg.17, ff.1-2], and in other contemporary
      registers.
2.   In the institutions throughout this section, it may be assumed
      that, unless otherwise indicated, mandates for induction were
      issued on the same day as the institution, to the archdeacon
      of York, or his Official.

78. [ff.16–16v] Letter to br. Robert Grene, prior of Bolton in Craven, absolving him from accusations of perjury made by M. Richard Skypse, rector of Slaidburn, during the visitation made on the authority of the dean and chapter of York during the vacancy of the see (1). Rest, 17 August 1398.

79. [f.16v] Memorandum of a licence granted during pleasure to the prior of the Charterhouse near Coventry, to farm out the rectory of Ecclesfield and appear by proxy at synods at York, and for divine service for the parishioners of Ecclesfield to be celebrated by a suitable chaplain or chaplains within the limits of the parish in St Michael's chapel. Rest, 23 August 1398.

80. Memorandum of a licence for non-residence for one year, to study at the university of Oxford, granted to Robert Duffeld, rector of Keighley. He may farm out his church, and be represented by proxy at synods. Rest, 30 August 1398.

81. Institution of br. Richard Roby, an Augustinian canon, to the vicarage of Wighill, by dispensation, on the presentation of the prior and convent of Healaugh Park. Ind. (2). n.d.

82. Institution of Robert Bryan, priest, to the rectory of All Saints, Peasholme, York, following an exchange with Thomas Wylardby for the chantry of St Mary in the church of St Crux, Fossgate, York, on the presentation of John de Depeden, knt., Robert Wyclyff, rector of Hutton Rudby, and Thomas Thurkyll of York. Ind: Rest, 6 September 1398.

83. Institution of Richard de Rievall, priest, to the perpetual chantry of St Thomas the Martyr in the church of All Saints, Pavement, York, vacant by the death of Henry de Basefford, on the presentation of William de Sallay, citizen of York, patron by reason of his guardianship of John de Acastre, a minor, son and heir of Richard de Acastre, deceased, late citizen of York. Ind: Rest, 11 September 1398.

84. [ff.16v–17] Mandate to the Official of the archdeacon of York, to order processions every fourth and sixth day of the week in every church throughout the archdeaconry, with litanies and special prayers during the mass, for the deliverance of the king, people, and church in England from pestilence and other miseries. The archbishop grants an indulgence of forty days to all who participate in these activities. Rest, 10 September 1398.

85. [f.17] Memorandum of similar commissions issued to the Officials of the archdeacons of the East Riding, Cleveland, Nottingham, and Richmond. Rest, 10 September 1398.

---

1. B.I., Reg.5A, ff.239–239v, 245v.
2. In the induction clause, the Christian name is given as 'Robert'.

86. Institution of William Kydlambe, chaplain, to the perpetual
chantry of St Mary in the church of St Michael, Ousebridge,
York, vacant by the death of William de Collom, on the
presentation of William de Sallay, citizen of York.   Ind:
Rest, 13 September 1398.

87. Institution of M. Robert de Appilton, jurisperitus, to the
rectory of St Wilfrid, York, vacant by the death of William de
Neuton, on the presentation of the abbot and convent of St
Mary's, York.   Ind: Rest, 24 September 1398.

88. Institution of Thomas de Longeley, priest, to the rectory of
Castleford, on the presentation of John [of Gaunt], duke of
Aquitaine and Lancaster, earl of Derby, Lincoln, and Leicester,
High Steward of England.   Ind: Rest, 26 September 1398.

89. Memorandum of a licence for non-residence for three years
granted to the above Thomas de Longeley. He may farm out the
rectory, and is excused personal appearance at synods.
26 September 1398.

90. Memorandum of a dispensation granted in accordance with the
constitution Cum ex eo, to M. Adam Wygan, rector of St Saviour,
York, to attend an English university. He may farm out his
rectory, and is excused personal appearance at synods held at
York.   26 September 1398.

91. Memorandum of a licence for non-residence for two years
granted to William Spygurnell, canon of the royal free chapel
within Windsor Castle, dioc. Salisbury, and rector of Normanton,
to reside in the royal chapel. He may farm out his rectory, and
is excused appearance at synods.   Rest, 29 September 1398.

92. Memorandum of letters dimissory granted to M. Richard Rasyn,
subdeacon, to receive deacon's and priest's orders.   Rest,
1 October 1398.

93. Appointment during pleasure of M. John de Thornton, vicar of
St Mary, Pontefract, as sequestrator within the archdeaconry
of York, except for the probate of wills over £10.   Rest,
6 October 1398.

94. [ff.17-18] Inspeximus and confirmation of the establishment of
a chantry in the chapel of Elland, in the parish of Halifax, by
John Herle, rector of Tankersley, John de Wath, vicar of
Huddersfield, John de Dissheford [Disford], chaplain, and
William de Heton.   Their charter of foundation is recited
(dated at Elland, 10 September 1398, and witnessed by John Scot,
Thomas Flemyng, and John Warde, knts., Richard Elvet, rector of
Almondbury, Henry de Dransfeld, rector of Kirkheaton, John de
Thornhill, rector of Thornhill, Richard de Lyversege, vicar of
Birstall, Henry Sayvill, lord of Thornhill, John de Heton and
Adam de Mirfeld, esqs., and others), setting out that the
chantry is to be founded in honour of Jesus Christ, by licence

94.   from King Richard II, and with the consent of Richard
      [le Scrope], archbishop of York; for the health of John
      [of Gaunt], duke of Aquitaine and Lancaster, John Sayvill, knt.,
      Isabella his wife, and their children, while they lived, and
      thereafter for their souls; and for the souls of Henry of
      Lancaster, late earl of Lancaster, John Sayvill and Margery
      his wife (the parents of John Sayvill), Thomas de Eland and
      Joan his wife (the parents of Isabella Sayvill), John Bylay and
      Thomas Crosse, chaplains, Richard Schepard of Elland, and the
      friends and benefactors of John and Isabella Sayvill, and for
      all the faithful departed.   The chantry is to be endowed with
      eight marks a year, to be paid in equal portions at Martinmas
      and Whitsun, out of the manor of Wyke, near Oakenshaw, one
      messuage, two hundred acres of land, twenty acres of meadow and
      six acres of wood and appurtenances at Hemsworth.   The chantry
      priest is to have a messuage and its appurtenances at Elland
      for his habitation.   If the payments are in arrears by forty
      days, the priest may enter upon the lands set out in the royal
      licence [those of the endowment] and distrain for payment, with
      costs.   The presentation of a chaplain to the ordinary for
      institution and induction is to be made within fifteen days of
      the vacancy by John and Isabella Sayvill while they live, and
      thereafter by their heirs.   Should they not present, the
      presentation passes for the next fifteen days to the vicars of
      Halifax and Huddersfield, acting together.   Failing
      presentation by them, the patronage passes to the prior and
      convent of St Oswald, Nostell, for the next fifteen days,
      failing presentation by whom it lapses to the chapter of York,
      reserving always the patronal rights of the heirs of John and
      Isabella Sayvill in later vacancies.   The incoming chaplain is
      to take an oath of residence and fulfillment of his obligations.
      While John and Isabella Sayvill live, the chaplain is to include
      the prayer Deus, qui caritatis dona in his services for the
      healths of them and the above named; this is to be replaced by
      the collect Inclina, domine, aurem tuam after their deaths, for
      their souls.   The offices for the dead are to be recited on
      the anniversaries of the deaths of John and Isabella Sayvill.
      Each incoming chaplain is to make out a full inventory of the
      ornaments of the chantry, in the form of an indenture with the
      patron, which is to be authenticated by seal, or attested by a
      notary public.   The royal licence (dated at Westminster,
      10 July 20 Richard II [1396]) (1) is also recited, allowing the
      lands of the endowment (which are not held of the Crown) to be
      alienated, in return for £20 paid into the Hanaper by John
      Sayvill, knt., and setting out that the messuage at Elland was
      valued at 2s. a year, as appeared from the inquisition held by
      Peter de Bukton, escheator of Yorkshire, recorded in Chancery.
      Cawood Castle, 30 October 1398.

---

1.   Calendar of Patent rolls, 1396-9, 9-10.

95.   [f.18] Memorandum of letters dimissory granted to Richard
      Wryde of Everingham, to receive all orders.   Rest, 8 October
      1398.(1)

96.   Note of similar letters dimissory granted to Thomas Saxton,
      clerk.   Cawood, 5 November 1398.

97.   Institution of Alexander Raudon, chaplain, to a chantry
      chaplaincy in the college of seven chaplains and the alms-
      house of the Holy Trinity at Pontefract, on the presentation of
      Robert Knolles, knt., the founder.   Cawood Castle, 12 November
      1398.

98.   Note of the institution of William Hall, chaplain, to the same,
      on the same presentation.   Cawood Castle, 12 November 1398.

99.   Note of the institution of Robert Freston, chaplain, to the
      same, on the same presentation.   Cawood Castle, 12 November
      1398.

100. Ind: for the above three chaplains to their chantries.
      Cawood Castle, 12 November 1398.

101. Memorandum of a licence for non-residence for one year granted
      to M. John de Ʒork, rector of Sessay.   He may farm out his
      rectory and is excused appearance at synods.   Cawood,
      28 October 1398.

102. [f.18v] Memorandum of a licence granted to John Cauthorn,
      rector of a mediety of High Hoyland, to celebrate private
      masses for two years and receive a suitable salary, on account
      of the poverty of his benefice, provided that the cure of souls
      there is not neglected.   Cawood, 14 November 1398.

103. Note of a licence for non-residence granted to William Canon,
      rector of Edlington.   He may farm out the rectory and be
      represented by proxy at synods held at York.   Cawood,
      14 November 1398.

104. Licence for non-residence during pleasure, to John de Wyndhill,
      rector of Arncliffe, in the service of Henry Percy, earl of
      Northumberland.   He may farm out the rectory.   Cawood,
      11 December 1398.

105. Note of a licence granted to John Snytall, vicar of Leeds, to
      hear confessions and grant absolution for one year, except in
      certain reserved cases.   Cawood, 22 December 1398.

---

1.   Marginal note that this entry is misplaced, and should be
      entered under the archdeaconry of the East Riding.

106. Note of a licence for non-residence for one year granted to Richard Degyll, rector of Bolton Percy. He may farm out the rectory, and be represented by proxy at synods, but must provide for the services of the church during his absence. Cawood, 3 January 1398/9.

107. Note of a similar licence granted to William de Gysburn, rector of St Helen, Stonegate, York. Cawood, 5 January 1398/9.

108. Memorandum of a licence granted to William Stalmyn, rector of Giggleswick, to act as penitentiary throughout the archdeaconry of York for one year, even in cases reserved to the archbishop (other than violation of the liberties and immunities of the minsters at York, Beverley, Ripon, and Southwell, invasion of the archbishop's parks and poaching of game, perjury in assizes and indictments, matrimonial and divorce cases, and cases involving disinheritance, loss of life or limb, or the greater part of goods). Cawood, 22 January 1398/9.

109. Licence for non-residence for one year, to attend a university, granted to br. John de Usflet, prior of Drax. He may be represented by proxy at synods, but must provide a suitable person to govern the house in his absence. Cawood Castle, 3 February 1398/9.

110. Note of a licence for non-residence for one year, in order to study, granted to John Wyles, rector of a mediety of Linton in Craven. He may farm out the rectory, and be represented by proxy at synods; but in order that the cure of souls is not neglected, he must provide a proctor to serve the church. Cawood Castle, 3 February 1398/9.

111. [ff.18v-19] Commission to the prior and convent of Monk Bretton, following letters from King Richard II (1), to act as collectors within the archdeaconry of York for the half tenth according to the new taxation which had been granted to the king at the provincial convocation held by Robert [Waldby], late archbishop of York, in York Minster on 6 October 1397, and which was to have been paid in two instalments at the feasts of the Invention of the Holy Cross [3 May] and St Michael [29 September] then next following. The subsidy is to be levied on dignities, prebends, offices, personalties and other ecclesiastical persons and benefices, as well as the temporalities annexed to spiritualities, and all ecclesiastical persons and benefices whether exempt or non-exempt throughout the archdiocese, subject to the following exemptions: the nunneries throughout the

---

1. These are presumably the letters of 27 January 1398/9 which are recited in a later commission to the bishop of Durham (ff.149v-150; to be calendared in vol.2). These do not appear in the printed calendars of the patent or close rolls.

111.   province and the monasteries of Egglestone and Rufford, on
        account of their poverty, the churches of Northumberland,
        Cumberland and Westmorland which had been destroyed by the
        Scots, benefices taxed at ten marks or less, and lands
        affected by flooding of the Humber and other rivers in
        Holderness and Marshland belonging to the archbishop, the
        abbots of St Mary's, York, Selby and Meaux, or to other
        religious places or private ecclesiastical persons. The prior
        and convent are responsible for the delivery of the money to the
        treasurer and barons of the royal exchequer no later than the
        quindene of Easter next following [13 April]. Cawood Castle,
        3 February 1398/9.

112.   [f.19] Notes of similar commissions issued to the abbot and
        convent of Rievaulx to act as collectors within the
        archdeaconry of Cleveland; to the prior and convent of Warter
        to act as collectors within the archdeaconry of the East Riding;
        to the abbot and convent of Welbeck to act as collectors within
        the archdeaconry of Nottingham; and to the abbot and convent
        of Fountains to act as collectors within the archdeaconry of
        Richmond.   3 February 1398. (1)

113.   Note of a licence granted to John Thornton, vicar of St Mary,
        Pontefract, to act as penitentiary throughout the archdeaconry
        of York for one year, except in cases as specified in no.108.
        Cawood Castle, 6 February 1398/9.

114.   Note of licences granted to Thomas [de Bilton], vicar of
        Tickhill, William de Derfeld, vicar of Darfield, and John
        [de Rozer], vicar of Sandal Magna, to act as penitentiaries
        for one year; of a similar licence granted to Henry
        [de Brammelay], vicar of Sheffield, to act as penitentiary
        within Hallamshire for one year; and of a licence granted to
        Thomas Garton, rector of St John the Baptist (alias St John del
        Pike), York, to act as penitentiary during pleasure, in all
        cases excepting the above reserved cases. Cawood Castle,
        6 February 1398/9.

115.   Note of a licence for non-residence for three years granted to
        Robert de Santon, rector of Aston. He may farm out the
        rectory and be represented by proxy at synods. Cawood,
        23 February 1398/9.

_____

1.   It is probable that this entry and no. 111 are misplaced, and
        should appear with the other material relating to convocations
        in the section of diverse letters. If the normal practice
        recorded there also prevailed in this instance, the commissions
        to act as collectors within the archdeaconries also extended to
        cover collecting within the appropriate peculiar jurisdictions.

116. [f.19–19v] Certificate of abbot Thomas [Pigot] and the convent of St Mary's, York, reciting an archiepiscopal commission (dated at Rest, 21 July 1398) to grant an annual pension to John Pygot, junior, as the archbishop's nominee, according to the custom on the election of a new abbot, which had occurred during the vacancy of the archbishopric; and reciting the grant (dated at St Mary's abbey, 24 July 1398) of a pension of 100s. a year payable in equal parts at Martinmas and Whitsun, until the abbey could provide Pygot to a suitable rectory. Chapter House, St Mary's abbey, York, 24 July 1398.

117. [f.19v] Institution of John Hesilwode, son of John Henryson of Hazelwood, to the chantry in the chapel of St Leonard, Hazelwood, vacant by the resignation of William Golde, on the presentation of Henry Vavasour, esq. Ind: Cawood Castle, 1 March 1398/9.

118. Commission to Hugh de Wombewell of the parish of Darfield, to administer the goods of Helen, his late wife, who had died intestate. Cawood Castle, 5 March 1398/9.

119. Memorandum of letters dimissory granted to Thomas Gaunt, clerk, to receive all remaining orders. Cawood, 12 March 1398/9.

120. Note of a licence granted to [William Hemmyng](1), rector of Kirk Sandal, an octogenarian, excusing him from personal appearance at synods held in York Minster for one year, on account of his age. Cawood, 9 April 1399.

121. Note of a licence for non-residence for one year granted to Thomas Hoede, rector of a mediety of Burnsall. He may farm out the rectory and be represented by proxy at synods held at York. Cawood, 17 April 1399.

122. [ff.19v–20] Certificate of M. John de Suthwell, receiver at York, reciting an archiepiscopal commission (dated at Cawood Castle, 25 February 1398/9) to inquire into the vacancy and patronage of the perpetual chantry founded for the souls of Ralph de Horneby, late citizen and merchant of York, and Joan, his late wife, at the altar of St Michael in the church of St Helen, Stonegate, York, to which William Hornby [de Horneby], citizen of York, had presented William Smyth of Welton. An inquisition had been held in St Helen's on 27 February 1398/9, attended by Thomas Garton, rector of St John del Pike, York, John, rector of St Helen on the Walls, York(2), Richard Carnaby, parson in York Minster, John de Bilton, William de Melton, parochial chaplain of St Helen, Stonegate, and John Bolleron, John de Richmund, and John Birkhawe of York, chaplains. They had declared that the chantry was vacant by the death of Edmund de Balderston, which had occurred on 21 February last, and that Hornby was the rightful patron.

---

1. Blank in ms.
2. The surname is uncertain, the rectors of both medieties being called John at this date.

122.   Smyth having been found suitable, Suthwell had caused him to be
        instituted and inducted to the chantry.   Sealed with the seal
        of the Official of the court of York, quia sigillum meum
        pluribus est incognitum.   York, 28 February 1398/9.

123.   [f.20] Dispensation to br. William Burnham, canon of St
        Oswald's priory, Nostell, to leave that house and go ad alium
        pium locum.   Cawood Castle, 29 April 1398/9.

124.   Institution of John Thomasson, priest, to the vicarage of
        Barnby Dun, on the presentation of the provost and brethren
        of the college of Cotterstock. (1)   Ind: Cawood Castle,
        3 May 1399.

125.   [f.20v] Moderation and dispensation to William Swerde, priest,
        of the chantry of St Mary in the church of All Saints, Pavement,
        York, that because of the insufficiency of his endowment he need
        celebrate masses only on Tuesday, Thursday, and Saturday in each
        week, for seven years.   Bishopthorpe, 13 May 1399.

126.   Vow of chastity [in English] of Katherine de Melton of Aston,
        taken before the archbishop.   n.d. (2)

127.   Institution of Thomas de Chaworth, priest, to the chantry of St
        John the Baptist in the chapel of Chapel Haddlesey, vacant by
        the resignation of William de Sprotburgh, on the presentation
        of John FiltzWilliam.   Ind: Cawood Castle, 23 May 1399.

128.   Institution of Thomas (3) de Toneton of Birkin to the perpetual
        chantry of the Holy Trinity in Birkin church, vacant by the
        resignation of Thomas de Cheworth, on the presentation of
        [John] de Everyngham, knt.   Ind: Cawood Castle, 5 June 1399.

129.   Note of letters dimissory granted to Thomas Lewer, having his
        first clerical tonsure, to receive remaining orders.   Cawood,
        20 June 1399.

130.   Note of the appointment of M. John de Suthwell, LL.B.,
        receiver at York, as coadjutor to William Gysburn, rector of
        St Helen, Stonegate, York.   Cawood, 20 June 1399.

131.   Institution of Ralph de Balderby, priest, to the vicarage of
        Calverley, vacant by the resignation of John Esseholt in
        exchange for the vicarage of Batley, on the presentation of
        Roger Weston, sacrist of the chapel of St Mary and the Holy
        Angels, York.   Ind. Rest, 26 July 1399.

1.   Called in the text a provostship or chantry.
2.   Printed in J. Raine (ed.), Testamenta Eboracensia, iii
        (Surtees Society 45, 1864), 316.
3.   Named 'William' in the induction clause.

132.   [f.21] Institution of John Esseholt, priest, to the vicarage
        of Batley, vacant by the resignation of Ralph de Balderby in
        exchange for the vicarage of Calverley, on the presentation of
        the prior and convent of St Oswald, Nostell.   Ind: Rest,
        26 July 1399.

133.   Institution of br. Robert de Emesay, canon of Drax, to the
        vicarage of Bingley, vacant by the death of Laurence de Dawtre,
        on the presentation of the prior and convent of Drax.   Ind.
        Rest, 28 July 1399.

134.   Appointment of John Adewyk, vicar of Ferry Fryston, to act as
        coadjutor to John Wylgyn, rector of Mirfield, stricken with age
        and debility.   He must prepare inventories of the goods of
        Wylgyn and of the church.   Robert de Stokes, a parishioner, is
        to assist him in caring for Wylgyn.   Rest, 23 August 1399.

135.   Note of a licence granted to John de Laton, rector of
        Romaldkirk, to act as penitentiary for two years, even in
        reserved cases.   Lodgings at London, near Westminster,
        3 October 1399.

136.   Note of the vow of chastity of Isabella, widow of John Savill,
        knt., administered by William [Northbrugge], bishop Pharensis
        and suffragan.   Chapel of the manor of Newstead, near the
        priory of St Oswald, [Nostell].   17 November 1399. (1)

137.   Note of the appointment during pleasure of M. Richard Rasyn,
        LL.B., as sequestrator within the archdeaconry of York, except
        for the probate of wills of over £10.   Bishopthorpe,
        26 November 1399.

138.   Institution of Thomas de Carnaby, priest, to the perpetual
        chantry founded for the soul of John Beng, priest, at the
        altar of St Mary in the church of All Saints, North Street,
        York, vacant by the death of John Brynyston, on the present-
        ation of Adam de Lychefeld, rector of the church, and Adam del
        Bank, Richard de Alne, William de Alne, Henry de Bolton, Henry
        de Burton, and John de Wraneby, parishioners.   Ind:
        Bishopthorpe, 4 December 1399.

139.   [f.21-21v] Institution of Walter Areshom, priest, to the
        vicarage of All Saints, Huntington, on the presentation of the
        warden and vicars choral of York Minster.   Ind: Official of
        Cleveland.   Bishopthorpe, 10 December 1399. (2)

---

1.   Raine, Testamenta Eboracensia iii, 316-7.
2.   Marginal note (f.21) that this entry is misplaced and should
        be entered under the archdeaconry of Cleveland.

140.   [f.21v] Institution of Henry de Raveneswath, priest, to the
        rectory of St Cuthbert, York, vacant by the death of John de
        Moubray, on the presentation of the prior and convent of Holy
        Trinity, York.   Ind: Bishopthorpe, 23 December 1399.

141.   Institution of M. John de Suthwell, LL.B., to the rectory of
        St Denys, York, vacant by the death of William de Yreland, on
        the presentation of the master and brethren of St Leonard's
        Hospital, York.   Ind: Bishopthorpe, 31 December 1399.

142.   Vow of chastity [in English] of Margaret of Slyngesby, taken
        before the archbishop during the solemnization of mass.
        Bishopthorpe Chapel, 1 January 1399/1400. (1)

143.   Note of a licence for non-residence for one year, to attend a
        university, granted to Geoffrey de Midelton, rector of
        Castleford.   He may be represented by proxy at synods, but
        retains responsibility for the maintenance of the chancel and
        rectory buildings, and must not neglect the cure of souls.
        Bishopthorpe, 17 January 1399/1400.

144.   [ff.21v-22v] Confirmation of the appropriation of Healaugh
        parish church to Healaugh Park priory.   The advowson had been
        granted by John Depeden, knt., and Elizabeth his wife, acting
        under a licence from King Richard II (recited in full, and
        dated at Westminster, 24 October 21 Richard II [1397], and
        setting out that, in return for a payment of 20 marks made to
        the Hanaper, they may alienate the advowson to the priory,
        together with two messuages and twelve acres of land at
        Catterton, none of the above being held of the Crown), in order
        to provide for the maintenance of two canons in priest's orders,
        in addition to the five already at the priory.   The archbishop,
        following inquiry, and with the consent of the chapter of York
        and the advice of lawyers, ordains that on the death or
        resignation of the present rector, William Polowe, the prior
        and convent may appropriate the church.   The fruits shall be
        used for the maintenance of an additional two canons who shall
        be priests, and who shall celebrate daily at the altar of St
        John the Evangelist and St Anne within the priory church, for
        the health of John and Elizabeth while they live, and there-
        after for their souls, and for the souls of their ancestors,
        successors, and all the faithful departed, and for the health
        of the lords of the manor of Healaugh for the time being;
        except on those days when, according to the rules of the priory,
        it shall be their weekly turn to celebrate at the main altar of
        the priory.   The parish of Healaugh is to be served by a
        perpetual vicar, who shall be a canon of the priory.   The
        prior and convent are to present the vicars to the archbishop
        for institution and induction or to the dean and chapter of
        York if the see is vacant.   The vicar is to receive his

---

1.   Printed in Raine, <u>Testamenta Eboracensia</u> iii, 317.

144.   common allowances as a canon, plus 20s. a year, payable in
         equal portions at Martinmas and Whitsun.   The priory is to be
         responsible for all other charges.   After the deaths of John
         and Elizabeth, an annual obit is to be celebrated in the priory
         church, during which the prior and convent shall distribute 13d.
         to the poor of the parish.   On the Sunday prior to the obit,
         due notice of it shall be given by the vicar in the parish
         church during the celebration of mass.   The prior and convent
         are to distribute 40d. to the poor of the parish annually.   The
         prior and convent are to inform the archbishop and chapter if
         the fruits of the living become reduced in value, and prove
         insufficient to maintain this ordination.   The prior and
         convent shall also provide 10s. a year in pensions, 6s. 8d.
         being paid to the archbishop, or to the dean and chapter of
         York is the see is vacant;   the remaining 40d. being paid to
         the dean and chapter of York, or to the chapter alone if the
         dean is absent, in equal portions at Martinmas and Whitsun.
         Each new prior must take an oath to observe this ordination.
         Cawood Castle, 5 February 1398/9. (1)

145.   [f.22v] Institution of br. Peter de Bridsall, canon of Healaugh
         Park priory, to the vicarage of Healaugh, on the presentation of
         the prior and convent of Healaugh Park.   Ind: Bishopthorpe,
         31 January 1399/1400.

146.   [ff.22v-24] Inspeximus and confirmation of the foundation of a
         chantry for one chaplain in honour of God the Father, St Mary,
         and all saints, at the altar of St Nicholas in the chapel of
         St Nicholas in Tadcaster parish church, by William Barker of
         Tadcaster and Agnes his wife.   The charter of endowment
         (undated) is recited.   This includes the licence of King
         Richard II (dated at York, 22 December 19 Richard II [1395])
         setting out that, in return for 20 marks paid by William Barker
         and Agnes his wife, they may endow their chantry with seven
         messuages, fifteen acres of land, five acres of meadow, and 20s.
         of rent in Tadcaster, none of which is held of the Crown.   The
         charter also recites a licence from Henry de Percy, earl of
         Northumberland and lord Percy, dated at Spofforth 20 August
         18 Richard II [1394], permitting the chantry to be endowed
         with all lands, rents, and services held of him in Tadcaster.
         An indenture dated at Tadcaster, 5 January 22 Richard II
         [1398/9], and witnessed by John de Depeden and Nicholas de
         Midelton, knts., John de Normanvill, John de Brerehaghe, and
         William de Driffeld, is also recited, confirming a fine levied
         in the Court of King's Bench, 22 Richard II, and making over the
         endowment to Henry Turnour, chaplain, the first chantry
         chaplain, in return for daily services for the health of
         William and Agnes Barker while they live, and thereafter for

---

1.   For other related documents, see J.S. Purvis (ed.), The
       chartulary of the Augustinian Priory of St John the Evangelist
       in the park of Healaugh (Yorkshire Archaeological Society
       Record Series 92, 1936), 55-6.

146.   their souls, and for the souls of their parents and ancestors
        and all the faithful departed.   According to the ordination
        the chantry is to be served by a priest.   The founders shall
        present the priests to the diocesan for institution and
        induction while they live; after their deaths the patronage
        is to be held by the earl of Northumberland and lord of
        Tadcaster for the time being.   They shall present within
        twenty days of the vacancy, failing which the collation lapses
        to the diocesan.   The chantry is not to be resigned or
        acquired by exchange.   The priest is to take an oath of
        personal residence and service and that he shall be absent for
        no more than three weeks, whether continuous or intermittent,
        in each year.   He must also swear to perform the services:
        the services for the dead, with commendations, every second,
        fourth and sixth weekday; and on Sundays and festivals to
        join in singing the canonical hours and parochial mass in the
        choir of the church.   Following the deaths of the founders,
        an annual obit is to be observed on the feast of St Nicholas
        the Confessor, with the services for the dead with nine
        lessons on the preceding day, and on the day after the
        commendation of souls, an appropriate mass for the dead.   At
        the obit, the priest shall be assisted by three chaplains,
        who shall receive 6d. each, and three clerks, who shall
        receive 3d. each.   If, in his oath, the priest adds or
        subtracts from the above, his institution is to be null.
        The daily services are to include prayers for the founders,
        and for Henry de Percy, his son and heir, progenitors and
        successors; and after the deaths of the founders, for the
        souls of their parents and benefactors and of all the faith-
        ful departed, especially Henry de Barton, sometime canon of
        York, and Thomas de Thorp.   If the priest becomes negligent,
        or criminal, or intolerably and incorrigibly lax, the diocesan
        or his commissary shall inquire into any allegations by
        inquisition of six trustworthy inhabitants of Tadcaster, and
        if he is found guilty, expel him.   For lesser crimes, the
        priest shall be subjected to canonical punishment by his
        superiors.   The charter is to be in triplicate, one copy
        being held by the earl of Northumberland, another by the
        chaplain, and the third by the founders while they live, and
        thereafter by the vicar of Tadcaster.   Bishopthorpe,
        21 January 1399/1400.

147.   [f.24] Note of letters dimissory granted to Robert
        Boresworth, in the first clerical order, to receive all
        orders.   Bishopthorpe, 2 March 1399/1400.

148.   Note of letters dimissory granted to John Stitenham, scholar,
        to receive all orders.   Bishop Burton, 17 March 1399/1400.

149.   Institution of Robert de Emmeswell, priest, to the rectory of
        St Helen, Fishergate, York, vacant by the death of John de
        Knayton, on the presentation of the prior and convent of Holy
        Trinity, York.   Ind: York, 31 March 1400.

150.   [ff.24-24v] Dispensation to Robert Roos, clerk, dioc. York, in
        accordance with a commission from Francis [Carboni], cardinal
        priest of St Susanna and papal penitentiary (recited in full,
        and dated at St Peter's, Rome, 22 May 1399), to receive
        remaining orders and acquire a benefice, notwithstanding that
        he was the son of a single man and a single woman, and had
        concealed the fact when acquiring clerical status.   Bishop
        Burton, 9 April 1400.

151.   [f.24v] Note of a licence granted to Robert Pelle, vicar of
        Kirkburton, permitting representation by proxy at synods at
        York for one year, on account of infirmity.   Bishop Burton,
        20 April 1400.

152.   Note of a licence for non-residence for one year granted to
        Richard Hadilsay, vicar of Whitkirk.   He may farm out his
        benefice, and be represented by proxy at synods.   Bishop
        Burton, 25 April 1400.

153.   Institution of br. Thomas de Hengham, canon of West Dereham,
        dioc. Norwich, to the vicarage of Kirkby Malham, vacant by the
        resignation of br. Hugh de Cressyngham, on the presentation of
        the abbot and convent of West Dereham.   Ind: Bishop Burton,
        12 May 1400.

154.   Note of a licence granted to the abbot of West Dereham, dioc.
        Norwich, permitting appearance by proxy at synods held at York
        to answer for churches within the diocese appropriated to his
        monastery, for three years.   Bishop Burton, 27 April 1400.

155.   Institution of Robert de Hill, priest, to a chantry chaplaincy
        in the college of seven chaplains and almshouse of the Holy
        Trinity, Pontefract, on the presentation of Robert Knolles, knt.,
        the founder.   Ind: Bishop Burton, 18 May 1400.

156.   [ff.24v-25] Dispensation to Henry Wavesur [Wavasur] and
        Margaret Skypwith, in accordance with a commission from Francis
        [Carboni], cardinal priest of St Susanna and papal penitentiary
        (recited in full, and dated at St Peter's, Rome, 20 June 1399),
        to confirm their marriage, which had been contracted in
        ignorance of the impediment caused by Margaret's earlier
        marriage to Hugh Cressy, son of John Cressy, an uncle to Henry,
        which had been terminated by divorce on the grounds of
        impotence.   Bishopthorpe, 7 July 1400.

157.   [f.25] Note of a dispensation granted in accordance with the
        constitution Cum ex eo to Thomas Croka, subdeacon, rector of
        Cowthorpe, to remain as a subdeacon while attending an English
        university for one year, provided that the services and cure of
        souls are not neglected.   Bishopthorpe, 8 July 1400.

158.   Commission from Henry [Beaufort], bishop of Lincoln, to the
        archbishop, for an exchange of benefices between William [de]
        Asshebury [Asshbury], rector of [a mediety of] High Hoyland,
        and David Qwytcherche, vicar of Tathwell, dioc. Lincoln.   He

158.   is to receive Qwytcherche's resignation and institute
         Asshebury to Tathwell, on Beaufort's collation.   n.d.

159.   [ff.25-25v] Collation (by virtue of the above commission) of
         the vicarage of Tathwell, dioc. Lincoln, vacant by the
         resignation of David Owytcherche (sic) by reason of the above
         exchange, to William Asshbury, priest.   Cawood, 23 July 1400.

160.   [f.25v] Institution of David Qwhitcherche, priest, to the
         [mediety of the] rectory of High Hoyland, vacant by the
         resignation of William Asshbury by the above exchange, on the
         presentation of John Scot, knt.   Ind: Cawood Castle,
         23 July 1400.

161.   Certificate of the dean and chapter of York, reciting an
         archiepiscopal commission (dated at Cawood Castle, 27 July
         1400) for an exchange of benefices between Robert Rossedale
         [Rosdall], rector of Whiston, and M. Robert Ragenhill, parson
         in York Minster.   They had received Rossedale's resignation,
         and had instituted Ragenhill to Whiston, on the presentation
         of Thomas de Nevill, lord Furnivall.   Chapter House, York,
         28 July 1400.

162.   Ind: for Ragenhill to Whiston.   Cawood, 29 July 1400.

163.   [ff.25v-26] Institution of M. William Thurbache, subdeacon,
         to the rectory of Methley, vacant by the resignation of
         Nicholas Dawbeney, in the person of John Welton, clerk, dioc.
         York, his proctor, following an exchange for the church of
         Holme Pierrepont; and on the presentation of King Henry IV
         in right of his duchy of Lancaster.   Ind: Cawood Castle,
         5 August 1400.

164.   [f.26] Collation of the rectory of Holy Trinity, Goodramgate,
         York, to William [Northbrugge], bishop Pharensis and suffragan
         of York, as permitted by apostolic dispensation (see no.354).
         Ind: Cawood Castle, 17 August 1400.

165.   Certificate of Henry [Beaufort], bishop of Lincoln, reciting
         [incompletely] an archiepiscopal commission (dated at Cawood
         Castle, 26 August 1400) for an exchange of benefices between
         Thomas Stanhurst, rector of Sausthorpe, dioc. Lincoln, and
         Richard Ossett, rector of Kirk Smeaton.   He had received
         Ossett's resignation, and had instituted Stanhurst to Kirk
         Smeaton, on the presentation of King Henry IV in his right as
         guardian of Edward de Hastynges, knt., a minor.   Liddington,
         1 September 1400.

166.   Mandate to the Official of the archdeacon of York, to induct
         Stanhurst to Kirk Smeaton.   Cawood Castle, 4 September 1400.

167.   Note of a licence for non-residence for two years granted to
         William Spigurnell, canon of the royal free chapel at Windsor,
         dioc. Salisbury, and rector of Normanton, provided that he

167. maintains his residence at the chapel. He may farm out the
      rectory, and is excused personal appearance at synods.
      Cawood Castle, 4 September 1400.

168. [f.26v] Institution of William de Morley [Morlay], priest,
      to the vicarage of Ledsham, vacant by the death of Nicholas
      de Duffeld, on the presentation of the prior and convent of
      Pontefract.   Ind: Cawood Castle, 6 September 1400.

169. Institution of M. Roger de Coryngham to the rectory of Campsall,
      on the presentation of King Henry IV.   Ind: Cawood Castle,
      16 September 1400.

170. Dispensation to Robert Drensfeld, clerk, dioc. York, in
      accordance with a commission from Francis [Carboni], cardinal
      priest of St Susanna and papal penitentiary (recited in full,
      and dated at St Peter's, Rome, 6 May 1400), to receive orders
      and acquire a benefice, notwithstanding that he is the son of
      a single man and a married woman, to whom his father was
      related in the fourth degree of consanguinity, and that he had
      concealed the fact when acquiring his first tonsure.   Cawood
      Castle, 15 September 1400.

171. Institution of Ralph Chestirfeld, priest, to a perpetual
      chantry in the church of St Peter le Willows, Walmgate, York,
      on the presentation of Robert de Halton, priest, the founder.
      Ind: York, 27 September 1400.

172. [f.27] Licence for non-residence for two years, granted to
      Thomas Stanyhurst, rector of Kirk Smeaton.   He may farm out
      his rectory, and be represented by proxy at synods.   Cawood
      Castle, 30 September 1400.

173. Note of a licence for non-residence for one year, granted to
      John Wyles, rector of a mediety of Linton in Craven.   He may
      farm out the rectory, and be represented by proxy at synods at
      York.   Cawood Castle, 30 September 1400.

174. Institution of John Humbelton, priest, to the vicarage of
      Weston, vacant by the death of Roger de Wymbelton, on the
      presentation of the chapter of York, the dean being absent.
      Ind: Dean of Otley.   Scrooby, 22 October 1400.

175. Institution of William Hexthorp, priest, to the chantry of
      St Nicholas in Doncaster parish church, vacant by the
      resignation of William de Hexthorp, on the presentation of
      Henry Westby.   Ind: Scrooby, 4 November 1400.

176. Copy of a grant of the patronage of a mediety of Holy Trinity,
      Goodramgate, York, to Walter [de Gray], archbishop of York
      (patron of the other mediety), by prior Thomas [de Melsonby]
      and the convent of Durham, the revenues of the separate medieties

176.   being insufficient to support two priests.
       [1235-45] (1)

177.   Petition [in French] of John de Ingelby, patron of Long
       Marston church, for a licence to rebuild the church, which is
       considerably decayed, on the site of the chapel.   n.d.

178.   [ff.27-27v] Licence to the parishioners and inhabitants of
       Long Marston to transfer their church as above, provided that
       the old cemetery is effectively closed off to prevent
       desecration or incursions by animals.   Scrooby, 8 January
       1400/1.

179.   [f.27v] Institution of Henry Clyderowe, priest, to the
       perpetual chantry in the chapel of St John the Baptist and
       St John the Evangelist in the church of St Mary, Castlegate,
       York, vacant by the death of John Hoton, on the presentation
       of Thomas Gra, son and heir of William, son of John Gra of
       York.   Ind: Scrooby, 9 January 1400/1.

180.   [ff.27v-28] Absolution to John Lokwode, clerk, dioc. York,
       in accordance with a commission from Francis [Carboni],
       cardinal priest of St Susanna and papal penitentiary
       (recited in full, and dated at St Peter's, Rome, 13 November
       1400) from the excommunication incurred by attacking John
       Wynk, priest, with intent to kill him, and so maiming him
       that he was unable to perform his duties.   The combatatants
       had since made their peace.   Because of wars and other
       dangers Lokwode had not been able to visit the apostolic see
       to obtain absolution.   Scrooby, 31 January 1400/1.

181.   [f.28] Institution of Henry Turnour, priest, to the chantry
       of St Nicholas in Tadcaster parish church recently founded by
       William Barker of Tadcaster, (2) on his presentation.   Ind:
       York, 13 February 1400/1.

182.   Dispensation to John Lokwode, clerk, dioc. York, in
       accordance with a commission from Francis [Carboni], cardinal
       priest of St Susanna and papal penitentiary (recited in full,
       and dated at St Peter's, Rome, 9 November 1400), to receive
       orders and acquire a benefice, notwithstanding that he was
       the son of a single man and a single woman, and had concealed
       the fact when acquiring clerical status.   Bishop Burton,
       25 February 1400/1.

---

1.   Printed in J. Raine (ed.), The register, or rolls, of Walter
       Gray, lord archbishop of York, with appendices of illustrative
       documents (Surtees Society 56, 1872), 174-5.   The location of
       the church derives from the marginal note.
2.   See above, no.146.

183.   Note of a licence for non-residence, granted during pleasure,
        to M. Roger Coryngham, rector of Campsall. He may farm out
        the rectory, and be represented by proxy at synods, but must
        arrange for a proctor to fulfil his spiritual duties at
        Campsall. Bishop Burton, 24 March 1400/1.

184.   [f.28v] Copy of a licence granted by King Edward III in
        return for 20 marks paid into the Hanaper by Robert, son of
        John, William Fery of Wakefield, and Robert de Heth, permitting
        William Kay and William Bull, chaplains, of Wakefield, to
        alienate to two chaplains £10 in rents from Wakefield, Stanley,
        Ossett, Horbury, Heckmondwike, Shafton, Darfield, Warmfield,
        Pontefract, Purston Jaglin, and Ferry Fryston, for the
        maintenance of daily services in the newly constructed chapel
        of St Mary on the bridge at Wakefield. Westminster, 13 May
        30 Edward III [1356].

185.   Similar licence, granted by King Richard II in return for a
        further 5 marks paid into the Hanaper by Edmund, duke of York,
        permitting him, Edward, earl of Rutland, Thomas Gerberg, knt.,
        Thomas Wroghton, clerk, William Gallander, clerk, and John
        Spenne, chaplain, to alienate the above rents as above, that
        licence not having been executed. Westminster, 30 May
        20 Richard II [1397].

186.   [ff.29-30v] Charter of foundation, enfeoffment, and ordination
        of the above chantry, granted by Edmund, duke of York, in
        accordance with the above licences. The duke, with Edward,
        earl of Rutland, Thomas Gerberg, knt., Thomas Worstan, clerk,
        William Galander, clerk, and John Spenne, chaplain, had
        acquired the above rents from Robert Bull and William
        Hirvyng (1) and Alice his wife, who had quitclaimed them to
        them. The chantry was to be established for the health of
        the souls of the duke and of all the faithful departed, by
        royal licence and with the consent of Richard, archbishop of
        York, and the dean and chapter of York. John Spenne and Henry
        [de] Whetelay, chaplains, are presented as the chaplains of the
        first and second portions of the chantry respectively, for
        institution and induction. Future presentations are to be
        made to the ordinary by the duke or his heirs for admission
        within 40 days of the vacancy; if they do not present, the
        collation for that occasion lapses to the archbishop. He
        must collate within one month, otherwise the presentation
        reverts to the duke and his heirs. The chaplains are to take
        an oath of personal residence and service, only illness being
        sufficient cause for absence. They shall celebrate daily
        masses and offices for the dead, with commendations of souls,
        according to the Use of York. At the beginning of the mass,
        after the confession, and before proceeding any further, the
        chaplains shall exhort the congregation to offer prayers with
        angelic salutation consisting of one <u>Pater noster</u> and one <u>Ave</u>,
        for the health (while living) and soul (after death) of the

---

1.   Possibly Hirnyng.

186.   duke in particular, and for the other benefactors of the
        chantry in general.   This is to be done by the chaplains at
        every mass.   They are also to say a certain special collect
        for the health of the duke, his wife, the earl of Rutland,
        and their other children while living, and for their souls
        after death, and for the souls of the duke's progenitors, in
        particular; and in general for the souls of Robert son of
        John, William Fery, Robert de Heth, and other benefactors of
        the chantry, and all the faithful departed.   An obit is to
        be maintained on the morrow of the anniversary of the duke's
        death, with the offices for the dead with nine lessons to
        commemorate his soul and the souls of the above, and with the
        singing of a mass for the duke's soul.   The chaplains are to
        be responsible for maintaining the chantry's possessions
        without diminution, dilapidation, or decay, to which end each
        successive chaplain after induction shall draw up an indented
        inventory of the possessions, one copy to be retained by the
        duke and his heirs, the other to be held by the chantry
        priests.   The inventory shall be authenticated by a notary
        public, or at least by seals.   The chaplains are not to act
        contrary to the interests of the rector or vicar of the parish
        church, by encouraging the parishioners to refuse tithes,
        offerings, or mortuaries; nor are they to incite discord
        between the vicar and his parishioners, but are to participate
        in the masses and canonical hours celebrated in the parish
        church on Sundays and festivals, and obey the lawful
        instructions of the vicar.   If any chaplain is absent for
        more than a fortnight continuously, or a month intermittently,
        or if he is present but does not fulfil his duties for any
        reason other than illness, or if he does not prepare the
        inventory of possessions, or despoils and neglects the chantry's
        goods, or is a criminal, or is suspended for irregularity, or
        is mutilated so as to be incapable of performing his duties,
        he may be summarily deprived by the diocesan after due process
        of law.   However, if his obligations are interrupted by
        illness or other urgent and reasonable cause, he may retain
        the chantry, provided that he fulfils as much of his duties
        as possible, by prayer.   If the chaplains prove morally lax,
        or engage in unworthy or forbidden activities, they may be
        deprived by the diocesan.   At his institution, every chaplain
        shall take an oath to obey this ordination (including that he
        will not alienate or despoil the chantry property), and to
        draw up the inventory of the chantry's possessions.   If the
        oath is not taken, the institution is to be void.   This
        ordination is to be in the form of a bipartite indenture, of
        which one copy is to be held by the duke, and the other by
        the successive chaplains.   It is also to be entered in the
        registers of Richard, archbishop of York, and of the chapter
        of York. (1)   Sealed with the seals of the duke, the
        archbishop, and the chapter of York.   20 August 1398.

        Confirmation of the above.   Cawood, 20 September 1398.

_____

1.   York Minster Muniment Room, M2(5), ff.148-150.

187.	Note that the Official of the archdeacon of York, acting on an archiepiscopal commission dated at Scrooby, 5 February 1400/1, had instituted and inducted William Irby, priest, to the chantry of St Mary in Holy Trinity church, Rothwell, vacant by the death of Robert Hunt, on the presentation of John Fox, son and heir of the late William Fox, and following an inquisition into the patronage. Wakefield parish church, 2 March 1400/1.

188.	Collation of the vicarage of Brodsworth, vacant by the resignation of Adam de Louth in exchange for the parish church of Kirton, to John Addestoke, priest. Ind: Bishop Burton, 6 May 1401.

189.	[f.31] Institution of William [de] Rodes, priest, to the vicarage of Bradford, vacant by the resignation of William, on the presentation of William de Wynceby, rector of Bradford. Ind: Cawood Castle, 4 June 1401.

190.	Certificate of Henry [Beaufort], bishop of Lincoln, reciting [incompletely] an archiepiscopal commission (dated at Cawood Castle, 3 June 1401) for an exchange for benefices between William Asshebery, vicar of Tathwell, dioc. Lincoln, and John Addestoke, vicar of Brodsworth. He had received Addestoke's resignation, and had instituted Asshebery to Brodsworth on the archbishop's collation. Lyddington, 9 June 1401.

191.	Ind: for Asshebery to Brodsworth. Cawood, 15 June 1401.

192.	[f.31-v] Mandate to the archbishop from Lewis [Aliotti], bishop of Volterra, papal nuncio and collector in England, to relax the sequestration imposed on the monastery of Kirkstall and its appropriated parish churches of Kilnsea, Birstall, Owthorne, Aldbrough, Paull, Skeckling, and Withernsea for non-payment of first fruits to Rome. London, 30 April 1401.

193.	[f.31v] Institution of William Smyth, priest, to the vicarage of Askham Richard, vacant by the resignation of William Bramham in exchange for the vicarage of Cantley, on the presentation of the prioress and convent of Nun Monkton. Ind: Cawood Castle, 7 July 1401.

194.	Institution of William Bramham, priest, to the vicarage of Cantley, vacant by reason of the above exchange, on the presentation of the prioress and convent of Wallingwells. Ind: Cawood Castle, 7 July 1401.

195.	Institution of William Cressop, priest, to the perpetual chantry founded by Thomas de Alwarthorp in the church of All Saints, Pavement, York, for the souls of Robert Haget, his wife Helen, the said Thomas, his sister Isabel, their ancestors, and all the faithful departed, on the presentation of John de Kenlay, citizen of York. Ind: Palace at York, 26 July 1401.

196.   [ff.31v-32] Institution of Peter Bird, priest, to the
         perpetual chantry of St John the Evangelist and St John the
         Baptist founded at the altar of those saints in the church of
         St Mary, Castlegate, York, by John, son of Richard Gra
         (grandfather of the present patron), and augmented by William
         Gra (father of the present patron), vacant by reason of an
         exchange for the chantry founded by Richard Toller, late
         citizen of York, in the chapel of St John the Baptist and
         St Katherine the Virgin in the church of St Martin,
         Micklegate, York; on the presentation of Thomas Gra, son and
         heir of William Gra, citizen of York.   Ind: Cawood Castle,
         19 August 1401.

197.   [f.32] Institution of Henry Clyderowe, priest, to the chantry
         of St John the Baptist and St Katherine the Virgin founded by
         Richard Toller, late citizen of York, in the church of St
         Martin, Micklegate, York, vacant by reason of the above
         exchange, on the presentation of William Crispyn, chaplain,
         of York, attorney for William May of Cottesmore, dioc.
         Lincoln, domicellus.   Ind: Cawood Castle, 19 August 1401.

198.   Institution of William Basely, priest, to the vicarage of
         Bishopthorpe, vacant by the resignation of John del Bryg, on
         the presentation of the prioress and convent of Clementhorpe.
         Ind: Rest, 7 September 1401.

199.   Proclamation of the excommunication of Margaret, wife of
         Robert Lofthows of York, at the instance of Robert de Folketon,
         priest, of York.   Rest, 6 October 1401.

200.   [ff.32-32v] Certificate of Henry [Beaufort], bishop of
         Lincoln, reciting [incompletely] an archiepiscopal commission
         (dated at Bishopthorpe, 16 October 1401) for an exchange of
         benefices between Arnold Wyke, vicar of Hambleton, dioc.
         Lincoln, and William Bryan, vicar of Ecclesfield.   He had
         received Bryan's resignation and instituted Wyke to
         Ecclesfield, on the presentation of the prior and convent of
         the Charterhouse of St Anne near Coventry.   Oxford,
         24 October 1401.

         Ind: for Wyke to Ecclesfield.   Bishopthorpe, 28 October 1401.

201.   [f.32v] Institution of John Clyveland, priest, to the
         rectory of St Cuthbert, Peaseholme, York, vacant by the
         resignation of Henry Raveneswath, on the presentation of the
         prior and convent of Holy Trinity, Micklegate, York.   Ind:
         Bishopthorpe, 14 November 1401.

202.   [ff.32v-33] Ordination of a perpetual vicarage at Mitton,
         the church being appropriated to the monastery of Cockersand,
         to replace the ordination made by archbishop William

202. [Melton] (1), which is annulled, the insufficiency of the small
tithes and other portions allowed to the vicar having caused
dissensions between him and his parishioners, and between him
and the abbot and convent.   This new ordination is made by
agreement between the abbot and convent (represented before
the archbishop on the matter by br. John de Lancastre, canon
and cellarer) (2), and the present vicar (who had appeared in
person). The vicarage is to be held by a professed canon of
Cockersand, who is to be presented by the abbot and convent
to the archbishop for institution and induction, or to the dean
and chapter of York, if the see is vacant.   The vicar is to
have for his portion a suitable rectory house with adjoining
gardens, and four bovates of land as glebe with their benefits
and produce, together with an annual payment of twenty marks
from the abbey, payable in equal portions at Easter, the
Nativity of St John the Baptist, Michaelmas, and Christmas, or
within twenty days thereof.   If any payment is delayed, for
each term of delay the abbey must pay five marks towards the
fabric of York Minster.   The fruits of Mitton will be
sequestrated until payment is made to the vicar, with
reparations and costs.   The abbey is to retain all other
income of the benefice, and to bear the ordinary and extraordinary burdens of the church.   If any attempt is made to
evade this ordination, the party concerned shall pay £20 to
the archbishop, or to the dean and chapter of York, if the see
is vacant, towards the fabric of York Minster.   The previous
ordination of the vicarage is annulled, and both parties
renounce any papal privileges or indulgences which may
interfere with the operation of this ordination.
Bishopthorpe, 7 January 1401/2.

The abbot and convent of Cockersand append their seal to the
above to signify their approval.   n.d.

203. [f.33] Institution of Adam de Louth, priest, to the rectory
of Ryther, vacant by the resignation of Thomas Porter in
exchange for the church of Kirton, on the presentation of
William de Rither, knt.   Ind: Cawood Castle, 11 March 1401/2.

204. [f.33v] Dispensation to John de Bradforth, scholar, dioc.
York, in accordance with a commission from Francis [Carboni],
cardinal priest of St Susanna and papal penitentiary (recited
in full, and dated at St Peter's, Rome, 26 March 1398), to
receive orders and acquire a benefice, notwithstanding that he
was the son of a married man and a single woman.   He had
concealed the fact when being ordained to his first tonsure and
as acolyte.   Cawood Castle, 17 March 1401/2.

---

1.   B.I., Reg.9A, f.218-v, summarised in N.K.M. Gurney and Sir C.
     Clay (eds.), Fasti Parochiales iv (Yorkshire Archaeological
     Society Record Series, 133, 1971), 99-100.
2.   For the procuration itself, see no.279 below.

205.   Mandate to the Official of the archdeacon of York, to cite
         the abbeys of St Mary, York, Selby, Sawley, Roche and
         Kirkstall, and the priories of St Oswald, Nostell, Bolton in
         Craven, Monk Bretton, Drax, Pontefract, Healaugh Park, Holy
         Trinity, York and St Andrew, York and all other abbeys and
         priories having churches or pensions within the archdeaconry(1),
         to attend at the chapel of the manor of Cawood on the Thursday
         after the Sunday of Quasi modo next following [6 April], to
         show their titles to those appropriated churches and pensions.
         Cawood, 13 March 1401/2.

206.   [f.34] Memoranda that similar mandates were issued to the
         archdeacons of Nottingham, the East Riding, and Cleveland, to
         cite the abbeys and priories within their archdeaconries. n.d.

207.   Institution of John de Broghton, priest, to the chantry of St
         John the Baptist in the chapel of Elland, on the presentation
         of Isabella Sayvill, widow of John Sayvill, knt., the elder.
         Ind: York, 13 April 1402.

208.   Note of a licence for non-residence for one year granted to
         William de Beroby, rector of Garforth. He may farm out the
         rectory, and be represented by proxy at synods. Rest,
         24 April 1402.

209.   Note of a licence for non-residence for one year granted to
         Richard Hadilsay, vicar of Whitkirk, as above. Rest,
         25 April 1402.

210.   Note of a licence for non-residence for two years granted to
         John Hanlay, rector of Hooton Roberts, as above. Rest,
         28 May 1402.

211.   Confirmation of the appropriation to Kirkstall abbey of the
         churches of Barnoldswick, Bracewell, Birstall, Paull,
         Skeckling, Kilnsea, Withernsea, Owthorne, and Aldbrough,
         following examination of title; and approval of the vicarages
         instituted therein other than that at Barnoldswick. Rest,
         31 May 1402.

212.   [f.34v] Institution of John Cave, priest, to the rectory of
         St Cuthbert, Peasholme, York, in the person of Robert
         Marschall, priest, his proctor, on the presentation of the
         prior and convent of Holy Trinity, Micklegate, York. Ind:
         Rest, 2 June 1402.

213.   Institution of John Maltster, priest, to the chantry of St
         Thomas the Martyr in the church of St Saviour, York, vacant
         by the death of William Sparowe, on the presentation of John
         de Moreton, son and heir of Roger de Moreton, late citizen of
         York. Ind: Rest, 2 June 1402.

---

1.   The scribe at this point has mistakenly given the
         archdeaconry as that of Cleveland.

214.   Certificate of the chapter of York, the dean being absent,
reciting [incompletely] an archiepiscopal commission (dated
at Rest, 23 May 1402), for an exchange of benefices between
Adam Bukler, vicar of the prebendal church of Strensall, and
Robert Elmeswell, rector of St Helen, Fishergate, York.
They had received Elmeswell's resignation, and instituted
Bukler to St Helen, on the presentation of the prior and
convent of Holy Trinity, York.   Chapter House, York, 10 June
1402.

215.   Ind: for Bukler to St Helen's.   Rest, 14 June 1402.

216.   [f.35] Commission to the prior of Pontefract, to enclose
Margaret Lakenby as an anchorite with Emmota Sherman at
Pontefract, with the consent of the prioress of Arthington,
and of Emmota.   He is to ensure that the action is voluntary,
that Margaret has sufficient sustenance, and that after
retirement she does not wish to return to secular life.
Rest, 11 July 1402.

217.   Institution of William Bergh, priest, to the perpetual chantry
recently founded in honour of St Anne, mother of St Mary, in
the church of St Saviour, York, on the presentation of William
de Burton, citizen of York.   Ind: Rest, 3 August 1402.

218.   Institution of William Spede, priest, to the perpetual chantry
at the altar of St Mary in the church of St Saviour, York,
vacant by the death of Robert Bilton, on the presentation of
William Frost, mayor of York, and John Bolton, William Bowes,
William Burton, John Tuche, John Eston, John Percy, Roger de
Barton, Peter Buggcy, Thomas de Bracebryg, William Wadman,
Hugh Straunges, John Gerard, and Hugh Gislay, parishioners of
the church.   Ind: Rest, 3 August 1402.

219.   [ff.35-35v] Confirmation of the appropriation to Holy Trinity
priory, York, of the church of Holy Trinity [Micklegate], York,
the chapels of Bilbrough and St James without the walls,
York (1), the church of Leeds, and a mediety of Hooton Pagnell
church, with pensions of £10 from the vicarage of Leeds, ten
marks from Adel church, five marks from Wintringham church,
16s. from the church of Newton upon Ouse, 40s. from a mediety
of Crambe church, and 20s. from the church of All Saints,
North Street, York, together with two parts of the tithes of
four carucates of land in the parish of Aberford, and two
parts of the demesne tithes within the church of Barton le
Street, all following examination of title.   Rest, 5 August
1402.

---

1.   The chapel of St James, formerly on The Mount, York.   See A.
Raine, Mediaeval York (1955), 307-9.   For a possible
identification of the chapel's precise location, see Royal
Commission on Historical Monuments, City of York, vol.3:
South and West of the Ouse (H.M.S.O., 1972) 66.

220.   [f.35v] Certificate of Walter [Skirlaw], bishop of Durham,
        reciting [incompletely] an archiepiscopal commission (dated at
        Rest, 18 August 1402) for an exchange of benefices between
        William Marnhull, rector of Whitburn, dioc. Durham, and Thomas
        Popilton, rector of Barwick in Elmet.   He had received
        Popilton's resignation, and instituted Marnhull to Barwick, on
        the presentation of King Henry IV in right of his duchy of
        Lancaster.   Howden, 19 August 1402.

        Ind: for Marnhull to Barwick in Elmet.   Beverley, 22 August
        1402.

221.   Institution of William Thornehill, priest, to the rectory of
        Thornhill, vacant by the death of John de Thornehill, on the
        presentation of Henry Sayvyll of Thornhill.   Ind: Rest, 26
        August 1402.

222.   Collation of the vicarage of Silkstone, vacant by the death of
        Ralph Elis, to M. Richard Ullerston, sacre pagine professor.
        Ind: Rest, 27 August 1402.

223.   [f.36] Institution of Thomas de Whiston, clerk to the rectory
        of Ackworth, in the person of M. John Thorneton, vicar of
        Pontefract, his proctor, on the presentation of King Henry IV.
        Ind: Scrooby, 27 November 1402.

224.   Institution of br. John de Foston, canon of West Dereham, dioc.
        Norwich, to the vicarage of Kirkby Malham, vacant by the death
        of br. Thomas de Hengham, on the presentation of the abbot and
        convent of West Dereham.   Ind: Scrooby, 7 December 1402.

225.   Institution of Richard Baron, priest, to the vicarage of
        Radford.   Scrooby, 31 December 1402. (1)

226.   Institution of br. Thomas Ferrour, canon of Bolton in Craven,
        to the vicarage of Skipton, on the presentation of the prior
        and convent of Bolton.   Ind: Scrooby, 30 January 1402/3.

227.   Institution of John de Scardeburgh, priest, to the vicarage of
        the chapel of Carlton in Craven, on the presentation of the
        prior and convent of Bolton in Craven.   Ind: Scrooby,
        30 January 1402/3.

228.   [ff.36-36v] Institution of John del Cotes, priest, to the
        vicarage of Featherstone, vacant by the death of William de
        Thorp, on the presentation of the prior and convent of St
        Oswald, Nostell.   Ind: Scrooby, 1 February 1402/3.

1.   The marginal title for this entry has been scratched out, and
        replaced by a note that it is misplaced, and should be entered
        under the archdeaconry of Nottingham.   It is also marked vacat
        in the inner margin.   The entry is repeated, in its correct
        position, below, no.560.

229. [f.36v] Institution of Thomas de Louther, priest, to the rectory of Treeton, on the presentation of Thomas Nevyll, lord of Hallamshire and patron in right of his late wife, Joan. Ind: Palace at York, 8 March 1402/3.

230. Certificate of John Barnet, canon of York, reciting an archiepiscopal commission (dated at Scrooby, 16 March 1402/3) for an exchange of benefices between M. William Gyloth, vicar of Lydd, dioc. Canterbury, and John [de] Oxeford, rector of Harthill. He had received Oxeford's resignation, given by John Elys, his proctor, by virtue of a notarial instrument subscribed by M. John Combe, clerk, of the city of London, notary public, and had instituted Gyloth to Harthill, on the presentation of the prior and convent of Lewes. Sealed with the seal of the Officiality of the court of Canterbury. London, 22 March 1402/3.

231. Ind: for Giloth (sic) to Harthill. Scrooby, 2 April 1403.

232. [f.37] Institution of William Sledmer, priest, to the vicarage of St Helen, Stonegate, York, on the presentation of the prioress and convent of Moxby. Ind: Scrooby, 10 April 1403.

233. Institution of John Nutteman, priest, to the vicarage of Womersley, on the presentation of the prioress and convent of Heynings, dioc. Lincoln. Ind: Scrooby, 11 April 1403.

234. Institution of William de Broughton, priest, to the recently established vicarage of Mirfield, (1) on the presentation of the prioress and convent of Kirklees. Ind: Scrooby, 12 April 1403.

235. Institution of Thomas Hulot, priest, to the vicarage of Kildwick, on the presentation of the prior and convent of Bolton in Craven. Ind: Scrooby, 18 April 1403.

236. Institution of William Ribstane, priest, to the perpetual chantry recently founded at the altar of St Katherine in the church of St Mary Bishophill Senior, York, on the presentation of Elizabeth, widow of Richard Basy. Ind: Scrooby, 26 April 1403.

237. Institution of John Skyres, priest, to the vicarage of Felkirk, vacant by the death of Hugh de Derfeld, on the presentation of the prior and convent of St Oswald, Nostell. Ind: Scrooby, 27 April 1403.

238. [f.37v] Institution of William atte Well, priest, to the perpetual chantry at the altar of St John the Evangelist in the chapel of Skelbrooke, vacant by the death of Adam de Derwent, on the presentation of the prior and convent of Monk Bretton. Ind: Scrooby, 6 May 1403.

1. See above, no.50.

36

239. [ff.37v-38] Certificate of the dean of Christianity of York, reciting an archiepiscopal commission (dated at York, 8 March 1402/3) (1) to inquire into the vacancy and patronage of the church of All Saints, North Street, York, to which the prior and convent of Holy Trinity, York, had presented their clerk, John Whitwell. An inquisition had been held in full chapter in York Minster on 9 March 1402/3, attended by the following rectors: Robert Lowther of Skelton, Richard Iwelay of St Mary Bishophill Senior, York, John Starfeld of Barningham, and Richard Uphall of Levisham; and by Thomas Qwhixlay, William Kedelham, Henry Cliderow, Robert Barbour, Thomas Hesill, Bernard Everton, Robert Cok, John Skelton, John Latoner, John Banen, William Crispin, Thomas Skelton, William Skelton, and John Preston, chaplains of the city of York. They had declared that the church was vacant by the death of Adam Lichefeld, which had occurred on 9 February last. The priory was the patron, but the King had made the presentation at the last vacancy, the temporalities being then in his hands. There was no dispute about the church as far as they knew, the presentee being the only claimant. The church was worth £20 a year, paying a pension of 20s. a year to the priory, and was taxed at eight marks. Whitwell was already vicar of Kirkby Grindalythe and was a suitable person to hold the church of All Saints. Sealed with the dean's official seal, and the seals of his witnesses, in the presence of M. Robert Ragnehill, advocate of the court of York, M. John Staynton, proctor of that court, M. John Bliburgh, M. John Foughler, and others. York, 9 March 1402/3.

240. [f.38] Institution of John Whtwell (sic), priest, to the rectory of All Saints, North Street, York, following the above inquisition. Ind: Scrooby, 3 June 1403.

241. Institution of John Horslay, priest, to the perpetual chantry founded for the soul of William Gra at the altar of St John the Baptist in a certain small chapel in honour of that saint in the church of St Mary, Castlegate, York, on the presentation of Thomas Gra, citizen of York, son of the said William. Ind: Scrooby, 18 June 1403.

242. Institution of Thomas Watton, priest, to the rectory of St Michael, Ousebridge, York, vacant by the death of M. [Richard] de Setryngton, on the presentation of the abbot and convent of St Mary, York. Ind: Cawood Castle, 21 August 1403.

243. Institution of John de Thornour, priest, to the rectory of St Wilfrid, York, vacant by the resignation of M. Robert de Apilton, on the presentation of the abbot and convent of St Mary, York. Ind: Cawood Castle, 27 August 1403.

---

1. The text gives the year as '1403'.

244.   Institution of William Couper, priest, in the person of M.
        Richard Rasyn, his proctor, to the vicarage of Doncaster,
        vacant by the resignation of William Farndale, on the
        presentation of the abbot and convent of St Mary, York.   Ind:
        Cawood Castle, 31 August 1403.

245.   [f.38v] Institution of Edmund Lacy, priest, to the rectory of
        Castleford, in the person of Robert Asshefeld, his proctor, on
        the presentation of King Henry IV in right of his duchy of
        Lancaster.   Ind: Cawood Castle, 4 September 1403.

246.   Ordination of the vicarage of Mirfield.   Cawood Castle,
        4 August 1403. (1)

247.   [f.39] Institution of William de Cloutherom to the vicarage
        of Mirfield, vacant by the resignation of William de Broughton,
        on the presentation of the prioress and convent of Kirklees.
        Ind: Cawood Castle, 18 September 1403. (2)

248.   Institution of John de Nafferton, priest, to the vicarage of
        St Andrew, Bishopthorpe, vacant by the resignation of William
        Basele, on the presentation of the prioress and convent of
        Clementhorpe.   Ind: Cawood Castle, 12 October 1403.

249.   [ff.39-40] Inspeximus and confirmation of the ordination of a
        chantry founded for the health of King Henry IV while he lives,
        and thereafter for his soul, and for the souls of his late wife,
        Hugh de Annesley, John Belewe the son, John Belewe the father,
        Cecilia Rosselyne, and William Michell, their ancestors and
        benefactors, and all the faithful departed, at the altar of
        St Mary in the church of Bolton upon Dearne, by Thomas de
        Hardewyk, clerk, Thomas de Annesley of Kinoulton, Thomas Hunt
        of Linby, Thomas de Kyrkeby, chaplain, and John Clerc [Clerk]
        of Hucknall Torkard, reciting their charter (dated at Bolton,
        All Saints day, 2 Henry IV [1 November 1400], and witnessed by
        John de Annesley, Nicholas de Strelley, John de Clifton, John
        de Burton, and Robert Cokfeld, knts.) enfeoffing Thomas Warde
        of Bolton, chaplain, and his successors in the chantry with a
        messuage called 'Hermytmanplace' and a garden in Bolton upon
        Dearne, and £5 of a rent a year derived from seven messuages,
        100 acres of land, and twenty acres of meadow in Bolton and
        Goldthorpe, as follows: 50s. from a messuage and forty acres
        of land and meadow formerly belonging to Cecilia Rosselyne in
        Bolton; 44s. from a messuage called 'Foxplace' in Bolton, with
        forty acres of land and meadow; 2s. from a messuage held by
        Henry Breton; 12d. from a messuage called 'Seustirplace';
        18d. from a messuage having the cemetery of Bolton to the west;

---

1.   This entry is a repeat of that at no.50.
2.   The scribe obviously became confused with the transfer to the
      new gathering.   Despite no.246, no.247 has a marginal note
      that hic deberet registrari ordinacio vicarie de Mirefeld' que
      registratur in primo quaterno de capitulis.

249.   and 18d. from ten acres of land at Goldthorpe, all which rents
were payable in equal portions at Whitsun and Martinmas.   The
priest may distrain on all the lands of the grantors in Bolton
and Goldthorpe if the rent is overdue for a fortnight, or if
any attempt is made to defraud him thereof, provided that the
services of the chantry have been maintained.   The presentation is to be made to the archbishop, or to the chapter of
York, if the see is vacant, within four weeks of the chantry
falling vacant, by Hugh de Annesley, son of Hugh de Annesley,
knt., and the heirs male of his body; failing whom the
patronage shall pass to Thomas de Annesley, son of Thomas de
Annesley of Kinoulton, and his heirs.   Should the patron (or
his guardian, if the patron be a minor) fail to present, the
collation on that occasion passes to the archbishop, or to the
chapter of York, if the see is vacant.   If the chaplain
becomes degenerate, and neglects his duties for eight days
without reasonable excuse, legal proceedings may be instituted
against him, and if he fails to reform within one month of
being warned, he may be expelled and replaced.   The chaplain
is to take up his position, provided that there is no
impediment, within six days of presentation.   He is to
celebrate matins and the canonical hours daily, and the offices
for the dead at least three times per week, in the church of
Bolton or in some other decent place if necessary.   All gifts
and oblations made to the chantry are to be handed over to
the parish church, so that the chantry shall be in no way
prejudicial to the finances thereof.   The chantry priest shall
pay to the parish church tithes due from the endowment of the
chantry.   He is not to do anything to reduce the endowment,
otherwise he must resign.   Scrooby, 4 December 1402. (1)

250.   [f.40] Institution of Richard Flemmyng, clerk, to the rectory
of St Andrew the Apostle, Slaidburn, vacant by the death of M.
Richard de Skipse, on the presentation of the prior and convent
of Pontefract.   Ind: Scrooby, 19 November 1403.

251.   Institution of John Prentys, clerk, to the rectory of Castleford, in the person of Thomas Oter, his proctor, on the
presentation of King Henry IV.   Ind: Scrooby, 22 November
1403.

252.   Institution of Thomas Wikireslay, priest, to the rectory of
Birkin, vacant by the resignation of John de Clifton in
exchange for the church of Gamston, on the presentation of
John Everyngham, knt., lord of Birkin.   Ind: Scrooby,
15 December 1403.

---

1.   This document is also calendared in Hamilton Thompson and Clay,
Fasti Parochiales, ii (Yorkshire Archaeological Society Record
Series, 107, 1943), 122-3.

253. [ff.40-40v] Certificate of John [Burghill], bishop of Coventry and Lichfield, reciting an archiepiscopal commission (dated at Scrooby, 7 January 1403/4) for an exchange of benefices between Robert Peyntour, rector of Caldecote, dioc. Coventry and Lichfield, and M. William de Stanley [Staneley], rector of Todwick. He had received Stanley's resignation, and had instituted Peyntour to Todwick on the presentation of John Wasteness, esq. Eccleshall Castle, 11 January 1403/4.

254. [f.40v] Certificate of Richard [Clifford], bishop of Worcester, reciting an archiepiscopal commission (dated at his lodgings in London, 18 February 1403/4) for an exchange of benefices between John Botyler [Botiler], rector of Winterbourne, dioc. Worcester, and John Prentys, rector of Castleford. He had received Prentys's resignation, and had instituted Botiler to Castleford, on the presentation of King Henry IV. Bishop's lodgings in London, 18 February 1403/4.

255. Ind: for Botiler to Castleford. 27 February 1403/4.

256. Institution of John Holmesfield, priest, to the perpetual chantry of St James in the church of Holy Trinity, Goodramgate, York, vacant by the death of William ʒong, on the presentation of Robert de Howm, son of Robert de Howm, deceased, citizen and merchant of York. Ind: Scrooby, 1 April 1404.

257. [f.41] Memorandum of a licence excusing appearance at synods for one year, granted to Robert de Lincoln, rector of Newton Kyme. Cawood, 14 April 1404.

258. Memorandum of a licence for non-residence and excusing appearance at synods for three years, granted to John Botiler, rector of Castleford. Cawood, 22 June 1404.

259. Collation of the chantry at Skellow to Roger Elys, priest. Ind: Cawood Castle, 6 July 1404.

260. Institution of John Bassett, priest, to the vicarage of Mirfield, vacant by the resignation of William Cloutherom, on the presentation of the prioress and convent of Kirklees. Ind: Cawood Castle, 13 July 1404.

261. Institution of William de Newerk alias Shepeley, clerk, in the person of M. Alan de Newerk, his proctor, to the rectory of Slaidburn, vacant by the resignation of Richard Flemyng, on the presentation of the prior and convent of Pontefract. Ind: Cawood Castle, 10 August 1404.

262. Institution of Richard de Elughton, priest, to the rectory of Edlington, vacant by the resignation of William Canon, on the presentation of Nicholas de Strilley, knt., Richard de Norton, John Tibbay, clerk, and Adam de Egleston, clerk. Ind: Cawood Castle, 18 September 1404.

263.   [f.41v] Certificate of M. Roger Coryngham, sacre pagine
        professor, dean of the royal chapel of Wimborne Minster, dioc.
        Salisbury, reciting an archiepiscopal commission (dated at
        Cawood Castle, 15 September 1404) for an exchange of benefices
        between William Cononum [Canonum], prebendary of Kentisburn in
        the said chapel, and William Marunhull, rector of Barwick in
        Elmet.   He had received Marunhull's resignation, and had
        instituted Cononum to Barwick, on the presentation of King
        Henry IV in right of his duchy of Lancaster.   Sealed with his
        seal and (quia sigillum meum quod ad manus habeo non est
        autenticum, sed pluribus incognitum) attested by John Selowe,
        clerk, dioc. York, notary public, in the presence of M. William
        Hull, LL.B., and M. John Apulton, B.Th., and others.   Queen's
        College, Oxford, 20 September 1404.

264.   [f.42] Ind: for Canonum to Barwick in Elmet.   25 September
        1404.

265.   Institution of Robert Halton, priest, to the perpetual chantry
        of St Mary in the church of St Peter, Walmgate, York, on the
        presentation of the prior and convent of Kirkham.   Ind:
        Cawood Castle, 27 September 1404.

266.   Institution of John Hogeson, priest, to the church of Bolton
        by Bowland, on the presentation of John de Pudsay, knt.
        Ind: Cawood Castle, 3 September 1404.

267.   [ff.42-42v] Certificate of the chapter of York, the dean
        being absent, reciting an archiepiscopal commission (dated at
        Cawood Castle, 23 September 1404) for an exchange of benefices
        between John Wace, chaplain of the chantry at the altar of St
        Nicholas in the church of Holy Trinity, Goodramgate, York,
        and Robert [de] Elmeswell, vicar of the prebendal church of
        Strensall.   They had received Wace's resignation, and had
        instituted Elmeswell (1) to the chantry, on the presentation
        of the mayor and community of the citizens of York.   Chapter
        House, York, 3 October 1404.

        Ind: for Elmeswell to the chantry.   6 October 1404.

268.   [f.42v] Certificate of John de Suthwell, receiver-general at
        York, reciting an archiepiscopal commission (addressed to him
        and to the Official of the archdeacon of York, and dated at
        Cawood Castle, 22 November 1404) to inquire into the vacancy
        and patronage of a perpetual chantry at the altar of St Mary
        in the church of St Sampson, York, to which Nicholas Holme,
        succentor of the college of vicars in York Minster, and Thomas
        Langton, Richard Horneby, Thomas Martyn, William de Tunstall,
        and other vicars of York Minster, and Robert Ledes, John
        Helmesley, Thomas Ruston, and William Scauceby, with other
        parishioners of St Sampson had presented William Forest, priest.

1.   The scribe became confused on turning the folio, and in the
        record of institution and note of the issue of the induction
        mandate, gives the christian name of Elmeswell as John.

268.   An inquisition had been held at the church, attended by M. John
        de Kyrkton, M. John de Lunde, Thomas de Scardeburgh, John de
        Swynton, and Robert Bryane (respectively rectors of the churches
        in York of Holy Trinity, King's Court; All Saints, Pavement;
        St Mary, Castlegate; St Edward and All Saints, Peasholme),
        with William [de Sledmer], vicar of St Helen, Stonegate, and
        Patrick de Aschburn, William de Welton, John Spenser, Thomas de
        Sutton, John de Foston, John de Clayton, and William Kydlame,
        chaplains of the neighbourhood. They had declared that the
        chantry was vacant by the death of Robert de Folketon, which
        had occurred on 12 November last. The presentation, according
        to the ordination, belonged to the rector and parishioners of
        St Sampson, Folketon having been presented by John Shirburn,
        then rector, with John de Scheffeld, William de Helmesley,
        John de Kyrkham, Simon de Waghen, and other parishioners.
        Forest was a suitable person to hold the chantry. Sealed with
        the seals of the commissary-general of the Official of the
        court of York, and of the inquisitors. York, 25 November 1404.

269.   Institution of William Forest, priest, to the above chantry,
        on the above presentation. Ind: Cawood Castle, 2 December
        1404.

270.   [f.43] Vow of chastity [in English] of Joan, sometime wife of
        Walter Calverley, knt., taken before William [Northbrugge],
        bishop Pharensis and suffragan of York. n.d. (1)

271.   Institution of br. John Kirkeby, canon of Healaugh Park priory,
        to the vicarage of Healaugh, vacant by the death of br. Peter
        Birdesall, on the presentation of the prior and convent of
        Healaugh Park. Ind: Cawood Castle, 13 December 1404.

272.   Commission to M. Alan de Newerk, advocate of the court of York,
        to cite all opponents of the election of br. John de Crofton as
        prior of Monk Bretton, following the resignation of br. William
        de Ardesley, to appear at the chapel of Cawood Castle on
        Tuesday, 23 December, next following, if it be a law-day, or on
        the law-day next following. Cawood Castle, 20 December 1404.

273.   [ff.43-43v] Certificate of M. Alan de Newerk, recording his
        execution of the above commission, which he had received on
        Sunday, 21 December. The citation had been published in the
        conventual church of the priory that same day. Sealed with
        the seal of the Officiality of the archdeaconry of York cuius
        custodiam habeo racione regiminis eiusdem archidiaconatus
        michi commissi. Monk Bretton priory, 21 December 1404.

274.   [f.43v] Confirmation of the election of br. John de Crofton
        as prior of Monk Bretton, and release to him of the temporalities
        and spiritualities of the house. n.d.

---

1.   Printed in Raine, Testamenta Eboracensia, iii, 318-9.

275.   Profession of obedience of br. John de Crofton as prior of
        Monk Bretton, n.d.

276.   Letters testimonial to br. John de Crofton, confirming his
        election as prior of Monk Bretton and releasing to him
        spiritualities and temporalities of the house.   Cawood Castle,
        23 December 1404.

277.   Mandate to the subprior and convent of Monk Bretton, to receive
        and obey br. John de Crofton as their prior.   Cawood Castle,
        23 December 1404.

278.   Mandate to the Official of the archdeacon of York, to install
        br. John de Crofton as prior of Monk Bretton.   Cawood Castle,
        23 December 1404.

279.   [ff.43v-44] Procuration by the abbot and convent of Cockersand,
        appointing br. John de Loncastre, canon of the monastery, to
        act on their behalf in dealing with the archbishop of York
        concerning the ordination of a vicarage at Mitton in Craven,
        the church there having been appropriated to their use.
        Chapter House, Cockersand abbey, 7 October 1401. (1)

280.   [f.44] Certificate of the dean of Otley, reciting an
        archiepiscopal commission (dated at Cawood Castle, 12 January
        1404/5) to inquire into the vacancy and patronage of the
        rectory of Leathley, to which the prior and convent of
        Healaugh Park had presented Richard de Wyghall, priest,
        following the death of John Campsall.   An inquisition had
        been held in full chapter at Otley on 20 January 1404/5,
        attended by M. Richard Marass, rector of Guiseley, Richard de
        Otteley, vicar of the same, William Byffyn, Richard Kyrkeby,
        William Newall, and John Marshall, priests.   They had
        declared that the rectory had been vacant since the death of
        Campsall on 9 January last, and that the priory held the
        patronage.   Wyghall having been found suitable, the dean had
        instituted and inducted him to the rectory.   Otley,
        20 January 1404/5.

281.   [f.44v] Grant of a pension of 40s. a year, payable in equal
        parts at Whitsun and Martinmas, to John Poleyn, clerk, of
        Sherburn in Elmet, by prior John [de Crofton] and the convent
        of Monk Bretton, because of the recent appointment of the prior,
        and until such time as they can provide him with a suitable
        benefice.   Chapter House, Monk Bretton priory, 23 January
        1404/5.

282.   Institution of John Sandall, priest, to the rectory of
        Armthorpe, vacant by the resignation of Richard Rouclyff, on
        the presentation of Thomas [Mowbray], Earl Marshall and earl of

---

1.   There is a marginal cross reference to the entry of the
        ordination of the vicarage in the previous gathering (above,
        no. 202).

282.   Nottingham, lord Mowbray, Segrave and Gower.   Ind: Cawood
Castle, 31 January 1404/5.

283.   Institution of John [de] Seggefeld [Seggesfeld], priest, in
the person of M. Robert Scurveton, his proctor, to the rectory
of Birkin, vacant by the resignation of Thomas Wykersley in
exchange for the parish church of Stokesley, on the presentation
of John Everyngham, knt.   Ind: Cawood Castle, 5 February
1404/5.

284.   Institution of John de Duggylby, priest, to the perpetual
chantry founded for the souls of William de Grantham, Matilda
his wife, William, son of Richard de Santon, and Arnold de
Ripon, deceased, at the altar of St John the Baptist in the
church of St Helen, Stonegate, York, vacant by the death of
Richard, son of Robert de Thornton, on the presentation of John,
son of Arnold de Ripon, executor of the will of William de
Grantham, citizen and merchant of York.   Ind: Cawood Castle,
14 February 1404/5.

285.   Institution of Thomas de Anlaby, priest, to the rectory of
Spofforth, on the presentation of Henry de Percy, earl of
Northumberland.   Ind: Cawood Castle, 23 February 1404/5.

286.   Institution of M. Robert Appylgarth [Appilgarth], priest, to
the rectory of St Michael, Coney Street, York, vacant by the
resignation of Thomas de Watton in exchange for the parish
church of Brafferton, on the presentation of the abbot and
convent of St Mary, York.   Ind: Cawood Castle, 24 February
1404/5.

287.   [f.45] Institution of br. William de Lyndesay, priest,
confrere of the house of St Robert near Knaresborough, to the
vicarage of Foston, vacant by the resignation of br. Richard
de Wakefeld, on the presentation of the minister and convent
of the said house.   Ind: Cawood Castle, 11 May 1405.

288.   Institution of John Burgeys, priest, in the person of Robert
Corbrygg, his proctor, to the wardenship of the free chapel of
Norton, vacant by the resignation of M. Alan de Newerk, on the
presentation of Edward de Hastynges, knt.   Ind: York, 27 May
1405.

289.   [ff.45-46v] Inspeximus and confirmation of amendments to the
foundation and ordination of a college for seven chaplains and
two clerks, together with an almshouse for thirteen poor people
and two servants, established by Robert Knolles, knt., citizen
of London, and Constance his wife, for their health   while
living, and for their souls after death, by licence from
Richard II, late king of England, and John [of Gaunt], late
duke of Lancaster, in honour of the Holy Trinity and St Mary,
on a site and messuage purchased from Thomas Schirwynd within
the parish of All Saints, Pontefract, within the duchy of
Lancaster, and commonly known as 'Knollesalmeshous'.   The

289.   archbishop refers to the original ordination, dated at London,
            4 October 1385, as entered in the register of the late
            archbishop Alexander [Neville] (1), and recites two later
            amending charters, made on the advice of lawyers to clarify
            certain obscurities in the original foundation.   The first,
            dated at Sculthorpe, dioc. Norwich, 20 May 1397, and sealed
            with the seals of Robert Knolles, the prior and convent of St
            Oswald, Nostell, and John de Neuthorp, master or warden of the
            almshouse, sets out that, while they live, the founders or the
            survivor of them are to have the nomination of the two chaplains
            to serve in the almshouse, and that after their deaths the
            nomination is to be made by the master or warden for the time
            being, who shall present the successive chaplains to the arch-
            bishop of York for admission.   The second charter, dated at
            Sculthorpe, dioc. Norwich, Trinity Sunday [10 June] 1403
            amends the clause relating to the selection of inhabitants and
            servants for the almshouse, which had not made clear by whom
            they were to be admitted after the deaths of the founders;   the
            clause setting out that the patronage of the mastership of the
            almshouse was to be held by the prior and convent of St Oswald,
            Nostell, after the deaths of the founders, and that the
            prospective master was to be presented to the archbishop within
            fifteen days of the vacancy, which had not made clear that the
            successive masters were to be chosen from among the chaplains
            of the college of chaplains; the clause which had provided that
            there should be a chest for the treasure and jewels, with two
            locks, one key for which was to be held by the prior of St
            Oswald, and the other by the master of the house, the chest not
            to be opened without the consent of the prior, which had not
            provided that a third key was to be held by the chaplains of
            the college, without the consent of whom, or a majority of
            them, the chest was not to be opened;   the clause which had
            provided that, after the deaths of the founders, each success-
            ive master was, within eight days of his promotion, to take an
            oath before the prior of St Oswald, in the presence of a notary
            and witnesses, to provide an annual inventory of the almshouse,
            and to render an annual account to the prior of his administr-
            ation of the house, which had not provided that the chaplains
            of the college should be present to hear the account;   the
            clause which had provided that the chaplains should together
            recite the services for the dead daily in the choir of the
            chapel, which had not provided that, on feast days according to
            the Use of York, they were to be excused these services in order
            to perform greater ones;   finally, the clause which had provided
            that the master of the house should have an official seal, which
            was to be kept in a chest with two locks, for which one key was
            to be held by the master and the other by the prior of St
            Oswald, by which seal the rents were to be farmed out etc., and
            which had not provided that a third key was to be held by the
            chaplains of the college.   The first clause is therefore
            amended to provide that, after the death of any chaplain, clerk,

_____

1.   B.I., Reg. 12, ff.97v-98v.

289.   pauper or servant, the master and chaplains, or a majority
thereof, shall appoint a replacement within a fortnight, with
preference to one who is destitute.   Should they fail to
appoint, the relevant portion of the income shall be distributed
by them to the poor of the town, especially those normally
living adjacent to the possessions of the college, under the
supervision of three or four worthy townsmen.   The second
clause is amended to provide that the most worthy of the
chaplains in the opinion of the prior shall, with the consent
of the other chaplains, succeed to the mastership.   The
appropriate amendment is made to the third clause, relating to
the keys to the treasure chest, so that the chest may not be
opened without the consent of the <u>maior et sanior pars</u> of the
chaplains.   The fourth clause is amended to permit the chaplains to hear the master's account, and challenge it if they
see fit.   The fifth clause, relating to the services, is
suitably amended so that the chaplains shall follow the Use and
Ordinal of York as much as possible.   The final clause is
amended, providing that one chaplain shall be appointed keeper
of the seal and of the third key by the <u>maior et sanior pars</u> of
his colleagues; that he shall, on appointment, take an oath
before the prior, master and chaplains, not to seal anything
prejudicial to the college without the consent of the chaplains,
or of the <u>maior et sanior pars</u>; and ordering that, should he do
so, he shall be expelled and otherwise punished by the ordinary,
as an example.   Cawood Castle, 5 October 1404.

290.   Collation of the rectory of Wheldrake, vacant by the
        resignation of. John Ikelyngton, to John de Holme, clerk.
        Ind: Southwell, 4 July 1398.

291.   Memorandum of letters dimissory granted to John Holme, clerk,
        rector of Wheldrake, to receive all orders.   Rest, 21 August
        1398.

292.   Institution of William Uphall to the rectory of Easington,
        vacant by the death of Thomas Seteryngton, on the presentation
        of the prior and convent of Guisborough.   Ind: Rest,
        3 September 1398.

293.   Certificate of the chapter of Southwell, reciting an
        archiepiscopal commission (dated at Rest, 24 September 1398)
        for an exchange of benefices between Thomas Paule, vicar of
        the prebendal church of South Muskham, and John [de] Cave,
        chaplain of the chantry at Wykeham.   They had received Cave's
        resignation, and had instituted Paule to the chantry, on the
        presentation of the prioress and convent of Wykeham.   They had
        also instituted Cave to South Muskham, on the presentation of
        John de Tibbay, the prebendary.   Chapter House, Southwell,
        30 September 1398.

        Ind: for Paule to the chantry.   2 October 1398.

294.   Institution of Walter Gyseburn, chaplain, to the rectory of
        Dunnington, on the presentation of Henry de Percy, earl of
        Northumberland.   Ind: Rest, 5 October 1398.

295.   Memorandum of a licence for non-residence for one year, granted
        to Richard Malton, rector of Thornton in Pickering Lythe.   He
        may farm out the rectory, and be represented by proxy at synods.
        Rest, 4 October 1398.

296.   [f.47v] Memorandum of a licence for non-residence for one
        year, granted to William Pek, rector of Middleton in Pickering
        Lythe.   He may farm out the rectory, and is excused personal
        appearance at synods.   Rest, 2 October 1398.

297.   Appointment of M. William de Uphall, B.Dec., as sequestrator
        and commissary-general within the archdeaconry of Cleveland.
        Rest, 8 October 1398.

---

1.   ff.47-48 have been transposed in rebinding.
2.   In the institutions throughout this section, it may be assumed
        that, unless otherwise indicated, mandates for induction were
        issued on the same day as the institution, to the archdeacon of
        Cleveland, or his Official, or either of them.

298.   Institution of Walter de Cowpeland, chaplain, to the vicarage
        of Stillingfleet, vacant by the death of Robert Pety, on the
        presentation of William de Donyngton, master or warden of St
        Mary's hospital, Bootham, York.   Ind: Cawood Castle,
        8 December 1398.

299.   Licence for non-residence, during pleasure, granted to Thomas
        Carnica, rector of Settrington, whilst in the service of Henry
        Percy, earl of Northumberland.   He may farm out his rectory.
        Cawood Castle, 11 December 1398.

300.   Institution of William Rolleston, chaplain, to the vicarage of
        Helmsley, vacant by the death of William de Dryffeld, on the
        presentation of the prior and convent of Kirkham.   Ind:
        Cawood Castle, 20 January 1398/9.

301.   Note of a licence for non-residence for one year, in order to
        study, granted to Thomas Kellow, rector of Lythe.   He may farm
        out his rectory, and be represented by proxy at synods.   Cawood,
        28 January 1398/9.

302.   Memorandum of a licence granted to John de Seggesfeld, parish
        priest of Guisborough, to act as penitentiary throughout the
        archdeaconry of Cleveland for one year, even in cases reserved
        to the archbishop (other than violations of the liberties and
        immunities of the Minsters at York, Beverley, Ripon, and
        Southwell; invasions of the archbishop's parks and poaching
        of game; perjury in assizes and indictments; matrimonial or
        divorce cases; and cases concerning disinheritance, loss of
        life or limb, or of the greater part of goods).   Cawood,
        22 January 1398/9.

303.   Memorandum of similar licences granted to John Paa, parish
        priest of Lastingham, and to Roger, parish priest of Whitby,
        to act as penitentiaries throughout the archdeaconry of
        Cleveland for one year.   Cawood, 22 January 1398/9.

304.   Note of a licence for non-residence for one year, in order to
        study, granted to M. Brian Farefax, rector of Gilling in
        Ryedale.   He may farm out the rectory, and be represented by
        proxy at synods held at York.   Cawood Castle, 3 February
        1398/9.

305.   [ff.47v-48] Licence to Thomas Spaunton, priest, of Guisborough,
        to act as penitentiary to Ralph de Lumle, knt., his wife, and
        twelve persons, clerical and lay, of both sexes, until Whitsun
        next following [18 May], even in cases reserved to the arch-
        bishop (other than injuries, violations, and offences against
        the archbishop and the church of York, attacks and inflictions
        on churches and their beneficed clergy, wounding of priests,
        mutilation of clerks and the spilling of their blood by
        violence, perjury in assizes both in secular courts and in
        matrimonial and other cases subject to ecclesiastical
        jurisdiction, homicide, and the corruption and carnal knowledge
        of nuns).   Cawood Castle, 4 March 1398/9.

306.   [f.48] Note of a licence for non-residence, during pleasure, granted to M. John Barnard, rector of Kirkleatham. He may farm out the rectory, and be represented by proxy at synods held in York Minster. Cawood, 9 April 1399.

307.   Note of letters dimissory granted to John Crosseby of Riccall, having his first tonsure, to receive remaining orders. Lodgings near Westminster, 10 November 1399.

308.   Note that the institution of the vicar of Huntington had been entered as the final entry of f.7 of the first quire relating to the archdeaconry of York. (1)

309.   [ff.48-48v] Certificate of the Official of the archdeacon of Cleveland, reciting an archiepiscopal commission (dated at Bishopthorpe, 11 December 1399) to inquire into the vacancy and patronage of the church of Crathorne, to which the prior and convent of Guisborough had presented Robert [de] Crathorn, clerk. An inquisition had been held in Crathorne church on Saturday, 13 December, attended by Thomas Bows and William Salisbyry, rectors of West Rounton and Kirkby in Cleveland, and Thomas Ermyn, William Shelford, and Thomas Ellerbek, chaplains of 'Castel', 'Wynton' (2) and Hutton Rudby. They had declared that Crathorne was vacant by the death of John Gretham, which had occurred on 8 December last; that Guisborough priory held the patronage and had presented Crathorn, who asserted that he was a clerk, although the inquisitors were ignorant of where and from whom he had received his first tonsure. The Official had instituted and inducted him to the rectory. Crathorne, 13 December 1399.

310.   [f.48v] Licence to John Symson, priest of a chantry in Wykeham chapel, to eat apart from his fellow chantry priest Thomas [Paule], on account of quarrels between them, but otherwise to perform all his chantry duties. Bishopthorpe, 26 February 1399/1400.

---

1.   i.e. f.21: see above, no.139.
2.   Unidentified. There is a Winton in Cleveland, but it seems too far away from Crathorne to be meant here. Wilton could be another possibility, particularly as it had a castle; while Castleton might serve to explain the first uncertain location. It is not clear from the text whether one or two places are intended to be named, although the latter seems more likely. There is also the possibility of a scribal error, either the omission of the actual castle name, or a total misreading from the original document, East Rounton perhaps being meant. I have not been able to find either Thomas Ermyn or William Shelford in James Torre's list of clergy for the archdeaconry of Cleveland [York Minster Muniment Room, L1 (9)].

311.   Note of letters dimissory granted to Thomas Bywell and Alan
        Elmeden, canons of Guisborough and subdeacons, to receive
        deacon's and priest's orders.   Bishopthorpe, 8 March 1399/1400.

312.   Acquittal of Robert Crathorn, rector of Crathorne, from the
        charge of having been instituted to his rectory prior to
        ordination.   Bishopthorpe, 30 June 1400.

313.   Licence for non-residence for one year, to attend the University
        of Oxford, according to the constitution Cum ex eo, granted to
        Robert Crathorn, rector of Crathorne, subdeacon.   He need not
        proceed to higher orders during the period of non-residence.
        He must provide a proxy for duties at Crathorne.   Bishopthorpe,
        2 July 1400.

314.   Institution of Richard de Thornton, priest, to the rectory of
        a mediety of South Otterington, on the presentation of John de
        Wadeslay, knt.   Ind: Cawood Castle, 4 August 1400.

315.   [ff.48v-49] Institution of John [de] Yngelby, priest, to the
        vicarage of Marske by the Sea, vacant by the death of William
        de Thorp, on the presentation of the prior and convent of
        Guisborough.   Ind: Cawood Castle, 20 August 1400.

316.   [f.49] Note of a licence for non-residence for three years,
        granted to John Midelton, rectory of Brandsby.   He may farm
        out the rectory, and be represented by proxy at synods.
        Cawood, 30 September 1400.

317.   Note of a similar licence for non-residence for two years,
        granted to Richard Malton, rector of Thornton in Pickering Lythe.
        Bishop Burton, 18 March 1400/1.

318.   Institution of br. William de Crayk, canon of Marton, to the
        vicarage of Sutton on the Forest, on the presentation of the
        prior and convent of Marton.   Ind: Cawood Castle, 5 July
        1401.

319.   Institution of Adam de Ebor', canon of Marton, to the vicarage
        of Sheriff Hutton, on the presentation of the prior and convent
        of Marton.   Ind: Cawood Castle, 9 July 1401.

320.   Note of a licence for non-residence for three years, granted
        to Edmund de Barton, rector of Barton le Street.   He may farm
        out the rectory, and be represented by proxy at synods.
        Bishopthorpe, 11 November 1401.

321.   Institution of M. John Fraunces, in the person of William de
        Salysberi, his proctor, to the rectory of Kirkby in Cleveland,
        vacant by the resignation of the said William, on the
        presentation of the abbot and convent of Whitby.   Ind: Cawood
        Castle, 25 February 1401/2.

322.   [ff.49-49v] Confirmation of the appropriation to Malton priory
        of the church of Malton and its chapels, the church of
        Wintringham and its chapel at Knapton, and the churches of
        Norton and Marton on the Forest, with part of the tithes of
        Brind, following examination of title, and approval of the
        arrangement whereby the churches of Malton, Wintringham, and
        Norton are served by members of the community or temporary
        secular priests rather than by perpetual vicars. Cawood
        Castle, 7 April 1402.

323.   [f.50] Confirmation of the appropriation to Guisborough priory
        of the churches of Guisborough, Danby, Skelton in Cleveland,
        Kirk Leavington, Ingleby Arncliffe, Kirkburn, Hessle, Sherburn
        in Harford Lythe, Ormesby, Marton in Cleveland, Stainton, and
        Marske by the Sea, and the chapels of Brotton, Yarm, East
        Harlsey, Eston, West Acklam, and Thornaby, together with
        pensions of 20s. from the church of Easington in Cleveland,
        five marks from the church of Welbury, half a mark from
        Crathorne church, and ten marks from Hessle church, following
        examination of title; and approval of the arrangement whereby
        the churches of Guisborough, Danby, Skelton in Cleveland, Kirk
        Leavington, and Ingleby Arncliffe are served by stipendiary
        priests without any vicarage being ordained.   Rest, 24 May
        1402.

324.   [ff.50-50v] Certificate of M. John de Suthwell, LL.B.,
        Receiver-general at York, reciting an archiepiscopal commission
        (dated at Rest, 12 June 1402), to receive the resignation of
        Henry Nundy, rector of Foston, and institute his successor.
        He had received the resignation in the presence of John de
        Lepyngton, clerk, notary public and Suthwell's scribe, and
        others.   He had also instituted M. Roger de Esyngwald, clerk,
        LL.B., to the rectory, on the presentation of the abbot and
        convent of St Mary, York, and had ordered the archdeacon of
        Cleveland or his Official to induct him.   Sealed with the
        seal of the Officiality of the court of York quod ad presens
        in custodia nostra habemus.   York, 17 June 1402.

325.   [f.50v] Notarial instrument recording the absolution of br.
        Robert de Esby, monk of Rievaulx, from the excommunication
        incurred for administering the sacraments to Roger Sissotson,
        from another parish, contrary to canonical sanctions.   He had
        appeared before the archbishop at Cawood to acknowledge his
        crime and submit to judgement.   Within a year he must obtain
        plenary remission from the Roman Curia, either in person or by
        proxy.   He must also personally say the Pater noster and Ave
        five times each on bended knee at the tomb of St William in
        York Minster and make an offering of one groat.   In the
        presence of M. Richard Conyngston, LL.D., archbishop's
        chancellor, Robert Oxton, canon of York, John Harwod, advocate
        of the court of York, Thomas Burstall, notary public, and
        John de Welton, notary public and scribe of the archbishop.
        Cawood, 7 August 1401.

326.   [ff.50v-51] Ordination for the union of two chantries, one in
       Stillingfleet church, the other in the chapel of St Nicholas,
       Naburn, at the petition of Henry Acclom, the patron.   Both
       chantries were originally established for the support of
       separate secular chaplains, but are now vacant, and their
       income so reduced as to be barely sufficient for the
       maintenance of one priest.   The united chantry is to be
       settled in the chapel of St Anne which Acclom had built near
       his manor of Moreby, the services being held there according
       to the original ordinations, except that the Tuesday masses in
       each week are to be said by the chaplain at the customary hours
       in the chapel at Naburn for the parishioners, so long as they
       provide a clerk and other ornaments for the celebration, while
       on double feasts and other major days (unless they fall on a
       Tuesday) the chaplain is to participate in the High Mass at
       Stillingfleet.   The method of presentation set out in the
       original ordinations is to be preserved.   Acclom and his heirs
       accept responsibility for the upkeep of the chapel of St Anne,
       and if they do not carry out any required repairs or rebuilding
       within two months of being cautioned, the chaplain may withdraw
       to continue his celebrations at either Stillingfleet or Naburn,
       on instructions from the archbishop or his successors, until the
       repairs are effected.   Other aspects of the original
       ordinations are to be retained without alteration.   Rest
       [blank] 1402.

327.   [f.51] Institution of John Midilsburgh, priest, to the rectory
       of Terrington, on the presentation of Thomas Metham, knt.
       Ind: Scrooby, 26 September 1402.

328.   Memorandum of a licence for non-residence for three years
       granted to John Seggefeld, rector of Stokesley.   He may
       farm out the rectory, and is excused personal appearance at
       synods, but must ensure that the services and cure of souls
       are not neglected.   Rest, 12 August 1402.

329.   [ff.51-51v] Confirmation of the appropriation to Whitby abbey
       of the churches of Seamer, Hackness, Whitby, Great Ayton,
       Ingleby Greenhow and Middlesbrough, with their dependent chapels
       together with parts of the tithes of sheaves at Nafferton and
       Foxholes, and pensions of 40s. from the church of Hutton Buscel,
       6s. 8d. from the church of Sutton on Derwent, 66s. 8d. from the
       church of Kirkby in Cleveland, 13s. 4d. from Slingsby church,
       13s. 4d. from Huntington church, and 13s. 4d. from Skirpenbeck
       church, following examination of title.   Rest, 18 September
       1402.

330.   [f.51v] Institution of br. Roger de Budesby, canon of Marton,
       to the vicarage of Sheriff Hutton, on the presentation of the
       prior and convent of Marton.   Ind: York, 16 January 1402/3.

331.   Certificate of Henry [Beaufort], bishop of Lincoln, reciting an
       archiepiscopal commission (dated at Scrooby, 11 June 1403) for
       an exchange of benefices between William Fawdon, rector of Brant

331.   Broughton, dioc. Lincoln, and William Peek, rector of Middleton
          in Pickering Lythe.   He had received Peek's resignation, and
          had instituted Fawdon to Middleton, on the presentation of
          Elizabeth Juliers, countess of Kent.   Lincoln, 24 June 1403.

          Ind: for Fawdon to Middleton in Pickering Lythe.   Scrooby,
          28 June 1403.

332.   [f.52] Institution of Thomas de Wykersley to the rectory of
          Stokesley, vacant by the resignation of John Seggefeld, in
          exchange for the parish church of Birkin, on the presentation
          of the abbot and convent of St Mary, York.   Ind: Cawood
          Castle, 5 February 1404/5.

333.   Institution of John Sandon, priest, in the person of John Kelk,
          his proctor, to the rectory of Kirkleatham, vacant by the
          resignation of M. John Bernard, on the presentation of William
          Trescour and William Marcheford, citizens of London.   Ind:
          Pontefract Castle, 1 July 1404.

334.   Institution of M. John Bernard, priest, lic.leg., to the
          rectory of Kirkleatham, vacant by the resignation of John
          Sandon, priest, on the presentation of William Marcheford and
          William Trescour, citizens of London.   Ind: Cawood Castle,
          6 January 1404/5.

          Memorandum that Bernard swore to observe the ordination
          concerning the above church, in the presence of M. Richard
          Conyngeston, archbishop's chancellor, and M. John Gylby,
          archbishop's registrar.   Cawood Castle, 6 January 1404/5.

335.   Institution of Thomas de Watton, priest, to the rectory of
          Brafferton, vacant by the resignation of M. Robert Appilgarth
          in exchange for the parish church of St Michael, Coney Street,
          York, on the presentation of the prior and convent of Newburgh.
          Ind: Cawood Castle, 24 February 1404/5.

336.   [ff.52-52v] Certificate of M. Thomas Weston, lic.leg., canon
          of York, reciting an archiepiscopal commission (dated at Cawood
          Castle, 1 February 1404/5) to inquire into the vacancy and
          patronage of the church of Kirkby in Cleveland, to which the
          abbot and convent of Whitby had presented John Bollesore,
          clerk, following the resignation tendered by John Savage as
          proctor for M. John Franceys, the last rector.   Following an
          inquisition, Weston had instituted Bollesore to the rectory,
          had caused him to be inducted, and received the oath of
          obedience.   Sealed with the seal of M. John Barnet, Official
          of the court of Canterbury, having been summoned for the
          purpose.   London, 23 February 1404/5.

          [ff.53-54v: MISSING]

337.   Institution of William son of John son of Roger of South
         Dalton, to the perpetual chantry of the Holy Trinity, Etton,
         vacant by the death of Patrick Scott, on the presentation of
         William Jakelyn of Etton.   Ind: York (under the seal of the
         vicar-general), 28 June 1398.

338.   Memorandum of the appointment of William Ryell, parochial
         chaplain at the altar of St Martin in the Charnel at Beverley,
         as penitentiary within his parish for one year.   Rest, 5 July
         1398.

339.   Licence for non-residence for two years, in order to visit the
         Holy Sepulchre and the shrines of St Peter, St Paul, and
         St James, granted to John Mayson, vicar of Lund.   He may farm
         out the vicarage, and be represented by proxy at synods.   He
         must also arrange for a replacement to carry out his duties at
         Lund.   Rest, 29 July 1398.

340.   Commission from Roger [Walden], archbishop of Canterbury, to
         the archbishop of York, for an exchange of benefices between
         M. Henry Hamerton, rector of Lockington, and William Morewyk,
         rector of Biddenden, dioc. Canterbury.   He is to receive
         Morewyk's resignation, and institute Hamerton to Biddenden, on
         Walden's collation.   Croydon, 25 July 1398.

341.   Collation (by virtue of the above commission) of the rectory of
         Biddenden, dioc. Canterbury, vacant by reason of the above
         exchange, to M. Henry Hamerton, chaplain, in the person of
         William Sarle, deacon, his proctor.   Rest, 1 August 1398.

342.   Institution of William Morewyk, chaplain, to the rectory of
         Lockington following the above exchange, on the presentation
         of King Richard II in his right as guardian of the heir to
         Maule (2), a minor.   Ind: Rest, 1 August 1398.

343.   [f.55v] Commission to M. John de Neuton, LL.D., treasurer of
         York Minster and Official of the court of York, to inquire into
         the vacancy and patronage of the church of Sproatley, to which
         the prior and convent of Bridlington had presented Richard
         Ulverston, clerk.   If all is well, and Ulverston is found
         suitable, he is to institute him and order his induction.
         Rest, 11 August 1398.

---

1.   In the institutions throughout this section it may be assumed
       that, unless otherwise indicated, mandates for induction were
       issued on the same day as the institution, to the archdeacon of
       the East Riding, or his Official, or either of them.
2.   This heir was Peter de Mauley VIII, who had succeeded his
       grandfather in 1383.

54

344.   Memorandum of a licence for non-residence for one year granted
        to John de Newburgh, rector of Roos. He may farm out the
        rectory, and is excused appearance at synods.   Rest, 19 August
        1398.

345.   Memorandum of the appointment during pleasure of br. John
        ʒereslay and br. William Sleghtholme, canons of Bridlington, as
        penitentiaries, particularly for their fellow canons, other than
        in reserved cases.   Rest, [blank], 1398.

346.   Institution of Thomas Martyn, chaplain, to the rectory of Hotham,
        vacant by the death of Ralph Wresill, on the presentation of
        Joan, widow of John Ask, domicellus.   Ind: Rest, 30 August
        1398.

347.   Memorandum of a dispensation granted to John de Howme, clerk, in
        accordance with apostolic letters, to receive orders and acquire a
        benefice, notwithstanding that he was the son of a single man and
        a single woman.   Rest, 17 September 1398.

348.   Note of a licence for non-residence for one year granted to John
        Colne, rector of Rowley.   He may farm out the rectory, and is
        excused appearance at the archbishop's synods.   Rest, 2 October
        1398.

349.   Note of the appointment of Richard Askam, vicar of Scarborough,
        as penitentiary within the town of Scarborough, other than in
        reserved cases.   Rest, 4 October 1398.

350.   Memorandum of a licence for non-residence for one year granted
        to William Wyndefeld, rector of Thorpe Bassett.   He may farm
        out the rectory, and may be represented by proxy at synods.
        Rest, 5 October 1398.

351.   [ff.55v-56] Commission to William Fulman, chaplain, to act as
        coadjutor to Roger Py, vicar of Rillington, on account of his
        illness.   Rest, 4 October 1398.

352.   [f.56] Memorandum of a licence for non-residence for two years,
        in order to go on pilgrimage and visit the shrines of St Peter
        and St Paul, granted to William Leke, vicar of Wharram Percy.
        He may farm out the vicarage, and may be represented by proxy at
        synods at York.   Cawood, 14 November 1398.

353.   Institution of John Clerk of Sheriff Hutton, chaplain, to the
        vicarage of Sancton, on the presentation of the prior and convent
        of Watton.   Ind: Cawood Castle, 10 December 1398.

354.   Bull of Pope Boniface IX to William [Northbrugge], bishop
        Pharensis, recording that he had been provided to his see by
        Urban VI, but because of the difficulties of access and its
        distance, he had been unable to exercise administration or
        maintain his episcopal dignity.   Therefore he, a professor of
        the order of friars preachers, is given licence to acquire a

354.   benefice.   St Peter's, Rome, 27 September 1396.

355.   Collation of the vicarage of Nafferton to William [Northbrugge],
        bishop Pharensis and suffragan of York, by virtue of the above
        papal licence.   Cawood Castle, 7 January 1398/9.

356.   [ff.56–56v] Memorandum of the appointment of John [Clerk],
        rector of Catwick, as penitentiary within the archdeaconry
        of the East Riding, even in reserved cases (other than
        violations of the liberties and immunities of the minsters at
        York, Beverley, Ripon and Southwell; invasions of the arch-
        bishop's parks and poaching of game; perjury in assizes and
        indictments, matrimonial and divorce cases, and cases
        concerning disinheritance, loss of life or limb, or the greater
        part of goods).   Cawood, 22 January 1398/9.

357.   [f.56v] Memorandum of the similar appointment of Thomas de
        Semer, rector of a mediety of Thwing, as penitentiary for one
        year.   Cawood, 22 January 1398/9.

358.   Memorandum of a licence granted to John Forster, chantry priest
        at the altar of St Nicholas in Lund parish church, to celebrate
        private masses elsewhere for one year, on account of the poverty
        of his benefice, provided that he maintains his chantry
        obligations as far as possible.   Cawood, 20 February 1398/9.

359.   Memorandum of letters dimissory granted to Robert Burne of
        Kirkburn, having his first tonsure, to receive minor and holy
        orders.   Cawood, 22 February 1398/9.

360.   Note of similar letters granted to John de Garton in Holdernes,
        acolyte.   Cawood, 22 February 1398/9.

361.   Note of similar letters granted to Richard Hardyng, acolyte.
        Cawood, 22 February 1398/9.

362.   Note of similar letters granted to William Downe, subdeacon.
        Cawood, 22 February 1398/9.

363.   Note of a licence granted to William Sawer, rector of Nuthill,
        to celebrate private masses and receive a salary, on account
        of the poverty of his benefice, provided that the church
        services are maintained as far as possible.   Cawood,
        23 February 1398/9.

364.   Commission to the archbishop from Francis [Carboni], cardinal
        priest of St Susanna and papal penitentiary, to inquire into
        the case of Thomas Dauncell of Pocklington, scholar, who wished
        to become a cleric, receive orders, and acquire a benefice,
        notwithstanding that he was the son of a married man and a
        single woman.   After inquiry the archbishop may, if he sees
        fit, grant the necessary dispensation.   St Peter's, Rome,
        17 March 1389/90.

56

365.   Notification that, following the above letters, the archbishop
        had granted the necessary dispensation to Thomas Dauncell, clerk.
        Cawood Castle, 27 February 1398/9.

366.   Licence for non-residence until the feast of St Martin next
        following, on account of illness, granted to Nicholas de Dighton,
        vicar of North Cave.   A proctor must take over his duties.
        Cawood Castle, 27 February 1398/9.

367.   [ff.56v-57] Notarial instrument recording the archbishop's
        nomination of M. John Hildiard to an annual pension from Kirkham
        priory, by reason of the vacancy of the priory, and confirmation
        of the election of a new prior which had occurred during the
        vacancy of the see.   In the presence of M. John de Neuton, LL.D.,
        treasurer of York Minster, and M. Robert [de] Appilton [Appelton],
        jurisperitus (they having been deputed by the chapter of York to
        attend the archbishop on certain matters), Robert Wlfeden,
        precentor of Lichfield cathedral, Thomas Hilton, canon of Lincoln,
        John de Harwode, advocate of the court of York, and Thomas
        Burstall and John Welton, notaries public.   A room contiguous to
        the chapel, Cawood Castle, 20 December 1398.

368.   [f.57] Institution of Richard Garton, priest, to the perpetual
        chantry in the chapel of St Mary, Molescroft, vacant by the
        death of Thomas Cokerell, at the nomination of Robert Ledes of
        York, and on the presentation of the chapter of Beverley Minster.
        Ind: Dean of Beverley.   Cawood Castle, 11 April 1399.

369.   Institution of Nicholas de Neuton, priest, to the vicarage of
        North Cave, on the presentation of the prior and convent of
        the Charterhouse of St Michael, Kingston upon Hull.   Ind:
        Cawood Castle, 16 April 1399.

370.   Institution of William de Sherburn, priest, to the perpetual
        chantry founded at the altar of St James the Apostle in
        Scarborough parish church for the souls of Robert Galon, Gregory
        de Brydlyngton, and Alice and Agnes their wives, vacant by the
        resignation of Robert de Bukton, on the presentation of Alan
        Waldife and Robert Shilbotell, bailiffs, and the commonalty of
        Scarborough.   Ind: Cawood Castle, 23 April 1399.

371.   Note of a licence for non-residence for one year granted to
        M. Peter de Stapilton, rector of Beeford.   He may farm out the
        rectory, and be represented by proxy at synods.   Cawood,
        2 June 1399.

372.   [f.57v] Institution of Ralph de Bottelom, priest, to the
        vicarage of Boynton, vacant by the death of Stephen de Ryse, on
        the presentation of the prior and convent of Bridlington.   Ind:
        Cawood Castle, 14 June 1399.

373.   Certificate of John Burbache, LL.D., canon of Lincoln and vicar-
        general of Henry [Beaufort], bishop of Lincoln, he being absent,
        reciting an archiepiscopal commission (dated at Cawood Castle,

373.   28 May 1399) for an exchange of benefices between John de
        Neuburgh, rector of Roos, and John Pygot, rector of Norton
        juxta Twycross, dioc. Lincoln.   He had received Neuburgh's
        resignation, and instituted Pygot to Roos on the presentation
        of the prior and convent of Kirkham.   Lyddington, 1 June 1399.

374.   Ind: for Pygot to Roos, obedience having been offered by
        William Wardell, vicar of Ellingham, dioc. Durham, his proctor.
        Pontefract priory, 16 June 1399.

375.   Institution of Robert Berdesay priest, to the vicarage of Paull,
        on the presentation of the abbot and convent of Kirkstall.
        Ind: Cawood Castle, 20 June 1399.

376.   Institution of Nicholas Harpame, priest, to the perpetual
        chantry in the chapel of St Mary, Molescroft, vacant by the
        resignation of Richard de Garton, at the nomination of Robert
        de Ledes of York, and on the presentation of the chapter of
        Beverley Minster.   Ind: Dean of Beverley.   Rest, 29 July
        1399.

377.   Note of a licence granted to Nicholas Harpame to celebrate
        private masses for two years and receive a suitable salary,
        provided that he does not neglect his chantry responsibilities
        at Molescroft.   Rest, 31 July 1399.

378.   [f.58] Institution of Thomas Clyff, priest, to the rectory of
        Goodmanham, vacant by the death of Robert Lewys, on the
        presentation of William Grymeston of Holderness, domicellus.
        Ind: Rest, 13 August 1399.

379.   Note of letters dimissory granted to Nicholas Hugon of
        Skeffling, having his first tonsure, to receive remaining orders.
        Lodgings near Westminster, 6 November 1399.

380.   Institution of John Broun, priest, to the perpetual chantry
        recently founded in the chapel of St Nicholas, Wansford, on the
        presentation of Richard Broune, priest.   Ind: Bishopthorpe,
        26 November 1399.

381.   Institution of John Sylesthorn, priest, to the chantry of
        St Stephen, protomartyr, in the church of St Mary, Scarborough,
        on the presentation of the bailiffs and burgesses of
        Scarborough.   Ind: Bishopthorpe, 2 December 1399.

382.   Dispensation to M. Richard Shropham, M.A., having his first
        tonsure, to receive holy orders notwithstanding a defect of
        sight.   Bishopthorpe, 18 December 1399.

383.   Note of the grant of letters dimissory to Robert Frauncyss,
        having his first tonsure, to receive remaining orders.
        Bishopthorpe, 20 December 1399.

384. Note of similar letters granted to John Walkyngton, subdeacon, to receive deacon's and priest's orders.   Bishopthorpe, 20 December 1399.

385. Institution of John Wryght, priest, to the rectory of Holme on Spalding Moor, vacant by the death of John German, on the presentation of Robert Conestabill, knt.   Ind: Bishopthorpe, 5 January 1399/1400.

386. [f.58v] Institution of Thomas Cotese, priest, to the perpetual chantry at Flamborough, vacant by the resignation of John Wryght, on the presentation of Robert Conestabill, knt.   Ind: Bishopthorpe, 7 January 1399/1400.

387. Institution of Nicholas Hugon of Skeffling, deacon, to the vicarage of Skeckling, vacant by the resignation of John Broune, on the presentation of the abbot and convent of Kirkstall. Ind: (1) Bishop Burton, 15 March 1399/1400.

388. Institution of Robert Grome, priest, to the chantry founded for the dean and canons of York and William de Roos and his successors, in the parish church of Lowthorpe, vacant by the resignation of Thomas Hobyn, in the person of John at Westend, priest, his proctor, in exchange for the chantry founded in the same church for the patron thereof, on the presentation of the chapter of York, the dean being absent.   Bishop Burton, 15 March 1399/1400.

389. Institution of Thomas Hobyn, priest, in the person of John at Westend, priest, his proctor, to the chantry founded for the patron in Lowthorpe parish church, following the above exchange, on the presentation of John de Hothom, knt.   Bishop Burton, 15 March 1399/1400.

   Ind: for Grome and Hobyn to their respective chantries, Hobyn having offered obedience by proxy, and Grome having done so in person.   Bishop Burton, 15 March 1399/1400.

390. Collation of the wardenship or mastership of the hospital of St Mary Magdalen, Killingwoldgraves, to William [Northbrugge], bishop Pharensis.   Ind: M. William Thurbache, archbishop's registrar.   Bishop Burton, 20 March 1399/1400.

391. Institution of Simon Wentislaw, priest, to the rectory of Cowlam, vacant by the death of Thomas Hassok, on the presentation of William de Grymston, domicellus.   Ind: Bishop Burton, 24 March 1399/1400.

392. [f.59] Letters testimonial to Isabella de Burton, confirming her election as prioress of Nunkeeling and releasing to her the spiritualities and temporalities of the house.   Bishop Burton, 31 March 1400.

---

1. His name is mistakenly given as Hugh in the induction clause.

392.   Note that a mandate was issued to the Official of the archdeacon of the East Riding to induct and install Isabella de
Burton as prioress of Nunkeeling.   Bishop Burton, 31 March
1400.

393.   Certificate of the Official of the archdeacon of the East
Riding, reciting an archiepiscopal commission (dated at
Bishopthorpe, 27 November 1399) to inquire into the vacancy and
patronage of the chapel at Argam, to which Richard Raper,
priest, had been presented by John de Ask, domicellus.   An
inquisition had been held in full chapter in Lowthorpe church
on 10 December 1399, attended by John Dyghton of Lowthorpe and
Thomas de Thyng (sic), rectors, and John Mounceux of Carnaby,
John Ward of Rudston, and William Burton of Ganton, vicars,
with the following priests of the neighbourhood: John Westende,
William Twng (sic), John Brasse of Lowthorpe, William Fosseton
of Carnaby, Peter Barker of Harpham, John Bugge of Rudston,
and William Scharpyng of Nafferton.   They had declared that
the chapel was vacant by the resignation of John Gresacre,
which had occurred on 21 November last; and that Ask was
patron in right of his wife, and had made the last presentation.
The Official had instituted Raper, and caused him to be
inducted.   Lowthorpe, 10 December 1399.

394.   Note of a licence granted to Thomas Martyn, [rector] of Hotham,
to be represented by proxy at the synod to be held at York
Minster after the following Easter.   Bishop Burton, 24 April
1400.

395.   Note of a licence for non-residence granted to Robert de Neuton,
rector of Kirby Underdale, whilst in the service of Stephen
Lescrop, knt., lord of Masham, brother to the archbishop.   He
may farm out his rectory, and be represented by proxy at synods.
Bishop Burton, 27 April 1400.

396.   Note of a licence granted to [John Colne] (1), rector of Rowley,
to be represented by proxy at the synods to be held at York at
Easter and Michaelmas next following.   Bishop Burton, 26 April
1400.

397.   [f.59v] Dispensation to John de Lekynfeld clerk, dioc. York,
in accordance with a commission from Francis [Carboni],
cardinal priest of St Susanna and papal penitentiary (recited
in full, and dated at St Peter's, Rome, 29 January 1399/1400)(2),
to receive orders and acquire a benefice, notwithstanding that
he was the son of a single man and a single woman.   He had
concealed the fact when being ordained to his first tonsure and
as acolyte.   Bishop Burton, 7 May 1400.

---

1.   MS: blank.
2.   In this commission the recipient is described as a scholar.

398. Dispensation to Edmund, son of Roger Constabile, clerk, dioc. York, in accordance with a commission from Francis [Carboni], cardinal priest of St Susanna and papal penitentiary (recited in full, and dated at St Peter's, Rome, 22 March 1398/9), to receive orders and acquire a benefice, notwithstanding that he was the son of a single man and a single woman. He had concealed the fact when being ordained to his first tonsure and as acolyte. Bishop Burton, 11 June 1400.

399. [f.60] Note that the Official of the archdeacon of the East Riding, acting on an archiepiscopal commission (dated at Bishopthorpe, 5 March 1399/1400), had instituted and inducted William Bromley, clerk, to the chapelries of Octon and Swaythorpe, vacant by the resignations of Marmaduke Stanell and Adam Cok because of the insufficiency of the income, and on the presentation of King Henry IV. This followed an inquisition into the vacancy and patronage, which had declared that Thomas Thweng, lord of Octon and Swaythorpe, had presented Stanell and Cok, but that the patronage had since reverted to the Crown by escheat. Filey parish church, 10 March 1399/1400.

400. Dispensation to William de Sutton, clerk, dioc. York, in accordance with a commission from Francis [Carboni], cardinal priest of St Susanna and papal penitentiary (recited in full, and dated at St Peter's, Rome, 22 December 1399) (1), to receive orders and acquire a benefice, notwithstanding that he was the son of a single man and a single woman. He had concealed the fact when being ordained to his first tonsure and as acolyte. Bishop Burton, 11 June 1400.

401. [ff.60-60v] Certificate of Henry [Beaufort], bishop of Lincoln, reciting [incompletely] an archiepiscopal commission (dated at Cawood Castle, 6 August 1400) for an exchange of benefices between John [de] Walkyngton [Walkington], rector of Sedgebrook, dioc. Lincoln, and John de Collum [Collom], rector of Rowley. He had received Collum's resignation, and had instituted Walkyngton to Rowley, on the presentation of King Henry IV by reason of the forfeiture of Thomas [Holand], late earl of Kent. Stow Park, 8 August 1400.

[f.60v] Ind: for Walkyngton to Rowley. Cawood, 10 August 1400.

402. Collation of the vicarage of Nafferton to William Morpath, priest. Ind: Cawood Castle, 17 August 1400.

403. Confirmation, following examination of title, of the appropriation to Watton priory of the church of Hutton Cranswick. Cawood Castle, 17 August 1400. (2)

---

1. In this commission the recipient is described as a scholar.
2. A space is left in the middle of this document for the insertion of the name of the monk who represented the priory as its proctor in this case.

404.   Collation of a perpetual chantry in Lowthorpe parish church
        vacant by the resignation of Peter Brid, to Stephen de
        Skeftling, priest.   Ind: Cawood Castle, 25 September 1400.

405.   Institution of Richard Smyth of Garton to the vicarage of
        Garton in Holderness, on the presentation of the abbot and
        convent of Thornton, dioc. Lincoln.   Ind: Cawood Castle,
        28 September 1400.

406.   Note of a licence for non-residence for three years granted to
        William Syxendale, rector of Nunburnholme.   He may farm out
        the rectory, and be represented by proxy at synods held at
        York.   Cawood, 30 September 1400.

407.   [f.61] Note that the Official of the archdeacon of the East
        Riding, acting on an archiepiscopal commission dated at Scrooby,
        19 October 1400, had instituted and inducted br. John de Barton
        to the vicarage of Hessle with the chapel of Holy Trinity,
        Kingston upon Hull, vacant by the death of br. Richard Marke,
        canon of Guisborough, on the presentation of the prior and
        convent of that house, and following an inquisition which had
        confirmed their patronage.   Holy Trinity chapel, Kingston
        upon Hull, 24 October 1400.

408.   Institution of John Croft, priest, to the vicarage of Garton in
        Holderness, vacant by the resignation of Richard Smyth, on the
        presentation of the abbot and convent of Thornton, dioc.
        Lincoln.   Ind: Scrooby, 27 November 1400.

409.   Note that the Official of the archdeacon of the East Riding,
        acting on an archiepiscopal commission dated at Scrooby,
        20 January 1400/1, had instituted and inducted Walter de
        Wynteryngham, priest, to the vicarage of Garton on the Wolds,
        vacant by the death of William [de] Attynwyk, on the
        presentation of the prior and convent of Kirkham, and following
        an inquisition which had confirmed their patronage.   Thwing
        parish church, 27 January 1400/1.

410.   [ff.61-61v] Notarial instrument, reciting the resignation by
        M. Richard Shropham, chaplain, M.A., of the chantry of St
        Stephen in the church of St Mary, Scarborough.   In the presence
        of M. John Fyfhide, M.A., canon of Lincoln, and M. John
        Wykyngeston,   M.A., perpetual fellow of St Michael's College,
        Cambridge.   Attested by Walter de Sutton, clerk, dioc.
        Worcester, notary public.   In the notary's lodgings within the
        parish of Holy Trinity, Cambridge, 16 December 1400.

411.   [f.61v] Presentation of John [de] Newton, chaplain, to the
        above chantry, following the above resignation, by the bailiffs
        and burgesses of Scarborough.   Scarborough, 3 January
        1400/1. (1)

---

1.   The MS. gives the year as anno domini millesimo tricentisimo
        quadringentisimo, 2 Henry IV.

412.   [ff.61v-62] Certificate of the Official of the archdeacon of
        the East Riding, reciting an archiepiscopal commission (dated at
        Scrooby, 7 January 1400/1) to inquire into the vacancy and
        patronage of the above chantry, following the above presentation
        of John de Neuton, priest.   An inquisition had been held in the
        church of St Mary, Scarborough, on 13 January 1400/1, attended
        by the rectors of Scarborough and Thwing, the vicars of Seamer,
        Willerby, Reighton, Burton Fleming, and Scarborough, and the
        parochial chaplains of Hackness and Scarborough.   They had
        declared that the chantry was vacant by the above resignation of
        M. Richard Shroppam, that the bailiffs and burgesses of
        Scarborough were the patrons, and that Neuton was a suitable
        person to hold the chantry.   The Official had accordingly
        instituted him, and caused him to be inducted.   Scarborough,
        13 January 1400/1.

413.   [f.62] Note that the Official of the archdeacon of the East
        Riding, acting on an archiepiscopal commission (dated at Scrooby,
        13 January 1400/1), had instituted and inducted Richard Raygate,
        priest, to the vicarage of Ganton, vacant by the resignation of
        Roger Ake, on the presentation of the prior and convent of
        Bridlington, and following an inquisition which had confirmed
        their patronage.   Folkton parish church, 20 January 1400/1.

414.   [ff.62-62v] Certificate of Thomas de Weston, lic. leg., arch-
        deacon of Durham and vicar-general of Walter [Skirlaw], bishop
        of Durham, reciting [incompletely] an archiepiscopal commission
        (dated at Bishop Burton, 25 March 1401) for an exchange of
        benefices between Thomas Whihot, vicar of Heighington, dioc.
        Durham, and John de Catton, vicar of Folkton.   He had received
        Catton's resignation, in the person of William Marchall, priest,
        of Durham, his proctor, and had instituted Whihot to Folkton in
        the person of William de Norham, his proctor, and on the
        presentation of Joan de Graystok, lady de Lucy.   Sealed with
        the seal of the archdeaconry of Durham.   Greatham, 29 March 1401.

415.   [f.62v] Ind: for Whihot to Folkton.   18 April 1401.

416.   Collation of the rectory of Nunburnholme, vacant by the death of
        William de Sixindale, to Alan de Humbleton, priest, clerk of the
        archbishop's household.   Ind: Bishop Burton, 20 April 1401.

417.   Note of a licence for non-residence for two years granted to
        William Wynfeld, rector of Thorpe Bassett.   He may be
        represented by proxy at synods held at York.   Bishop Burton,
        1 May 1401.

418.   Institution of John de Kylburne, priest, to the rectory of
        Folkton, in the person of Robert Goldale, priest, his proctor,
        and on the presentation of Joan de Graystok, lady de Lucy.
        Ind: Bishop Burton, 20 May 1401.

419. Institution of John Laschyn, priest, to a perpetual chantry in the chapel of the college of Sutton in Holderness, vacant by the death of William Pypyne, on the presentation of Robert de Hilton, knt. Ind: Bishop Burton, 24 May 1401.

420. [f.63] Institution of Thomas Parker, clerk of the archbishop's household, to the rectory of Huggate, vacant by the resignation of M. Robert Appilton, on the presentation of the abbot and convent of St Mary, York. Ind: Bishop Burton, 28 May 1401.

421. Certificate of Robert Manfeld, provost of Beverley Minster, reciting an archiepiscopal commission (dated at Bishop Burton, 26 May 1401) for an exchange of benefices between Robert Marton, priest of the chantry of the Holy Trinity in Etton parish church, and Robert Clifton [Clyfton], priest of the chantry of the Holy Trinity in Burton Fleming church. He had received Marton's resignation and had instituted Clifton to the chantry at Etton, on the presentation of William Jakelyn, domicellus. Sealed with the seal of the Officiality of the spirituality of the provostship. Beverley, 5 June 1401.

422. Ind: for Clyfton to the chantry at Etton. 8 June 1401.

423. [ff.63-63v] Dispensation from Pope Boniface IX to John Pygote, senior, rector of Roos (the value of which does not exceed 60 marks a year), permitting him to acquire another benefice or dignity, although incompatible, even if a dignity, parsonage, or an office in a metropolitan, cathedral, or collegiate church, or a dignity with cure, below the pontifical in a metropolitan or cathedral church, or the principal in a collegiate church. The dispensation is for life, with authority to exchange and resign at will, on condition that the services and cure of souls at Roos and the other benefice are not neglected. St Peter's, Rome, 1 January 1400/1. (1)

424. [f.63v] Certificate of the chapter of Southwell, reciting [incompletely] an archiepiscopal commission (dated at Cawood Castle, 18 June 1401) for an exchange of benefices between William Morpath, vicar of Nafferton, and John York, vicar of the prebendal church of Dunham. They had received the resignations of both priests (that of York being offered by proxy), and had instituted York to Nafferton on the archbishop's collation. Chapter House, Southwell, 28 June 1401.

Ind: for York to Nafferton. Cawood, 4 July 1401.

425. Note of a licence for non-residence for one year granted to William Morewyk, rector of Lockington. He may farm out the rectory, and be represented by proxy at synods. Cawood, 28 July 1401.

---

1. CPL, V, 372; see also ibid., 371, 396.

426. [ff.63v-64] Dispensation to John Fryston, deacon, dioc. York, in accordance with a commission from Francis [Carboni], cardinal priest of St Susanna and papal penitentiary (recited in full, and dated at St Peter's, Rome, 25 December 1400), to receive priest's orders and acquire a benefice, notwithstanding that he was the son of a single man and a single woman, and had concealed the fact when acquiring clerical status, and being ordained to minor orders and as subdeacon and deacon. Rest, 23 September 1401.

427. [f.64] Institution of Richard Gyllyot, priest, to the wardenship of a chantry in the chapel called the Charnel at Scarborough (1), vacant by the resignation of Robert de Neweby, priest, on the presentation of King Henry IV. Ind: Bishopthorpe, 11 December 1401.

428. [ff.64-64v] Institution of Thomas del Chamber, priest, to the chantry of St Mary, Molescroft, near Beverley, vacant by the resignation of Nicholas Harpham, at the nomination of Robert Ledes of York and on the presentation of the chapter of Beverley. Ind: Dean of Beverley. Bishopthorpe, 8 January 1401/2.

429. [f.64v] Confirmation, following examination of title, of the appropriation to Warter priory of the churches of Lund and Warter, and a mediety of the chapel of Seaton Ross. Cawood, 7 April 1402.

430. [ff.64v-65] Confirmation, following examination of title, of the appropriation to Meaux abbey of the churches of Nafferton, Skipsea, Easington, and Keyingham, and two chapels which had been erected in districts within the archbishop's jurisdiction, one of them being served by six monks acting as chaplains, and the other, which had been constructed in a wood, being served by two secular chaplains. (2) Cawood, 7 April 1402.

431. [f.65] Institution of John Whtwell (sic), priest, to the vicarage of Kirby Grindalythe, on the presentation of the prior and convent of Kirkham. Ind: York, 13 April 1402.

432. Institution of William de Langton, priest, to the vicarage of Westow, on the presentation of the prior and convent of Kirkham. Ind: Rest, 11 May 1402.

---

1. A marginal note records that the chantry had only recently been founded.
2. These were two chantry chapels, the first of which had been built at the gates of the monastery for the chantry established by Richard de Otringham, while the other housed the chantry founded by Peter de Mauley I. See E.A. Bond (ed.), Chronica monasterii de Melsa (3 vols., Rolls Series, 1866-8), i, 106; ii, 59-61, 294-6.

433.   Certificate of John [Fordham], bishop of Ely, reciting
[incompletely] an archiepiscopal commission (dated at Cawood
Castle, 16 March 1401/2) for an exchange of benefices between
Alan de Humbleton, rector of Nunburnholme, and Thomas Robert,
rector of Downham, dioc. Ely.   He had received Humbleton's
resignation, and had instituted Robert to Nunburnholme, on the
archbishop's collation.   Somersham, 16 April 1402.

Ind: for Robert to Nunburnholme.   Rest, 22 April 1402.

434.   [f.65v] Confirmation, following examination of title, of the
appropriation to Haltemprice priory of the churches of Kirk
Ella and Wharram Percy, with their annexed chapels.   Rest,
17 April 1402.

435.   Institution of br. William Hessay, canon of Haltemprice, to
the vicarage of Wharram Percy, vacant by the resignation of
Alexander Herle, on the presentation of the prior and convent
of Haltemprice.   Ind: Rest, 23 May 1402.

436.   Certificate of Walter [Skirlaw], bishop of Durham, reciting
[incompletely] an archiepiscopal commission (dated at York,
19 May 1402) for an exchange of benefices between Ralph
Graystok [Graystoke], rector of Morpeth, dioc. Durham, and
John Kylburn, rector of Folkton.   He had received Kylburn's
resignation, and had instituted Graystok to Folkton, on the
presentation of Joan de Graystoke [Graystok], lady de Lucy.
Howden, 20 May 1402.

Ind: for Graystok to Folkton, obedience having been offered
by proxy.   Rest, 4 June 1402.

437.   [f.66] Institution of Robert Writh, priest, to the vicarage
of Yedingham, vacant by the death of John Pokley, on the
presentation of the prioress and convent of Yedingham.   Ind:
[not named].   Rest, 29 June 1402.

438.   Confirmation, following examination of title, of the
appropriation to Ellerton priory of the churches of Ellerton
and Aughton, with the latter's dependent chapel of Thorganby;
and approval of the arrangement whereby Ellerton was served by
a stipendiary chaplain rather than a perpetual vicar.   Rest,
12 August 1402.

439.   Institution of John Tyryngton, priest, to the chantry which
John Forster, chaplain, held in Lund parish church, on the
presentation of John [Beaufort], earl of Somerset.   Ind:
Beverley, 23 August 1402.

440.   [ff.66-66v] Confirmation, following examination of title, of
the appropriation to Kirkham priory of the churches of Kirby
Grindalythe, Westow, Crambe, Garton on the Wolds, Helmsley,
and St Peter, Walmgate, York, with annual pensions of 40s. from
Roos church and one mark from Burythorpe church.   York,
5 August 1402.

441.   [f.66v] Confirmation, following examination of title, of the
        appropriation to Bridlington priory of the churches of Bridling-
        ton, Flamborough, Carnaby, Ottringham, Filey, Atwick, Boynton,
        Ganton, Willerby, and Scalby, with their chapels, and even though
        there were no vicarages ordained at Bridlington, Ottringham,
        Flamborough, and Filey, together with an annual pension of one
        mark from Beeford church, and certain tithes of the church of
        Hunmanby.   Rest, 5 September 1402.

442.   Confirmation, following examination of title, of the
        appropriation to Bardney abbey, dioc. Lincoln, of the church of
        Hunmanby and its annexed chapels.   Rest, 25 September 1402.

443.   [ff.66v-67] Institution of Thomas de Poynton, chaplain, to the
        mastership or wardenship of the collegiate church or chapel of
        St James, Sutton in Holderness, vacant by the death of William
        de Barneby, at the nomination of the chaplains of the college,
        and on the presentation of Peter de Malo Lacu [Mauley] VIII,
        lord of Mulgrave and Doncaster.   Ind: Scrooby, 19 November 1402.

444.   [f.67] Institution of Richard ʒork, priest, to one of the five
        chantries in the collegiate chapel of St James, Sutton in
        Holderness, vacant by the resignation of Thomas de Poynton, on
        the nomination of the master and chaplains of the chapel, and on
        the presentation of Peter de Malo Lacu [Mauley] VIII, lord of
        Mulgrave and Doncaster.   Ind: Scrooby, 25 November 1402.

445.   Institution of John Randson, chaplain, to the vicarage of
        Sherburn in Harford Lythe, vacant by the resignation of John de
        Grymston, on the presentation of the prior and convent of
        Guisborough.   Ind: Scrooby, 1 February 1402/3.

446.   Institution of M. William de Wissenden, priest, to the vicarage
        of Hutton Cranswick, on the presentation of the prior and convent
        of Watton.   Ind: Scrooby, 9 April 1403.

447.   Note of a licence for non-residence for three years granted to
        William Wynfeld, rector of Thorpe Bassett.   He may farm out the
        rectory, and is excused personal appearance at synods.   Scrooby,
        20 May 1403.

448.   Institution of Nicholas Wayte, priest, to the vicarage of
        Aldbrough, on the presentation of the abbot and convent of
        Kirkstall.   Ind: Scrooby, 12 May 1403.

449.   Institution of John de Dalton, priest, to the vicarage of
        Kirby Grindalythe, on the presentation of the prior and convent
        of Kirkham.   Ind: Cawood, 6 August 1403.

450.   [f.67v] Institution of Thomas de Norton, priest, to the rectory
        of Skirpenbeck, vacant by the resignation of John Lund in
        exchange for the vicarage of Edwinstowe, on the presentation of
        the abbot and convent of Whitby.   Ind: Cawood Castle,
        23 April 1404.

451.   Certificate of Walter [Skirlaw], bishop of Durham, reciting an
        archiepiscopal commission (dated at Cawood Castle, 16 June
        1404) for an exchange of benefices between John Kilburne
        [Kelburne], rector of Morpeth, dioc. Durham, and M. Peter de
        Stapilton, rector of Beeford. He had received Stapilton's
        resignation, and had instituted Kilburne to Beeford, on the
        presentation of br. Robert Normanton, locum tenens of the prior
        of the Hospital of St John of Jerusalem in England.   Howden,
        16 June 1404.

        Ind: for Kilburne to Beeford.   Cawood, 17 June 1404.

452.   [ff.67v-68] Institution of William Frankys, priest, to the
        vicarage of North Frodingham, vacant by the resignation of
        Robert Frakys, on the presentation of the abbot and convent of
        Thornton, dioc. Lincoln.   Ind: Cawood Castle, 28 July 1404.

453.   [f.68] Presentation by the prior and convent of Guisborough
        of Thomas de Hayton, chaplain, to the archbishop, for
        institution to the vicarage of Kirkburn, vacant by the
        resignation of John Melreth.   They also submit to the
        archbishop's ordination regarding an annual pension of two and
        a half marks to be paid from the church to Melreth until he is
        provided to a rectory.   Guisborough, 27 November 1404.

454.   Institution of Thomas Hayton, chaplain, to the vicarage of
        Kirkburn, following the above presentation.   Ind: Cawood
        Castle, 6 December 1404.

455.   Ordination of a pension of two and a half marks a year, to be
        paid in equal parts at the feasts of the Purification and St
        John the Baptist to John de Melreth, out of the church of
        Kirkburn, until he is given a suitable rectory (the suitability
        to be determined by the archbishop) by Guisborough priory.
        The succeeding vicars of Kirkburn are to swear to observe this
        ordination.   The payment is to be doubled if it becomes
        overdue, or if the ordination is contravened.   In the presence
        of M. Richard Conyngeston, archbishop's chancellor, Robert
        Wolvenden, canon of York, Walter Patyswyk, rector of Kippax,
        Richard de Hayton, esq., and John Welton, notary public.
        Chapel of the manor of Cawood, 6 December 1404.

456.   Note that Thomas Hayton, in the presence of the archbishop and
        the above witnesses, swore to pay the above pension to John
        Milreth or his attorney in York Minster, according to the above
        ordination.   Cawood, 6 December 1404.

457.   Commission to John Drax, rector of Leconfield and dean of
        Beverley, and Richard Santon of North Cave, to execute a writ
        of Levari facias on the goods and possessions of Richard de
        Rouley.   They will be held responsible for the delivery of the
        sum of £100 to the justices at Westminster at the term
        mentioned in the writ.   York, 12 November 1404.

458. [f.68v] Institution of Richard Broket, priest, in the person of William Wryght, parochial chaplain of Hovingham, his proctor, to the vicarage of Rillington, vacant by the death of Roger Pye, on the presentation of the abbot and convent of Byland. Ind: Cawood Castle, 21 April 1405.

[ff.69-70v: MISSING] (1)

---

1. These two folios now form the front flyleaves, on which the sixteenth century index to the Register is written. See the introduction.

459.   Institution of William Geffray, priest, in the person of
        Richard Clerk of Rossington, clerk, his proctor, to the
        perpetual chantry of St Helen, Bingham, on the presentation of
        William de Roos, lord of Hamlake. Ind: Southwell, 5 July
        1398.

460.   Institution of M. Thomas Ruggelay, (2) clerk, in the person of
        John Hornyngese, clerk, his proctor, to the rectory of Staunton
        in the Vale, vacant by the resignation of William de Mapyrlay,
        on the presentation of Thomas Mapyrlay of Nottingham, esq.
        Ind: Southwell, 5 July 1398.

461.   Commission to the dean of Nottingham to receive criminous
        clerks from the royal justices and place them in the archbishop's
        prison. Rest, 24 July 1398.

462.   Appointment of M. Richard Arnald, LL.B., as sequestrator within
        the archdeaconry of Nottingham during pleasure, other than for
        probates of wills over £10 in value. Rest, 30 July 1398.

463.   Memorandum of a licence for non-residence for three years
        granted to Richard Wetewang, rector of Kirkby in Ashfield. He
        may farm out the rectory, and is excused appearance at synods.
        Rest, 2 August 1398.

464.   Memorandum of a similar licence for non-residence for one year,
        granted to M. Thomas Ruggelay, rector of Staunton in the Vale.
        He may farm out the rectory and be represented by proxy at
        synods. Rest, 12 August 1398.

465.   [ff.71-71v] Certificate of Henry [Dispenser], bishop of Norwich,
        reciting an archiepiscopal commission (dated at Rest, 4 August
        1398) for an exchange of benefices between Hugh Sturmy, rector
        of Great Cressingham, dioc. Norwich, and Henry Merston, rector
        of East Bridgford. He had received Merston's resignation, and
        had instituted Sturmy to East Bridgford, in the person of John
        Bray, clerk, his proctor, and on the presentation of Robert
        Deyncourt, esq. South Elmham, 10 August 1398.

466.   [f.71v] Ind: for Sturmy to East Bridgford. 16 August 1398.

467.   Confirmation of the appropriation to Lenton priory of the
        churches of St Mary, Nottingham, Lenton, and Radford, and the
        chapel of Beeston, together with two parts of the tithes of

---

1.   In the institutions throughout this section it may be assumed
        that, unless otherwise indicated, mandates for induction were
        issued on the same day as the institution, to the archdeacon
        of Nottingham, or his Official, or either of them.
2.   The scribe initially wrote 'Ryggelay', but has corrected it
        simply by scratching out the tail of the first 'y'.

467.   sheaves, hay, lambs, and wool, and the mortuary payments within
         the territory of the church of Langar, with annual pensions of
         16s. from the church of St Peter, Nottingham, 15s. from the
         church of St Nicholas, Nottingham, 22s. and a salmon from
         Beeston chapel, 26s. 8d. from Lenton church, 6s. 8d. from Linby
         church, 14s. from Cotgrave church and the tithes of corn of the
         chapel of the manor; 2s. from Rempstone church, 2s. from Costock
         church, 5s. from the church of Barton in Fabis; a salmon from
         Radford church, and also two parts of the demesne tithes of the
         lordships of Bunny, Bradmore, Ruddington, West Bridgford, Thorpe
         in the Glebe, Towton, Attenborough, Chilwell, Bramcote, Basford,
         Langley, Watnall, and Stapleford; all following examination of
         title. M. William Dernton, notary public, had acted as their
         proctor. Rest, 5 August 1398.

468.   Memorandum of the appointment of Robert Thornton, vicar of
         Lenton, as penitentiary for one year, except in reserved cases.
         1 August 1398.

469.   Memorandum of a dispensation granted in accordance with the
         constitution Cum ex eo, to Hugh de Ker, rector of Headon, to
         study in the schools of England for two years. He may farm out
         the rectory. Rest, 6 September 1398.

470.   Institution of M. Richard Arnall, LL.B., to the rectory of
         Barton in Fabis, vacant by the death of William Conyngton, on
         the presentation of the prior and convent of Lenton. Ind:
         Rest, 29 September 1398.

471.   Institution of Robert Weloghby, chaplain, to the chantry founded
         at the altar of St Mary in the church of Willoughby on the Wolds,
         on the presentation of Hugh de Weloghby. Ind: Rest, 5 October
         1398.

472.   [f.72] Institution of br. William de Clonne, O.S.A., in the
         person of M. Robert Laghton, his proctor, to the vicarage of
         Walkeringham, on the presentation of the prior and convent of
         Worksop. Ind: Rest, 7 October 1398.

473.   Institution of John de Howby, chaplain, to the chaplaincy or
         wardenship of the perpetual chantry of St Mary, Sibthorpe, vacant
         by the resignation of Robert de Selby, on the presentation of
         Gilbert Nutebroun, Richard de Paddelay, and Henry Pepircorn,
         chaplains of the chantry. Ind: Rest, 18 October 1398.

474.   Institution of Richard Webster, chaplain, to the rectory of
         Kimberley, vacant by the resignation of William de Broughton,
         on the presentation of the prior and convent of Beauvale.
         Ind: Cawood Castle, 17 November 1398.

475.   Certificate of Henry [Beaufort], bishop of Lincoln, reciting an
         archiepiscopal commission (dated at Cawood Castle, 18 December
         1398) for an exchange of benefices between William de Patryngton,
         rector of Spridlington, dioc. Lincoln, and Thomas Coke, vicar of

475.   Clarborough. He had received Coke's resignation, and had
        instituted Patryngton to Clarborough, on the presentation of
        Roger Weston, sacrist of the chapel of St Mary and the Holy
        Angels, York.   Stow Park, 22 November 1398. (1)

        Ind: Dean of Laneham, for Patryngton to Clarborough.   Cawood,
        18 December 1398.

476.   [f.72v] Memorandum of a licence for non-residence for three
        years, in order to study at Cambridge university, granted to
        William Bedeman, rector of Bingham.   He may farm out the
        rectory, and be represented by proxy at synods.   Cawood,
        7 January 1398/9.

477.   Certificate of the Official of the archdeacon of Nottingham,
        reciting an archiepiscopal commission (dated at Cawood Castle,
        18 December 1398), which had been issued after representations
        had been made to the archbishop by Robert Laghton, clerk,
        acting as proctor for William Ʒonge, priest, who was seeking
        institution to the rectory of Grove following presentation
        thereto by Thomas Hercy, knt.   He had examined Ʒonge and found
        him a fit person, and had therefore instituted him to the
        rectory and received his oath of obedience.   Tollerton,
        23 December 1398.

478.   Memorandum of the appointment of John, rector of Arnold, as
        penitentiary within the archdeaconry of Nottingham for one year
        even in cases reserved to the archbishop, (other than violations
        of the liberties and immunities of the minsters at York,
        Beverley, Ripon, and Southwell, invasions of the archbishop's
        parks and poaching of game, perjury in assizes and indictments,
        matrimonial and divorce cases, and cases involving
        disinheritance, loss of life or limb, or of the greater part of
        goods).   Cawood, 22 January 1398/9.

479.   Commission from Roger [Walden], archbishop of Canterbury, to
        the archbishop of York, for an exchange of benefices between
        M. Thomas Ruggeley, rector of Staunton in the Vale, and William
        Hayward, rector of Eynsford, dioc. Canterbury.   He is to
        receive Hayward's resignation and institute Ruggeley to Eynsford,
        on Walden's collation.   Otford, 6 February 1398/9.

480.   Note that, following the resignation of M. Thomas Ruggeley,
        tendered by M. Roger Caldecote, LL.B., his proctor, and
        virtue of the above commission, the archbishop of York had
        instituted William Hayward, priest, in the person of Peter
        Blakwell, clerk, dioc. York, his proctor, to the rectory of
        Staunton in the Vale, on the presentation of Thomas Mapirley

---

1.   Sic.   It seems likely that the copyist has made a mistake with
        the date of the archiepiscopal commission recited in the text,
        the month for which should probably read November.

480. of Nottingham; and that a mandate for his induction had been issued to the Official of the archdeacon. 15 February 1398/9.

481. [ff.72v-73] Note that, following the resignation of William Hayward, tendered by Peter Blakwell, his proctor, the archbishop of York, acting on the above commission, had collated the rectory of Eynsford, dioc. Canterbury, to M. Thomas Ruggeley in the person of Roger Caldecote, his proctor, and had sent the appropriate certificate to the archbishop of Canterbury. 15 February 1398/9.

482. [f.73] Note of a licence for non-residence, whilst in the king's service, granted to William Rodyngton, rector of St Peter, Nottingham. He may farm out the rectory and be represented by proxy at synods. Cawood, 27 March 1399.

483. Licence to Margery Pensax, anchorite, of Hawton, to choose another place of abode, and to choose a prelate to seclude her. Cawood, 20 March 1398/9.

484. Note of a licence granted to the prior of Ulverscroft, rector of Bunny, to farm out the rectory for one year. Cawood, 9 April 1399.

485. Dispensation to John Russell, clerk, dioc. York, in accordance with a commission from Francis [Carboni], cardinal priest of St Susanna and papal penitentiary (recited in full and dated at St Peter's, Rome, 12 February 1395/6), to receive orders and acquire a benefice, notwithstanding that he was the son of a subdeacon and a single woman, and had concealed the fact when acquiring clerical status. Cawood Castle, 23 May 1399.

486. Commission to M. Richard Arnall, LL.B., rector of Barton in Fabis, to hear and proceed in a cause between Margaret Basset, lady of Fledborough, and the parishioners or inhabitants of the chapelry of Woodcoates on the one part, and Robert Grene, rector of Fledborough, on the other, concerning the rector's failure to provide a priest to celebrate three days each week in the said chapel. He is to submit a certificate of the proceedings within a month of their completion. Cawood Castle, 23 June 1399.

487. [ff.73-73v] Licence to John Thorp, vicar of Gringley, in accordance with letters of Pope Boniface IX dated at St Peter's, Rome, 5 September 1398 (1), to absent himself from his benefice for seven years in order to study, provided that the duties of the vicarage, the services, and the cure of souls are not neglected. He may be represented by proxy at synods. Cawood Castle, 26 June 1399.

---

1. Described in the text as '_unam ... graciosam ... et aliam executoriam_'. Presumably, one was the papal authorisation to Thorp to absent himself, but the addressee of the other is unknown.

488.   [f.73v] Commission, during pleasure, for William Hunston,
John de Byngham, and John de Lichefeld, burgesses of
Nottingham, to receive rents for the subvention of a priest
to celebrate masses of St Mary in the church of St Mary,
Nottingham, according to ancient provision.   Cawood Castle,
3 July 1399.

489.   Certificate of Henry [Dispenser], bishop of Norwich, reciting
an archiepiscopal commission (dated at Bishopthorpe, 4 December
1399) for an exchange of benefices between Nicholas Fuller of
Fulbourn, rector of Thorpe next Norwich, dioc. Norwich, and
Thomas Revell, rector of Hockerton.   He had received Revell's
resignation, and had instituted Fuller to Hockerton in the
person of Thomas Playford of 'Banburgh', clerk, his proctor,
and on the presentation of John Breggeford [Bregeford],
domicellus. Blofield, 15 December 1399.

Ind: for Fuller to Hockerton.   Bishopthorpe, 2 January
1399/1400.

490.   [ff.73v-74] Certificate of Henry [Beaufort], bishop of Lincoln,
reciting an archiepiscopal commission (dated at Bishopthorpe,
6 December 1399) for an exchange of benefices between Robert
[de] Wylughby, rector of Harlaxton, dioc. Lincoln, and John
Normanton, rector of Clifton.   He had received Normanton's
resignation, and had instituted Wylughby to Clifton on the
presentation of John [de] Gaytford, Hugh Cressy of Oldcoates
and Thomas Strelley [Strylley] of Woodborough, esqs.,
Lyddington, 12 January 1399/1400.

491.   [f.74] Ind: for Wylughby to Clifton, after obedience had been
offered by John Welton, clerk, his proctor.   Bishopthorpe,
16 January 1399/1400.

492.   [ff.74-74v] Dispensation to M. Hugh Martill, rector of
Tollerton, in accordance with a commission from Pope Boniface IX
(recited in full, and dated at St Peter's, Rome, 26 February
1399/1400), permitting him to resume the celebration of divine
service and retain his benefice, notwithstanding that he had,
unintentionally, caused the death of John Smytheman of
Ruddington, a layman.   The death had occurred following a
dispute over certain lands belonging to the church.   After an
argument Martill, with two companions, had confronted Smytheman
in a field.   He, following harsh words, had attacked the
priest with a hammer.   Martill had defended himself with a
sword, and struck Smytheman on the head, causing a wound from
which he died within eight days.   Since hearing of the death
he had voluntarily abstained from his priestly functions.
In the presence of M. Richard Conyngston, LL.D., archbishop's
chancellor, William Bulkote, lic. [leg.], John de Garton, LL.B.,
all dioc. York.   Attested by John de Welton, clerk, dioc. York,
notary public.   Chapel of the archbishop's lodgings or manor
near Westminster, London, 11 October 1399.

493.   [f.74v] Institution of William Thurbache, clerk, to a mediety of the rectory of Eakring, vacant by the resignation of William Askeby, on the presentation of William de Roos, lord of Hamlake. Ind: Bishopthorpe, 17 January 1399/1400.

494.   Notarial instrument, reciting the resignation by William Askeby [Askby] from the above mediety of Eakring.   In the presence of John [Sharpe], vicar of Newark, and William Burnby, dean of Nottingham.   Attested by William Dernton, clerk, dioc. Durham, notary public.   Newark Castle, 8 January 1399/1400.

Memorandum that William Thurbache delivered his deeds of presentation to the archbishop, together with the above resignation, and was admitted to the mediety of Eakring in the presence of M. Richard Conyngston, canon of York and archbishop's chancellor, and Robert Wolvenden, precentor of Lichfield cathedral.   Bishopthorpe, 17 January 1399/1400.

495.   [f.75] Note of letters dimissory granted to Hugh de Ker, subdeacon, rector of Headon, to receive deacon's and priest's orders.   24 February 1399/1400.

496.   Ordination for the union of two chantries in Edwinstowe parish church to form one chantry, at the petition of the prior and convent of Newstead, the patrons.   The revenues of the separate chantries are now insufficient to sustain two priests, and barely enough to support one.   When either of the chantries next falls vacant, the union is to take effect.   Bishopthorpe, 1 March 1399/1400.

497.   [ff.75-75v] Certificate of John [Burghill], bishop of Coventry and Lichfield, reciting an archiepiscopal commission (dated at Bishop Burton, 20 March 1399/1400) for an exchange of benefices between Thomas Tewer [Tewar], rector of Holme Pierrepont, and M. William Thurbache, rector of a mediety of Eakring and prebendary of a prebend lately held by Thomas Aderley in the collegiate church of St Chad, Shrewsbury, dioc. Coventry and Lichfield.   He had received both resignations, with William Brunby, priest, acting as proctor for Thurbache, and Thomas Wyght, priest, acting for Tewer.   Thurbache, in the person of Brunby, had been instituted to Holme Pierrepont on the presentation of Edmund Perpount, knt.   Tewer, in the person of Wyght, had been instituted to the mediety of Eakring on the presentation of William de Roos, lord of Hamlake;   the prebend in the collegiate church had also been collated to him in the person of Wyght.   Mandates had been issued to the archdeacon of Nottingham or his Official, and to the dean of the collegiate church, to induct Brunby and Wyght, in their proctorial capacities, to the exchanged benefices.   Bishop's palace, Lichfield, 20 April 1400.

498.   [f.75v] Note that the Official of the archdeacon of
Nottingham, acting on an archiepiscopal commission dated at
Bishop Burton, 15 April 1400, had admitted and inducted
Gregory de Upton, priest, to the vicarage of Headon, vacant by
the resignation of John Leverton, on the presentation of Hugh
de Ker, rector of Headon, and following an inquisition of
neighbouring rectors and vicars, who had asserted that Leverton
had been presented to the vicarage by Gregory Fayrefax, late
rector and predecessor of Ker, and had confirmed the rector's
patronage of the vicarage.   Retford, 29 April 1400.

499.   [ff.75v-77v] Charter of John de Plumptre of Nottingham,
establishing and ordaining a chantry for two priests at the
altar of the Annunciation in the chapel of the hospital for
thirteen poor women which he had founded in honour of God and
the Annunciation at the end of Nottingham Bridge.   The chantry
is to be for the health of the king, the founder, and his wife,
while they live, and thereafter for their souls; for the
safety of the community of Nottingham; and for the souls of
the founder's successors and those from whom he had received
goods to establish prayers and other charitable works, and for
the souls of all the faithful departed, especially those who
shall make bequests to the hospital or found oratories at the
above altar.   One of the priests is to be designated master or
warden, the other is to be styled chaplain.   Daily, one of them
shall say the mass of the day, the other the mass of St Mary or
Requiem; before mass, one shall make a memorial of the Trinity,
the other a memorial of the Holy Spirit or Holy Cross; after
mass they shall together say the gospel, Missus est angelus
Gabriel.   The division of services is to be arranged by
agreement, failing which the warden is to have the first choice.
Both priests are to include the Collects, Deus, qui caritatis
[dona] per gratiam sancti spirito, and Inclina, domine, aurem
tuam ad preces nostras, with the appropriate Secrets and Post-
communions.   In the canon of the mass they are first to
mention the founder, and Emma his wife, and then their parents.
The priests are also to say alternate hourly masses at the
chapel.   Daily, before the mass, they shall kneel and say the
Pater noster and Ave, recommending the founder and his wife to
God and St Mary.   Daily, at nightfall or thereabouts, one or
other of the priests, or a deputy appointed by them, shall ring
the hospital bell five times, that the hearers may say a five-
fold Angelus for the health of the founder and all people while
he lives, and thereafter for the souls of the founder and his
wife and of all the faithful departed.   Every Saturday at
sunset the priests are to say or sing the antiphone of St Mary
in the chapel of the hospital, with a suitable versicle and
collect, with at least one raised lamp or wax candle, and
afterwards they are to say together the De profundis with the
collect Deus, qui caritatis dona per gratiam during the life
of the founder and his wife, or after their deaths the collect,
Inclina, domine, aurem tuam or any other that the priests may
choose for their souls and the souls of their benefactors.
The priests are to sing placebo and dirige together daily, with

76

499.   commendations of the dead, unless there shall be some impediment
to their singing together, in which case they shall sing
separately.   They are to be excused these services on the major
double feasts of Christmas, Epiphany, Easter, Ascension, and
Whitsun, on which days and on Sundays and festivals, they are to
assist in mattins, mass, and vespers in the parish church of the
chantry or chapel of the hospital.   They are to maintain an
annual obit for the founder on the anniversary of his death,
solemnly saying placebo and dirige with notation on the
preceding day, with solemn commendation of the dead and requiem
mass with notation and at least two elevated wax candles during
the following octave.   The priests are to abstain from taverns
and games, and are to visit the poor women of the hospital and
maintain their dwellings, so that they may be a symbol and
instruction to them in the catholic faith.   The priests are not
to reduce the property or divert it to other uses, on pain of
expulsion and replacement.   The founder reserves the right to
nominate the priests during his lifetime, and to present them to
the diocesan, or to the custodian of the spiritualities of the
see of York if it is vacant.   After the founder's death, the
patronage is to pass to the prior and convent of Lenton, who must
make a presentation within fifteen days of the vacancy becoming
known in both Nottingham and Lenton, failing which the collation
for that time lapses to the diocesan, or to the custodian of the
spiritualities if the see is vacant.   The chaplains are to be
secular priests, literate, and of good conduct and repute.   They
shall not hold other benefices, and their temporal patrimony shall
not exceed 40s. a year, nor shall they be physically decrepit.
If a candidate does not fulfil these conditions, he shall not be
admitted; if he does gain the chantry, although unfit, he shall
be removed.   If the priests, although initially suitable, later
degenerate, then they may be removed if they do not amend their
ways within one month of a canonical warning issued by a
competent judge.   To prevent the appointment of unsuitable
priests, presentations are to be made in person rather than by
proxy, so that the candidate may be personally examined.   The
priests are to commence their duties within four days of
presentation.   Thomas Tawburn, priest, is nominated to the
wardenship, and John de Coventre, priest, is named chaplain.
The priests are to inhabit two messuages within the hospital.
By royal licence they are to receive a stipend of 100s. from the
rents of the following ten tenements and two tofts: a tenement
of six messuages under the same roof situated in the little marsh
in Nottingham, with the end of the bridge to the east and the
tenement of Agnes Remay to the west; a messuage in the street
called Incole [?Finkhill Street], leading from the church of St
Peter to the friars minor, with the tenement on the corner
(belonging to Nicholas de Hopton) to the north, and the messuage
of Henry de Plumptre to the south; a tenement of three messuages
under one roof, situated in an alley opposite the north door of
the church of St Peter, with the founder's capital tenement to
the north, and the tenement of John Sheepe to the east; one
messuage in Cook Stool Row, with the founder's tenement to the
west and the messuage of Henry de Wilford to the east; one

499.   messuage with a garden situated in Barkergate, on the south
        side of the road, with the messuage of St Mary held by John del
        Ile on the corner to the east, and the messuage of William
        Tynet to the west; two messuages lying together in Fishergate,
        on the north side of the road, with the tenement of Cecilia de
        Emlay (held by William Taylour) to the east, and the tenement
        of John Samon to the west; four messuages lying together on
        the south side of Fishergate, with the chantry to the west and
        the tenement of John Samon (held by Geoffrey de Skelton) to the
        east, which four messuages extend with their gardens from the
        highway to the butt green, towards the south; one messuage
        with a garden in Fishergate, near to Penny Foot Street, with
        the messuage of John Samon to the west and the lands of St Mary
        to the east.   Any rent in excess of 100s. is to be reserved to
        the uses of the chantry, as the founder may in future direct.
        The oblations and other receipts of the chantry are to be used
        towards the upkeep of the inhabitants and fabric of the hospital,
        according to the agreement with the priory of Lenton; but the
        priests may retain a third of the oblations as remuneration for
        their labours.   They are to supervise the workmen and household
        in the hospital.   The founder reserves to himself while he
        lives the disposition and administration of the goods of the
        chantry, and the power to remove any priest who opposes him.
        After his death the priests, especially the warden, are to be
        responsible for the upkeep of the chantry.   There is to be no
        diminution or alienation of the goods, on pain of expulsion.
        To prevent maladministration there is to be no common seal, but
        the priests are to use separate private seals.   In cases of
        temporary illness, the sick priest is to be provided for out of
        the common funds.   If the sickness is perpetual and contagious,
        the priest is to be provided with a separate room, and is to be
        ministered to at his own expense.   If the sickness is perpetual
        but not contagious, he is to be looked after by the common
        servants unless he makes other arrangements.   These provisions
        are not to apply in cases of sickness or incapacity resulting
        from crime or notable sin, in which case the priest may be
        deprived, except in cases where the illness or defect is
        temporary and may be speedily remedied.   During illnesses, in
        recompense for the omission of masses, the priests are to say
        the canonical hours, placebo and dirige with commendations of
        the dead, and other devout intercessions, as well as they are
        able notwithstanding their sickness.   The chaplain who is well
        is to visit and cheer his sick colleague.   Those having the
        presentation of poor women to the hospital are not to present
        so many that the chantry has responsibility for more than
        thirteen.   The chaplains are to be personally resident, and are
        to fulfill their duties; they are not to incur any injury to
        the chantry or bring it into disrepute.   To ensure knowledge
        and observation of the ordination, the warden and chaplain are
        to collate their copies of the documents each Quarter Day.
        Each new chaplain shall acquire a copy of the ordination at
        his own expense within forty days of institution, and study and
        understand it.   There is to be a great chest in the chapel of
        the hospital, or in any safe place within the hospital building,

499.   with two locks and two different keys, of which the warden and
       the chaplain are to hold one each.   The chest is to hold the
       muniments and other things relating to the chantry, the priests
       being responsible for their safe-keeping.   Although the prior
       and convent of Lenton will hold the patronage, the nomination to
       a vacancy shall be made by the surviving priest within ten days
       of the vacancy becoming known in Nottingham.   If the nominee is
       unsuitable, the nomination on that occasion shall pass to the
       prior and convent of Lenton.   The founder reserves the right to
       clarify any obscurities and generalisations which may be
       discovered in the ordination during his lifetime.   The priests
       are to have their meals in common with the poor women of the
       hospital.   Sealed with the founder's seal and (quia pluribus est
       incognitum) the seal of the mayoralty of Nottingham.   Witnesses:
       John de Tannesley, mayor of Nottingham, William de Stookys and
       Thomas Fox, bailiffs of Nottingham, John Samon, William de
       Thrompton, Henry de Wilford, Hugh de Lyndby, Henry de Normanton,
       Henry de Plumptre, William Leeche, and others, burgesses of
       Nottingham.   Nottingham, 12 July 1400.

       [f.77v] Confirmation of the above ordination.   Cawood Castle,
       22 July 1400.

500.   Institution of Thomas Tawburn, priest, to the wardenship or
       mastership of the above chantry, on the presentation of John de
       Plumptre of Nottingham.   Ind: Dean of Nottingham.   Cawood,
       22 July 1400.

501.   [ff.77v-78] Institution of John de Coventre, priest, to the
       chaplainship of the above chantry, on the above presentation.
       Ind: as above.   Cawood, 22 July 1400.

502.   [f.78] Institution of Nicholas Dawbeney, priest, in the person
       of John de Welton, clerk, his proctor, to the rectory of Holme
       Pierrepont, vacant by the resignation of M. William Thurbache in
       exchange for the parish church of Methley, on the presentation of
       Edmund Pierpount, knt.   Ind: Cawood Castle, 5 August 1400.

503.   Note of a licence for non-residence for three years, to attend
       the university of Oxford, granted to M. William Segrave, sacre
       pagine professor, rector of Sutton Bonington.   He may farm out
       the rectory, and be represented by proxy at synods.   Cawood
       Castle, 16 August 1400.

504.   Note of a similar licence for non-residence for one year, to
       attend a university, granted to Hugh del Ker, rector of Headon.
       Cawood Castle, 8 September 1400.

505.   Dispensation to John Melton, clerk (1), dioc. York, in
       accordance with a commission from Francis [Carboni], cardinal
       priest of St Susanna and papal penitentiary (recited in full and

---

1.   Described as a scholar in the recited commission.

505. dated at St Peter's, Rome, 15 January 1398/9), to receive
further orders including those of acolyte, and acquire a
benefice, notwithstanding that he was the son of a single man
and a single woman. He had concealed the fact when acquiring
his first tonsure. Cawood Castle, 18 September 1400.

506. [f.78v] Institution of William Martha, priest, to the
perpetual chantry at the altar of Corpus Christi in Newark
parish church, vacant by the death of John de Dureham, on the
presentation of br. John Sharp, vicar of Newark, and Nicholas
Kayser, Richard Sayvyll, John de Bekyngham, and Thomas Ferrour,
all of Newark. Ind: Cawood Castle, 5 October 1400.

507. Collation, by lapse of time, of the parish church of Broxtow (1),
to John Dowbrygg, priest. Ind: Scrooby, 25 October 1400.

508. Institution of Simon Gaunstede, clerk, in the person of Peter
Cameryngham, clerk, his proctor, to the rectory of Sutton
Bonington, on the presentation of King Henry IV as guardian of
the lands and heir of the late Thomas Moubray, duke of Norfolk,
who had been a tenant in chief of the former King R[ichard] II.
Ind: Scrooby, 24 December 1400.

509. Certificate of Henry [Beaufort], bishop of Lincoln, reciting
[incompletely] an archiepiscopal commission (dated at Scrooby,
7 December 1400) for an exchange of benefices between Henry
Langham, rector of Friesthorpe, dioc. Lincoln, and John Tantot,
vicar of Mattersey. He had received Tantot's resignation and
had instituted Langham to the vicarage at the archbishop's
collation. Liddington, 11 January 1400/1.

510. Ind: for Langham to Mattersey. Scrooby, 16 January 1400/1.

511. Institution of Thomas Watton, priest, to the rectory of
Hawksworth, on the presentation of the prior and convent of
Thurgarton. Ind: Bishop Burton, 19 February 1400/1.

512. [f.79] Institution of William Tyllyng, priest, to the
vicarage of Walesby, vacant by the resignation of John Fryston,
in exchange for the chantry founded at the altar of the Holy
Trinity in the church of St Swithin, East Retford, on the
presentation of Richard Felde, clerk, warden of the free chapel
of Tickhill. Ind: Bishop Burton, 23 February 1400/1.

513. Institution of John de Fryston, priest, to the perpetual chantry
founded at the altar of the Holy Trinity in the church of St
Swithin, East Retford, vacant by the resignation of William

---

1. No longer a separate parish, having been united with Bilborough
in 1458 by reason of its poverty (K.S.S. Train, Lists of the
clergy of central Nottinghamshire,(Thoroton Society Record
Series 15, part 1, 1953), 28).

513. Tyllyng by reason of the above exchange, on the presentation of the bailiffs and community of East Retford. Ind: Dean of Laneham. Bishop Burton, 23 February 1400/1.

514. Certificate of Robert [Braybrooke], bishop of London, reciting [incompletely] an archiepiscopal commission (dated at York, 16 February 1400/1) for an exchange of benefices between John Lughton, rector of South Ockenden, dioc. London, and Ralph de Forthington, rector of Widmerpool. He had received Forthington's resignation and instituted Lughton to Widmerpool, on the presentation of John Eynesford, knt. Bishop's palace, London, 26 February 1400/1.

515. Mandate to the Official of the archdeacon of Nottingham, to induct John Lughton to the rectory of Widmerpool, following the above exchange. Bishop Burton, 15 March 1400/1.

516. [ff.79-v] Institution of Robert Sybthorp, priest, to the vicarage of South Leverton, vacant by the death of John de Belton, on the presentation of John de Shepeye, dean of Lincoln cathedral. Ind: Beverley, 28 March 1401.

517. [f.79v] Institution of John [de] Marton, priest, in the person of M. Roger de Burton, clerk, his proctor, to the vicarage of West Markham, vacant by the resignation of John de Hendeley, on the presentation of Richard de la Feld, clerk, warden or master of the royal free chapel of Tickhill. Ind: Beverley, 31 March 1401.

518. Note of the resignation of the church of Widmerpool, tendered by Ralph Forthington, rector of South Ockendon, dioc. London, acting as proctor for John Lughton, rector of Widmerpool. In the presence of William Toppcliff, clerk, Robert Crase of Bishop Burton, and others. Bishop Burton, 8 April 1401.

519. Institution of Richard atte Kyrk [Kyrke] of Thurlestone, clerk, to the rectory of Widmerpool, vacant by the resignation of John Loughton, on the presentation of John Eynisford, knt. Ind: Bishop Burton, 8 April 1401.

Note of a licence for non-residence for one year, in order to study in the schools, granted to Richard atte Kyrke. He may farm out his rectory, and is excused personal appearance at synods. Bishop Burton, 8 April 1401.

520. [ff.79v-80] Certificate of Henry [Dispenser], bishop of Norwich, reciting [incompletely] an archiepiscopal commission (dated at Bishop Burton, 21 March 1400/1) for an exchange of benefices between William Benet, rector of Buckenham Ferry, dioc. Norwich, and John Juwell, rector of Screveton. (1) He had received

---

1. MS. reads Kyrketon iuxta Kyrkcolston and (in no.522) Kyrkton iuxta Kyrkecolston. The identification is derived from J.T. Godfrey, Notes on the churches of Nottinghamshire: Hundred of Bingham (London, 1907), 385.

520.   Juwell's resignation, and had instituted Benet to Screveton,
         on the presentation of John Boson, knt.   South Elmham,
         2 April 1401.

521.   [f.80] Ind: for Benet to Screveton.   Bishop Burton,
         12 April 1401.

522.   Note of a licence granted to Nicholas Daubeney, rector of
         Holme Pierrepont, to farm out his rectory for one year.
         Bishop Burton, 1 May 1401.

523.   Institution of Henry de Normanton, priest, to the rectory of
         Kelham, on the presentation of the abbot and convent of
         Welbeck.   Ind: Bishop Burton, 6 May 1401.

524.   Institution of Adam de Louth, priest, to the rectory of Kirton,
         vacant by the resignation of John Addestoke in exchange for the
         vicarage of Brodsworth, on the presentation of William la
         Zouche, lord of Totnes, knt.   Ind: Bishop Burton, 6 May 1401.

525.   Institution of William Steven, priest, to the vicarage of
         Misson, on the presentation of the prior and convent of
         Mattersey.   Ind: Bishop Burton, 16 May 1401.

526.   Institution of M. Robert Apilton, clerk, to the rectory of
         Sturton le Steeple, on the presentation of the abbot and
         convent of St Mary, York.   Ind: Bishop Burton, 20 May 1401.

527.   [ff.80-80v] Institution of William Mysne, priest, to the
         rectory of West Retford, on the presentation of Thomas Hercy,
         knt.   Ind: Cawood Castle, 14 June 1401.

528.   [f.80v] Institution of br. Thomas de Retford, canon of
         Mattersey, to the vicarage of Misson by dispensation for this
         occasion, and reserving to the archbishop his right to institute
         a secular priest at succeeding vacancies, on the presentation
         of the prior and convent of Mattersey.   Ind: Cawood Castle,
         13 July 1401.

529.   Certificate of Henry [Beaufort], bishop of Lincoln, reciting
         [incompletely] an archiepiscopal commission (dated at Cawood
         27 June 1401) for an exchange of benefices between Robert
         Bassyngham, vicar of Bitchfield, dioc. Lincoln, and John
         Gateles, rector of Kimberley.   He had received Gateles's
         resignation, and had instituted Bassyngham to Kimberley, in the
         person of Nicholas Tebawte, priest, his proctor, and on the
         presentation of the prior and convent of Beauvale.   Buckden,
         4 July 1401.

         Ind: for Bassyngham (1) to Kimberley.   12 July 1401.

---

1.   The scribe here became confused, the induction clause
         referring to prefatum dominum Johannem.

82

530.   Institution of William Bawdewyn, priest, to one of the chantries
       of St Mary at the altar of All Saints in Newark church, on the
       presentation of Richard Sayvill, warden of the fraternity of
       St Mary at Newark, br. John Scharp, vicar of Newark, and Nicholas
       Kayser and Simon de Sybthorp of Newark, members of the fraternity.
       Ind: Cawood Castle, 17 July 1401.

531.   [f.81] Institution of Robert Eddynglay [Edynglay], priest, to
       the rectory of Kilvington, vacant by the death of William
       Maundevyle, on the presentation of John del Ker of Stoke.   Ind:
       Palace at York, 27 July 1401.

532.   Note that the Official of the archdeacon of Nottingham, acting
       on an archiepiscopal commission dated at Bishop Burton, 2 May
       1401, had instituted and inducted Peter del Ker, priest, to the
       church of Headon, on the presentation of John Wastneys, esq.,
       following an inquisition held in full chapter by rectors, vicars,
       and other priests of the vicinity, which had confirmed Wastneys'
       patronage by reason of his inheritance of the manor there, and
       declared that he had made the last presentation.   Retford,
       12 May 1401.

533.   Institution of John Bowdon, priest, to the chantry in honour
       of Corpus Christi founded by Alan Flemyng of Newark in a chapel
       in Newark parish church, on the presentation of John Scharp,
       vicar of Newark, and John Billesthorp, Simon Sibthorp, John
       Bekyngham and William Seme, parishioners of Newark.   Ind:
       Cawood Castle, 28 August 1401.

534.   Institution of William, lord of Sandiacre, priest, in the person
       of William Brunby, priest, his proctor, to a mediety of the
       chantry in the parish church of Willoughby on the Wolds, vacant
       by the death of Robert de Wyloghby, on the presentation of Hugh
       de Wyloghby.   Ind: Cawood Castle, 31 August 1401.

535.   [ff.81-81v] Institution of Richard Chilwell, priest, to the
       vicarage of St Mary, Nottingham, vacant by the resignation of
       Robert de Retford, on the presentation of the prior and convent
       of Lenton.   Ind: [not named].   Sherburn in Elmet, 24 September
       1401.

536.   [f.81v] Institution of William Peek, priest, to the rectory of
       Holme Pierrepont, vacant by the resignation of Nicholas Daubeney,
       on the presentation of Edmund Perpond, knt.   Ind: Rest,
       5 October 1401. (1)

537.   Presentation by Edmund Perpond, knt., of William Peek, priest,
       to the archbishop, for institution to Holme Pierrepont, and
       petition that a life pension be reserved out of the revenues of
       the church for Nicholas Daubeney, the previous rector.   Holme
       Pierrepont, 1 October, 3 Henry IV [1401]. (1)

---

1.   Marginal letters indicate that the order of these entries should
       be reversed.

538.   [ff.81v-82] Certificate of Henry [Beaufort], bishop of
         Lincoln, reciting an archiepiscopal commission (dated at Rest,
         3 September 1401) for an exchange of benefices between John
         Cook, vicar of Skidbrook, dioc. Lincoln, and John Thoresby,
         rector of Gamston. He had received Thoresby's resignation,
         and had instituted Cook to Gamston, on the presentation of the
         prior and convent of Mattersey. Buckden, 29 September 1401.

         Ind: for Cook to Gamston. Bishopthorpe, 16 October 1401.

539.   [f.82] Institution of John Futtyng, priest, to the vicarage
         of Misson, on the presentation of the prior and convent of
         Mattersey.   Ind: Scrooby, 20 January 1401/2.

540.   Institution of Thomas Porter, priest, to the rectory of Kirton,
         vacant by the resignation of Adam de Louth in exchange for the
         parish church of Ryther, on the presentation of William la
         Zouche, knt., lord of Totnes.   Ind: Cawood Castle, 11 March
         1401/2.

541.   Institution of Henry de Elmesall, priest, to the mastership
         or wardenship of the hospital of St Mary Magdalene,
         Broadbusk (1), vacant by the resignation of Henry de Merston,
         priest, on the presentation of Roger de Swylyngton, knt.
         Ind: Cawood Castle, 20 March 1401/2.

542.   Institution of Henry Serle, priest, to the vicarage of Beeston,
         vacant by the death of Richard Mason, on the presentation of
         the prior and convent of Lenton.   Ind: Cawood Castle, 21 March
         1401/2.

543.   [ff.82-82v] Mandate to the Official of the archdeacon of
         Nottingham, to induct Ralph de Dalby, priest, to the vicarage
         of Ruddington, to which he had been instituted on the
         presentation of the prior and convent of Durham following an
         exchange with Roger de Saxton for the parish church of
         Egremont in Copeland, in the archdeaconry of Richmond.
         Cawood Castle, 23 March 1401/2. (2)

544.   [f.82v] Certificate of William de Norton, B.Dec., vicar
         general of Stephen Lescrop, archdeacon of Richmond, he being
         absent, reciting an archiepiscopal commission (dated at Cawood
         Castle, 24 January 1401/2) for an exchange of benefices between
         Roger de Saxton, vicar of Ruddington, and Ralph de Dalby, rector
         of Egremont in Copeland.   He had received Saxton's resignation
         and had instituted Dalby to Ruddington, on the presentation of
         the prior and convent of Durham.   Tanfield, 22 March 1401/2. (2)

---

1.   This place is now known as Spital.   As the present form is so
         obviously derived from the previous existence of the hospital,
         it has seemed preferable to retain the older alternative name.
2.   It is probable that the order of these two entries should be
         reversed; but on this occasion there are no marginal entries
         to indicate this.

545.   Note of a licence for non-residence for three years, in order to
        study, granted to Richard atte Kyrk, rector of Widmerpool. He
        may farm out the rectory, and be represented by proxy at synods.
        Rest, 31 March 1402.

546.   [ff.82v-83] Certificate of Robert [Braybrooke], bishop of
        London (addressed to the archbishop of York, or John de Neuton,
        LL.D., treasurer of York Minster and vicar-general of the
        archbishop), reciting [incompletely] a commission from Neuton
        (dated at York, 20 February 1401/2, and sealed with the arch-
        bishop's seal) for an exchange of benefices between John Holme,
        priest of the perpetual chantry established for the soul of
        Thomas Pilk in the parish church of All Saints, Barking, city and
        dioc. London, and William Tillyng, vicar of Walesby. He had
        received Tillyng's resignation, offered by Thomas Worsop,
        domicellus, his proctor, and had instituted Holme to Walesby, on
        the presentation of Richard Kyngeston, warden of the free chapel
        of Tickhill. Hadham, 7 March 1401/2.

547.   [f.83] Institution of Geoffrey de Oxton, priest, to the vicarage
        of Burton Joyce, on the presentation of the prior and convent of
        Shelford. Ind: Rest, 5 May 1402.

548.   [ff.83-83v] Certificate of John [Burghill], bishop of Coventry
        and Lichfield, reciting [incompletely] an archiepiscopal
        commission (dated at Rest, 20 April 1402) for an exchange of
        benefices between John Basage, rector of Hathersage, dioc.
        Coventry and Lichfield, and M. Hugh Martill, rector of Tollerton.
        He had received Martill's resignation, and had instituted Basage
        to Tollerton in the person of Henry Clerk of Tollerton, his
        proctor, and on the presentation of Robert Barre, knt. Coleshill,
        24 April 1402.

        [f.83v] Ind: for Basage to Tollerton. Rest, 4 May 1402.

549.   Certificate of the Official of the archdeacon of Nottingham,
        reciting an archiepiscopal commission (dated at Rest, 2 October
        1401) to inquire into the vacancy and patronage of the rectory
        of Linby, to which the prior and convent of Lenton had presented
        William Vale of Linby, priest. An inquisition had been held of
        neighbouring rectors, vicars, and chaplains, who had confirmed
        the patronage. The Official had instituted and inducted Vale to
        the rectory, vacant by the death of John Syleby. Linby,
        5 October 1401.

550.   Certificate of Henry [Beaufort], bishop of Lincoln, reciting
        [incompletely] an archiepiscopal commission (dated at Rest,
        27 May 1402) for an exchange of benefices between John Sharp,
        vicar of East Wykeham, dioc. Lincoln, and Henry de Sutton, vicar
        of Elkesley. He had received Sutton's resignation, and had
        instituted Sharp to Elkesley on the presentation of the abbot and
        convent of Welbeck. Stamford, 31 May 1402.

551.   [f.84] Ind: for Sharp to Elkesley. Rest, 2 June 1402.

552. Ratification of a papal dispensation to William Peek, rector of Holme Pierrepont (1) and vicar of Flintham, to hold both benefices in plurality, following appearance by proxy in the chapel of the archbishop's manor of Rest, 6 June 1402. Rest, 6 June 1402.

553. Institution of Thomas de Muskham, priest, to the recently founded chantry at the altar of the Holy Trinity in the church of St Mary Magdalene, Newark, on the presentation of Thomas Ferrour and Thomas Mawdeslay of Newark. Ind: Rest, 19 June 1402. (2)

554. Institution of Thomas Aylif, priest, to the perpetual chantry at the altar of St Katherine the Virgin in Newark parish church, on the presentation of John Sharp, vicar of Newark, and Nicholas Kayser, John de Bekyngham, John Bron, and John Lake, of Newark. Ind: Rest, 20 June 1402.

555. [ff.84-84v] Certificate of John [Bottlesham], bishop of Rochester, reciting [incompletely] an archiepiscopal commission (dated at Rest, 20 May 1402) for an exchange of benefices between John Gote, vicar of Leigh, dioc. Rochester, and Robert Sibthorp [Sybthorp], vicar of South Leverton. He had received Sibthorp's resignation, and instituted Gote to South Leverton, on the presentation of M. John Shepeye, dean of Lincoln cathedral. Trottiscliffe, 1 June 1402.

556. [f.84v] Ind: for Gote to South Leverton. Rest, 22 June 1402.

557. [ff.84v-85] Notarial instrument, recording an inquisition held before Thomas [de Ouston], vicar of Walesby and dean of Retford, at which Richard de Cotump, John Lord, Robert Monk, John Kyng, and John de Totwyk, parishioners of Cottam, sought a decision as to whether the vicar of South Leverton was obliged to provide a chaplain to minister to the inhabitants of Cottam in the chapel there on three days in each week. Hugh Hake, aged sixty and more, had testified that a chaplain should be present on Sundays, Wednesdays, and Fridays, he having known them for the past forty years, and his father and relatives having told him that the arrangement had been in force even earlier, all sacraments being administered, from baptism to burial in the cemetery of the chapel. Thomas de Wyntlane, aged fifty and more, testified to the same, having known the chaplains for the past thirty years. William Person, chaplain, aged fifty-two years, testified that he had been chaplain there twenty years previously, and had acted for the vicar of South Leverton, and had never heard the arrangement denied. William de Stratton, aged seventy and more, testified that the vicar of South

---

1. The identification is provided by the marginal title, the text itself omitting the vital first word from the form 'Holme super Trent'.
2. The ordination of the chantry appears below, no.572.

557.   Leverton should provide a chaplain at Cottam, saying that he had
       known them there for forty years. Following this, the
       petitioners produced a mandate from John [de Thoresby], arch-
       bishop of York (recited in full, and dated at Bishopthorpe,
       20 May 1370), ordering the dean of Retford to inquire into the
       case, and determine whether he, who held the fruits of the
       vicarage of South Leverton during its vacancy, should provide a
       chaplain for Cottam during the vacancy, and what stipend should
       be allowed him. If the dean found in favour of the parishioners,
       he was to appoint a chaplain. The dean found in favour of the
       parishioners. In the presence of br. Nicholas Wekyngham, canon
       of Worksop, M. Thomas de Edynstow, John Alas, chaplain.
       Attested by John, dictus de Hoveden, clerk, dioc. York, notary
       public. South Leverton church, 25 May 1372.

       [f.85] Note that the Official of the archdeacon of Nottingham
       fixed his seal to the above document, in the presence of John de
       Landford, [vicar] of a mediety of Gedling, and John Row, clerk.
       Gedling, 30 May 1372.

558.   Mandate of Simon [Langham], cardinal priest of St Sixtus and
       papal nuncio, to the dean of Retford, to warn Thomas [de Langwath],
       vicar of South Leverton, to provide a chaplain to serve in the
       chapel of Cottam on Sundays, Wednesdays, and Fridays in each week,
       following complaints from Richard Cotum, John Lord of Cottam and
       other parishioners of Cottam, that no chaplain had been provided.
       The vicar is to be warned every five days, and if he has not
       complied within fifteen days of the original warning, is to be
       proceeded against by ecclesiastical censure. London, 7 June
       1372.

559.   [ff.85-85v] Confirmation following examination of title, of the
       appropriation to Thurgarton priory of the churches of Thurgarton,
       Owthorpe, Tithby, Hoveringham, Sutton in Ashfield, Granby, Cotham,
       and Radcliffe on Trent. Scrooby, 9 December 1402.

560.   [f.85v] Institution of Richard Baron, priest, to the vicarage of
       Radford, vacant by the resignation of William Alferton, on the
       presentation of the prior and convent of Lenton. Ind: Scrooby,
       31 December 1402.

561.   Note of a licence for non-residence for one year granted to
       M. Richard Killom, rector of a mediety of Gedling. He may farm
       out the rectory, and is excused appearance at synods. Scrooby,
       11 November 1402.

562.   Note of a licence for non-residence for one year granted to Henry
       Fox, rector of Stanford on Soar. He may farm out the rectory,
       and is excused appearance at synods. Scrooby, 1 October 1402.

563.   [ff.85v-86] Certificate of John [Burghill], bishop of Coventry
       and Lichfield, reciting an archiepiscopal commission (dated at
       Scrooby, 28 December 1402) for an exchange of benefices between
       John Osmund [Osmud], vicar of Crich, dioc. Coventry and Lichfield,

563.   and William Garton [Carton] of Driffield, rector of Bulwell.
          He had received Garton's resignation in the person of Thomas
          Arnall, his proctor, and had instituted Osmund to Bulwell on
          the presentation of King Henry IV.   Eccleshall Castle,
          1 January 1402/3.

564.   [f.86] Ind: for Osnund (sic.) to Bulwell.   7 January 1402/3.

565.   Memorandum of a commission to William [Northbrugge], bishop
          Pharensis and suffragan, to receive the resignation of Helen
          de Bollesovere as prioress of Wallingwells, and to confirm
          the election of her successor.   7 January 1402/3.

          Note that, by virtue of the above commission, the election of
          Isabella de Durham, subprioress, as prioress of Wallingwells,
          had been confirmed, and that she had professed obedience.
          17 January 1402/3.

566.   Certificate of Robert [Braybrooke], bishop of London, reciting
          an archiepiscopal commission (dated at York, 10 January
          1402/3) for an exchange of benefices between Thomas de Thorp,
          rector of Fairstead, dioc. London, and Robert Cumberton, vicar
          of Blyth.   He had received Cumberton's resignation, and had
          instituted Thorp to Blyth, on the presentation of the prior and
          convent of Blyth.   Palace at London, 22 January 1402/3.

567.   [f.86v] Ind: for Thorp to Blyth.   Scrooby, 3 February 1402/3.

568.   Confirmation following examination of title, of the
          appropriation to Worksop priory of the churches of Worksop,
          Gringley, Walkeringham, Normanton, West Burton, Sutton on Trent,
          Car Colston, Willoughby on the Wolds, and Wysall, a third of the
          church of Sheffield, and the chapel of Osberton, with an annual
          pension of 6s. 8d. from Wickersley church.   Scrooby,
          21 February 1402/3.

569.   Confirmation following examination of title, of the
          appropriation to Welbeck abbey of the churches of Norton
          Cuckney, Whatton, Elkesley, Littleborough, and Flintham.
          Scrooby, 21 February 1402/3.

570.   [f.87] Confirmation following examination of title, of the
          appropriation to Shelford priory of the church of Shelford and
          chapel of Newton, the church of Burton Joyce and chapel of
          Bulcote, the church of Saxondale, and medieties of the churches
          of Gedling with the chapel of Stoke Bardolph, North Muskham
          with the chapel of Bathley, and Holme; with annual pensions of
          8s. from the church of Radcliffe on Trent, 14s. from the church
          of Car Colston, and 2s. from the other mediety of Gedling.
          Scrooby, 21 February 1402/3.

571.   [ff.87-87v] Confirmation following examination of title, of the
          appropriation to the priory of St Katherine, Lincoln, of the
          church of Newark.   Scrooby, 19 October 1402.

572.   [ff.87v-88v] Inspeximus and confirmation of the ordination of
        a chantry at the altar of the Holy Trinity in the church of St
        Mary Magdalene, Newark, established by John [de] Leek, knt.,
        Richard Sayvill [Savull], Thomas Ferrour [Ferrur], and Roger
        del Chaumber of Newark, reciting their charter of ordination
        (dated at Newark, 8 April 1402, with the attestation of M.
        Robert Attekirk of South Scarle, clerk, dioc. York, notary
        public, appended in Newark parish church, 31 October 1402, in
        the presence of John Sharp, vicar of Newark, William Mook, John
        Manthorp, and Thomas Colyngham, priests, dioc. Lincoln and York).
        By licence of King Henry IV (recited in full, and dated at
        Westminster, 20 August 2 Henry IV [1401]) (1) granted in return
        for a payment of £22 by the licensees, and with the consent of
        the brothers and sisters of the fraternity of the Holy Trinity
        in Newark, and in return for daily services for the health of
        Richard [le Scrope], archbishop of York, the founders, and the
        present and future members of the fraternity of the Holy Trinity
        while they live, and thereafter for their souls, and especially
        for the health of Thomas Ferrour and Beatrice his wife while
        they live, and thereafter for their souls, and for the souls of
        Matilda, Ferrour's late wife, Margaret, his late daughter and
        his parents, brothers, sisters and benefactors and all the
        faithful departed, they enfeoff Thomas [de] Muscham [Muskham,
        Muskcham], chaplain, custodian of the altar of the Holy Trinity
        in Newark church, with six messuages, three cottages and 40d
        worth of rent, namely: a messuage in Castle Gate, with the
        tenement of John Tymworth to the south and that of John de
        Wadyngton to the north; a messuage in Castle Gate, between the
        tenements of Stephen Mynyers and John Wakman; a cottage in
        Middle Gate, between the tenements of Ed[mund] Pierpount, knt.,
        and the prioress of Heynings; a messuage on the corner of
        le Cokeraw, with the tenement of John de Beby to the south, and
        abutting on the tenement of the prior of St Katherine's [Lincoln]
        to the west; a messuage in Carter Gate, with the tenement of
        Thomas de Kelum to the north, and with the well called le Dikewell
        to the south; a cottage in Mill Gate, with the tenement of John
        de Burton to the south, and that of John de Lesingham to the
        north; a cottage in the Market Place, with the tenement of
        Richard Bykerstaf to the north, and that of John Skirlington to
        the south; a messuage in Mill Gate, with the tenement of Hugh
        Osmundthorp to the south and that of William Osmundthorp to the
        north; a messuage in Carter Gate, with the tenement of John
        Bosom, knt., to the north, and that of Henry Acclum to the south;
        and 40d. worth of rent derived from a messuage in the Market
        Place, lying between the tenements of Richard Wakefeld and
        William Seme. During the lifetime of Ferrour he, or the provost
        or keeper of the fraternity of the Holy Trinity acting on his
        nomination, shall present the successive priests to the arch-
        bishop of York for institution, or to the dean and chapter,
        (or chapter alone should the dean be absent) if the see is
        vacant. After Ferrour's death, the presentation is to be made

1.   Calendar of Patent Rolls, 1399-1401, 535.

572.   within fifteen days of the vacancy by the provost or keeper in
         conjunction with six worthy members of the fraternity at
         Newark, a majority decision being acceptable if there is
         disagreement.   If they do not present, the presentation passes
         for the succeeding fifteen days to the vicar of Newark or his
         deputy, failing presentation by whom the collation lapses to
         the archbishop, or to the dean and chapter (or chapter alone
         should the dean be absent) if the see is vacant.   The priest
         is to maintain and repair the houses and buildings thus granted
         at his own expense; but if he cannot or will not, then after
         due warning having been given the patron who presented him
         shall carry out the repairs from the rents of the property.
         The priest is to hold no other benefice or office and must
         maintain his residence.   He must daily say mattins, mass and
         the other canonical hours and the services of the dead,
         comprising placebo and dirige, with commendation of souls.
         Daily, when possible, he shall make a special memorial of the
         living and dead named above, and during the week shall say the
         Requiem mass for the dead and on every other Sunday the mass or
         memorial of the Holy Trinity.   Every other weekday during the
         year, except on the feasts of saints as set out in the Ordinal,
         he is to say the Trentale of St Gregory.   The priest is to
         join the other chaplains of the parish church, surpliced, for
         mattins, mass, vespers and compline every day, unless there are
         reasonable grounds for not so doing.   Every incoming chaplain
         is to take an oath before the archbishop, to observe this
         ordination.   Like the other chaplains, the priest is to be
         subject to the vicar of the parish church, who shall not
         impose additional duties on him.   If the priest is absent
         from his duties for six consecutive days without reasonable or
         legitimate excuse, or neglects the ordination, or breaks his
         oath, or is accused of moral laxity, and is found guilty by a
         competent judge, he is to be deprived and replaced.   One half
         of the indenture is to remain with Muscham and the successive
         chaplains, the other half with the provost or warden and
         members of the fraternity.   Scrooby, 26 November 1402.

573.   [f.89] Institution of Thomas de Algarkyrk, priest, to the
         vicarage of Misterton, on the presentation of the chapter of
         York Minster.   The archbishop reserves the right to ordain
         the vicarage. (1)   Ind: Scrooby, 2 April 1403.

574.   Institution of John de Swafeld, priest, to the perpetual chantry
         at the altar of St James in Newark parish church, vacant by the
         death of Robert de Lyndesey, on the presentation of br. John
         Sharp, vicar of Newark, and Thomas Mawdesley, John de
         Bildesthorp, John de Bekyngham, and Richard de Wakefeld,
         parishioners of Newark.   Ind: Scrooby, 18 April 1403.

---

1.   For the ordination, see above, no.55.

575.   Certificate of Henry [Beaufort], bishop of Lincoln, reciting
        [incompletely] an archiepiscopal commission (n.d.) for an
        exchange of benefices between Thomas Normanton, rector of
        Somerby near Grantham, dioc. Lincoln, and Thomas Thorp, warden
        of the chantry or college of St Mary, Sibthorpe. He had
        received Thorp's resignation, and had instituted Normanton to
        the wardenship, on the presentation of Richard Routh and John
        Adam, chaplains of the chantry. Torksey, 25 April 1403.

576.   Ind: for Normanton (1) to the wardenship of the chantry at
        Sibthorpe. 25 April 1403.

577.   [f.89v] Profession of obedience of br. William de Beverlaco,
        master of the Order of Sempringham, in respect of all parish
        churches within the diocese of York appropriated to priories or
        other houses of the Order, saving papal privileges, liberties,
        exemptions, and immunities. In the presence of Robert
        Wolveden, canon of York, M. John Gilby, LL.B., and John Welton,
        notary public, with others of the archbishop's household.
        Chapel of the manor of Scrooby, 29 April 1403.

578.   Institution of John Scrimschire, priest, to the vicarage of a
        mediety of North Muskham, vacant by the resignation of Thomas
        Saxendale, on the presentation of the prior and convent of
        Shelford. Ind: Scrooby, 13 July 1403.

579.   [ff.89v-90] Certificate of Robert [Braybrooke], bishop of London,
        reciting an archiepiscopal commission (dated at Scrooby,
        15 June 1403) for an exchange of benefices between Roger
        Walpoole of Uffington, rector of All Saints, Chingford, dioc.
        London, and Nicholas Fuller of Fullbourn, rector of St Nicholas,
        Hockerton. He had received Fuller's resignation, and had
        instituted Walpoole to Hockerton, on the presentation of John
        Briggeford [Bryggeford], domicellus, of Hockerton. Lower Stoke,
        4 July 1403.

580.   [f.90] Ind: for Walpoole to Hockerton. 9 July 1403.

581.   Certificate of William [of Wykeham], bishop of Winchester,
        reciting an archiepiscopal commission (dated at Cawood, 2 August
        1403) for an exchange of benefices between Thomas de Wykersley,
        rector of Bentworth, dioc. Winchester, and John Coke, rector of
        Gamston. He had received Coke's resignation, and had
        instituted Wykersley to Gamston, on the presentation of the
        prior and convent of Mattersey. BishopsWaltham, 13 August 1403.

        Ind: for Wykersley to Gamston. Cawood, 2 September 1403.

---

1.   The MS. has the names confused, here giving the surname as Thorp.

582.   [ff.90-90v] Certificate of Richard [Mitford], bishop of
        Salisbury, reciting an archiepiscopal commission (dated at
        Cawood Castle, 15 September 1403) for an exchange of benefices
        between William Dalton, rector of Bromham, dioc. Salisbury,
        and Nicholas Haukerigg, rector of Normanton on Soar.   He had
        received Haukerigg's resignation, and had instituted Salton to
        Normanton, on the presentation of the prior and convent of
        Durham.   Wilton, 3 October 1403.

        [f.90v]   Ind: for Dalton to Normanton.   Cawood, 9 October
        1403.

583.   Institution of John Taylour, priest, to the rectory of
        Hawksworth, vacant by the resignation of Thomas Watton, on
        the presentation of Elias de Middelton, esq.   Ind: Scrooby,
        18 October 1403.

584.   Institution of William Peek, priest, to the wardenship of the
        chantry of St Mary, Sibthorpe, vacant by the resignation of
        Nicholas Seward in exchange for the vicarage of Flintham, on
        the presentation of Henry Pepurcorne and Robert Barneby,
        chaplains and brethren of the chantry.   Ind: Scrooby,
        17 October 1403.

585.   Institution of Nicholas Seward, in the person of William
        Wollaston, his proctor, to the vicarage of Flintham, vacant
        by the resignation of William Peek following the above
        exchange, on the presentation of the abbot and convent of
        Welbeck.   Ind: Scrooby, 18 October 1403.

586.   [ff.90v-91] Certificate of Henry [Beaufort], bishop of
        Lincoln, reciting an archiepiscopal commission (dated at
        Scrooby, 19 October 1403) for an exchange of benefices between
        William Bertham, vicar of Carlton le Moorland, near Bassingham,
        dioc. Lincoln, and John Randolf, vicar of Mansfield.   He had
        received Randolf's resignation, and had instituted Bertham to
        Mansfield, on the presentation of M. John Shepeye [Shepey],
        dean of Lincoln cathedral.   Lyddington, 23 October 1403.

        [f.91]   Ind: for Bertham to Mansfield.   Scrooby, 26 October
        1403.

587.   Institution of John de Clifton, priest, to the rectory of
        Gamston, vacant by the resignation of Thomas Wikireslay in
        exchange for the church of Birkin, on the presentation of the
        prior and convent of Mattersey.   Ind: Scrooby, 15 December
        1403.

588.   Note that the ordination of the vicarage of Misterton, the
        church being appropriated to the dean and chapter of York,
        had been registered in the second gathering of capitular
        material. (1)

_____

1.   Above, no.55.

92

589.   Vow of chastity [in English] of Alize, sometime 'John wyf
Jankynson', of Sturton, taken before the archbishop. n.d. (1)

590.   [f.91v] Institution of Thomas Beyekyrke, priest, to the
perpetual chantry of the altar of St James in Newark parish
church, vacant by the resignation of John Swafeld, on the
presentation of br. John Sharp, vicar of Newark, and Thomas
Maudesley, John Bildesthorp, John Bekyngham, and Richard de
Wakefeld, all of Newark.   Ind: (2) Scrooby, 4 April 1404.

591.   Institution of John Lunde, priest, to the vicarage of
Edwinstowe, vacant by the resignation of Thomas de Norton in
exchange for the church of Skirpenbeck, on the presentation of
the subdean and chapter of Lincoln cathedral, the dean being
absent.   Ind: Cawood Castle, 23 April 1404.

592.   Dispensation of Pope Boniface IX to John de Laghton, canon of
Worksop priory, confirming his election as prior, notwithstanding
that he was the son of a priest and a single woman.   St Peter's,
Rome, 9 September 1398.

593.   [ff.91v-92] Certificate of the dean of Retford, recording his
fulfillment of an archiepiscopal commission (recited in full
and dated at York, 17 April 1404) to cite all opponents of the
election of br. John [de] Laghton as prior of Worksop in
succession to br. Roger de Upton, deceased, to attend in the
chapel of the manor of Cawood on the Saturday after the feast
of St George [26 April] next following.   The citation had been
published in the conventual chapter of Worksop.   Southwell,
22 April 1404.

594.   [f.92] Confirmation of the election of br. John de Laghton as
prior of Worksop, and release to him of the spiritualities and
temporalities of the house.   n.d.

595.   Profession of obedience by br. John de Laghton as prior of
Worksop.   n.d.

596.   [ff.92-92v] Letters testimonial to br. John de Laghton,
confirming his election as prior of Worksop, and releasing to
him the spiritualities and temporalities of the house.
Cawood Castle, 26 April 1404.

597.   [f.92v] Mandate to the subprior and convent of Worksop, to
receive and obey br. John de Laghton as their prior.   Cawood
Castle, 26 April 1404.

598.   Mandate to the Official of the archdeacon of Nottingham, to
install br. John de Laghton as prior of Worksop.   Cawood Castle,
26 April 1404.

---

1.   Printed in Testamenta Eboracensia, iii, 318.
2.   The surname is incorrectly given as 'Swafeld' in the induction
clause.

599.   Institution of Richard Gosse, chaplain, to the perpetual
        chantry of the Holy Trinity in Newark parish church, vacant
        by the death of John de Thurleby, on the presentation of
        Elias Bakster of Newark, provost of the fraternity of the
        Holy Trinity at Newark.   Ind: Cawood Castle, 6 July 1404.

600.   [ff.93-93v] Certificate of Robert Trowell, vicar of Sutton
        on Trent and dean of Newark, and Robert Fyschlake, rector of
        a mediety of Treswell and dean of Retford, reciting an
        archiepiscopal commission (dated at Rest, 10 May 1402) to
        inquire into the possibility of uniting the parishes of
        Kneesall and Boughton, the archbishop having been made aware
        of their situation, when travelling through the archdeaconry
        of Nottingham.   An inquisition had been held in Boughton
        church on 12 July 1402, attended by the prior and convent of
        Blyth as patrons of Boughton, the rectors of the churches,
        and interested parishioners.   It had been found that the
        parishes were inextricably intermingled, so that the division
        and collection of tithes and other parochial dues frequently
        caused difficulties;   that because of the mingling of the
        parishes it was impossible to define their boundaries;   that
        the tenants of the temporal fee of Allerton, being
        parishioners of Kneesall, and the tenants of the fee of
        Tickhill, being parishioners of Boughton, were similarly
        mingled;   that the revenues of Boughton amounted to barely
        40s. a year, and were insufficient to maintain the rector
        and his duties;   and that the parishioners of Boughton might
        well be served by the church of Kneesall, three-quarters of
        the inhabitants of Boughton being already parishioners of
        Kneesall.   Sealed with the seals of br. Nicholas Anglia,
        prior of Blyth, of the convent of Blyth, and with the official
        seals of the deans.   Boughton, 4 August 1402.

601.   [ff.93v-94] Certificate of M. John Suthwell, receiver at
        York, and M. John Staynton [Stanton], proctor of the Court of
        York, reciting an archiepiscopal commission (dated at Scrooby,
        5 December 1403) naming them as his representatives to discuss
        with the dean and chapter of York the proposed union of the
        churches of Kneesall and Boughton, and to obtain their consent
        thereto.   On 30 December 1403, in the chapter house at York,
        they had recited the commission in the presence of M. John [de]
        Neuton, M. Thomas Walleworth, and M. William Waltham, the
        canons residentiary, who had appointed 7 January 1403/4 for a
        full chapter to discuss the matter.   On that date the same
        canons (the others having been duly cited, not having appeared,
        and having therefore been declared contumacious), discussed
        the archbishop's commission and the certificate of the
        inquisition on the proposed union with the commissaries and
        had given their consent to the project without requiring any
        indemnity.   Sealed with the seal of the dean of Christianity
        of York.   York, 7 January 1403/4.

602.   [f.94] Certificate of the chapter of York (the dean being absent) setting out that, after consideration of the archiepiscopal commission recited in the above document, and the certificate of the inquisition into the proposed union of the churches of Kneesall and Boughton, they had approved the project, without claiming any pension from the united parishes. Chapter House, York, 7 January 1403/4.

603.   [f.94v] Decree for the union of the parishes of Boughton and Kneesall.   After the resignation or decease of Thomas Vemelby, the present rector of Boughton, that church is to become a chapelry of Kneesall, and its revenues are to be annexed to those of Kneesall.   The rector of Kneesall is thereafter to arrange, either in person or by deputy, and at his own expense, for masses to be said at Boughton on Sunday, Wednesday and Friday in each week.   Archbishop's chapel,   Scrooby, 4 February 1403/4.

604.   [f.95] Certificate of Henry [Beaufort], bishop of Lincoln, reciting an archiepiscopal commission (dated at Cawood Castle, 25 April 1404) for an exchange of benefices between John Porter, rector of Gayton, dioc. Lincoln, and John Benet, rector of Winthorpe.   He had received Benet's resignation, and had instituted Porter to Winthorpe, on the presentation of the prior and convent of Elsham, dioc. Lincoln.   London, sub sigillo armorum nostrum, quia aliud ad manus non habemus de presenti, 6 June 1404.

Ind: for Porter to Winthorpe.   Cawood, 17 June 1404.

605.   [ff.95-95v] Certificate of Henry [Beaufort], bishop of Lincoln, reciting an archiepiscopal commission (dated at Cawood Castle, 20 June 1404) for an exchange of benefices between M. Robert [de] Oxton, rector of Meppershall, dioc. Lincoln, and William Caton, rector of Sutton Bonington.   He had received Caton's resignation, and had instituted Oxton to Sutton Bonington in the person of M. Richard Arnall, LL.B., his proctor, on the presentation of Thomas [de Mowbray], Earl Marshal, earl of Nottingham, lord Segrave and Mowbray.   Lyddington, 27 June 1404.

[f.95v] Ind: for Oxton to Sutton Bonington.   Cawood, 3 July (1) 1404.

606.   Certificate of William [of Wykeham], bishop of Winchester, reciting an archiepiscopal commission (dated at Cawood Castle, 16 June 1404) for an exchange of benefices between Henry Helmesale, rector of Weyhill, dioc. Winchester, and William Peek, rector of Holme Pierrepont.   He had received Peek's resignation, and had instituted Helmesale to Holme Pierrepont, on the presentation of Edmund Perpound, knt.   Bishops Waltham, 4 August 1404.

---

1.   The MS. gives the month, incorrectly, as June.

607.   [f.96] Ind: for Helmesale to Holme Pierrepont.   Cawood,
         26 October 1404.

608.   Institution of William Powger, priest, to the perpetual
         chantry of St Mary in the church of Willoughby on the Wolds,
         vacant by the death of Robert Alman, on the presentation of
         Hugh Wyloby, lord of Risley.   Ind: Cawood Castle,
         2 September 1404.

609.   Certificate of John [Burghill], bishop of Coventry and
         Lichfield, reciting an archiepiscopal commission (sealed with
         the seal of the dean and chapter of Lichfield, the
         archiepiscopal seal not being to hand, and dated at Lichfield,
         28 August 1404) for an exchange of Benefices between John [de]
         Accres, chaplain of a chantry in Chesterfield parish church,
         dioc. Coventry and Lichfield, and Thomas Tewere, rector of a
         mediety of Eakring.   He had received Tewere's resignation,
         and had instituted Accres to the mediety of Eakring, in the
         person of Gregory Neuport, clerk, his proctor, on the
         presentation of William de Ros, lord of Hamlake.   Eccleshall
         Castle, 12 September 1404.

         [ff.96-96v] Ind: for Accres to the mediety of Eakring.
         Lichfield, [blank] September 1404, the precise date being
         unknown because the business was concluded at Lichfield
         whilst the archbishop was attending the king's council.

610.   [f.96v] Certificate of Richard [Clifford], bishop of
         Worcester, reciting an archiepiscopal commission (dated at
         his lodgings in Coventry, 11 October 1404) for an exchange of
         benefices between William Dalton, rector of Normanton on Soar,
         and John Claypoll, rector of North Cerney, dioc. Worcester.
         He had received Dalton's resignation, and had instituted
         Claypoll to Normanton, on the presentation of the prior and
         convent of Durham.   Alvechurch, 12 October 1404.

         Ind: for Claypoll to Normanton.   November 1404, the precise
         date being unknown because the business was concluded whilst
         the archbishop was at the Parliament at Coventry.

611.   Institution of John de Berford, priest, to the rectory of
         Leake, on the presentation of John Mawvesyn, lord of Mavesyn
         Ridware.   Ind: November 1404, the precise date being unknown
         because the business was concluded whilst the archbishop was
         at the Parliament at Coventry.

612.   Memorandum of the state of Shelford priory at the time of the
         confirmation of the election of br. Robert Lyndeby as prior,
         1404.

Debts of the priory	80 marks
Perpetual pensions	£20
Corrodies	£40
Temporalities and spiritualities	
for the year	£120

613.   [f.97] Certificate of the dean of Nottingham, recording his
        fulfillment of an archiepiscopal commission (recited in full,
        and dated at Cawood Castle, 20 November 1404) to cite all
        opponents of the election of br. Robert de Lyndeby as prior of
        Shelford in succession to br. William de Kynalton, deceased,
        to attend at the chapel of the manor of Cawood on the Wednesday
        after the feast of St Katherine the Virgin next following
        [26 November].   The citation had been published in the
        conventual church.   Shelford, 23 November 1404.

614.   Confirmation of the election of br. Robert de Lyndby as prior
        of Shelford and release to him of the spiritualities and
        temporalities of the house.   n.d.

615.   Profession of obedience of br. Robert de Lyndby as prior of
        Shelford.   n.d.

616.   [f.97v] Letters testimonial to br. Robert de Lyndeby,
        confirming his election as prior of Shelford, and releasing to
        him the spiritualities and temporalities of the house.   Cawood
        Castle, 26 November 1404.

617.   Mandate to the subprior and convent of Shelford to accept and
        obey br. Robert de Lyndeby [Lyndby] as their prior.   Cawood
        Castle, 26 November 1404.

618.   Mandate to the Official of the archdeacon of Nottingham to
        install br. Robert de Lyndby as prior of Shelford.   [Cawood
        Castle], 26 November 1404.

619.   [ff.97v-98] Certificate of John [Burghill] bishop of Coventry
        and Lichfield, reciting an archiepiscopal commission (dated at
        Cawood Castle, 28 August 1404) for an exchange of benefices
        between James de Conyngeston, rector of Colston, dioc. Coventry
        and Lichfield, and John Barston, rector of Rempstone.   He had
        received Barston's resignation in the person of M. John Bacford,
        acting as substitute for M. Walter London, his original proctor,
        and had instituted Conyngeston to Rempstone in the person of
        John Kyddelow, his proctor, and on the presentation of the prior
        and convent of Lenton.   Eccleshall Castle, 7 November 1404.(1)

620.   [f.98] Certificate of the Official of the archdeacon of
        Nottingham, reciting an archiepiscopal commission (dated at
        Cawood Castle, 28 August 1404) to inquire into the vacancy and
        patronage of the vicarage of Radcliffe on Trent, to which the
        prior and convent of Thurgarton had presented br. Walter de
        Elmeton, canon of Thurgarton.   An inquisition of neighbouring
        rectors and chaplains had declared that the vicarage had been

---

1.   There is no record of the issue of a mandate for induction
        following this institution.   However, the entry is followed by
        a gap in the register, which was presumably intended to
        accommodate the appropriate note.

620.   vacated by John de Thurgarton, now rector of Knebworth, dioc.
        Lincoln, to which church he had been instituted and admitted
        by Henry [Beaufort], bishop of Lincoln, and inducted by the
        archdeacon of Lincoln; that the vacancy had begun on the
        feast of the Nativity of St John the Baptist [24 June] and
        that the prior and convent of Thurgarton were the rightful
        patrons.   Elmeton having been found suitable, the Official
        had instituted and inducted him to the vicarage.   Cotgrave,
        Thursday, the eve of the feast of the Presentation of St Mary
        [20 November] 1404. (1)

621.   [f.98v] Institution of John, son of Henry del Heth, to the
        rectory of Elston, on the presentation of Achilles Bosevyll,
        esq.   Ind: Cawood Castle, 20 December 1404.

622.   Certificate of Henry [Beaufort], bishop of Lincoln, reciting
        an archiepiscopal commission (dated at Cawood Castle,
        22 December 1404) for an exchange of benefices between Robert
        de Kelsay, rector of Firsby, dioc. Lincoln, and William
        Chester, chaplain of the chantry of the gild or fraternity of
        St Mary in Newark parish church.   He had received Chester's
        resignation, and had instituted Kelsay to the chantry, on the
        presentation of Richard Seyvell, warden of the gild or
        fraternity of St Mary of Newark, and Richard de Wakefeld, Elias
        Baxster, and John Bron [Broun], brethren of the fraternity.
        Lincoln, 30 December 1404.

        Ind: for Kelsay to the above chantry.   7 January 1404/5.

623.   Institution of Robert Smyth, priest, to the vicarage of
        Thorney, vacant by the resignation of William Ward, on the
        presentation of the prioress and convent of Broadholme.
        Ind: Cawood Castle, 9 January 1404/5.

624.   [f.99] Institution of John de Glentham, priest, in the person
        of Robert Trowell, vicar of Sutton on Trent, his proctor, to
        the chantry at the altar of St Katherine and St Margaret in
        Edwinstowe parish church, vacant following an exchange for the
        vicarage of Laxton, on the presentation of the prior and
        convent of Newstead.   Ind: Cawood Castle, 20 January 1404/5.

625.   Institution of William Umfray, in the person of Robert Weton,
        clerk, his proctor, to the vicarage of Laxton, vacant by the
        above exchange, on the presentation of Thomas Haxey, rector of
        Laxton.   Ind: Cawood Castle, 20 January 1404/5.

626.   Institution of John Bron, priest, to the vicarage of Basford,
        on the presentation of the prioress and convent of Catesby,
        dioc. Lincoln.   Ind: Cawood Castle, 29 January 1404/5.

---

1.   The text gives the feast as the Assumption, but this (which
        would make the date 14 August) is clearly incorrect.

627.   Institution of Roger Orchard, chaplain, to the vicarage of
       East Markham, on the presentation of Richard Kyngeston, warden
       of the free chapel within Tickhill castle.   Ind: Cawood
       Castle, 2 February 1404/5.

628.   [ff.99-99v] Certificate of the Official of the archdeacon of
       Nottingham, reciting an archiepiscopal commission (dated at
       Cawood Castle, 3 January 1404/5) to inquire into the vacancy
       and patronage of the rectory of Elton, to which the prior and
       convent of Blyth had presented Thomas Gernelle [Gernell],
       priest.   An inquisition of neighbouring rectors, vicars, and
       chaplains had declared that the rectory was vacant by the death
       of John Redmyld, which had occurred on the eve of the feast of
       the Circumcision [31 December] last;   and that the prior and
       convent of Blyth were the rightful patrons.   Gernell having
       been found suitable, the Official had instituted and inducted
       him to the rectory.   Bingham, Tuesday after the feast of
       Epiphany [12 January] 1404/5.

629.   [f.99v] Institution of M. John de Derlton to the vicarage of
       East Markham, vacant by the resignation of Roger Orchard, on
       the presentation of Richard Kyngeston, warden of the free chapel
       within Tickhill castle.   Ind: Cawood Castle, 13 April 1405.

630.   Memorandum of the appointment of John Dernyngton, parson in
          York Minster, as penitentiary within the archdeaconry of
          Richmond, during pleasure.   Rest, 1 August 1398.

631.   Note of the appointment of Nicholas Wartyll, prior of St Bees,
          as penitentiary within Copeland for one year.   Cawood,
          9 January 1398/9.

632.   Appointment of John de Brygnall, parson in York Minster, as
          penitentiary within the archdeaconry of Richmond for one year,
          even in reserved cases (other than violations of the liberties
          and immunities of the minsters at York, Beverley, Ripon, and
          Southwell, invasions of the archbishop's parks and poaching
          of game, perjury in assizes and indictments, matrimonial and
          divorce cases and cases involving disinheritance, loss of life
          or limb, or the greater part of goods).   Cawood, 17 January
          1398/9.

633.   Memorandum of a licence granted to John de Sandall, vicar of
          Clapham, to hear confessions upon the moors within the
          archdeaconry of Richmond for one year.   Cawood, 17 January
          1398/9.

634.   Note of letters dimissory granted to William Ayndyrgate,
          having his first tonsure, to receive acolyte's and other
          orders.   Cawood, 28 January 1398/9.

635.   Dispensation to br. Adam de Fyssewyk [Fissewyk], priest,
          O.P., in accordance with a commission from Francis [Carboni],
          cardinal priest of St Susanna and papal penitentiary (recited
          in full, and dated at St Peter's, Rome, 18 September 1398),
          to receive orders and acquire offices within his Order below
          that of prior provincial, notwithstanding that he is the son
          of a single man and a single woman.   Cawood Castle, 10 April
          1399.

636.   Note of letters dimissory granted to William Laiburn, to
          receive minor and holy orders.   York, 18 April 1399.

637.   Note of similar letters granted to John de Alton, clerk, dioc.
          York.   Cawood, 25 May 1399.

638.   Note of similar letters granted to Anthony de Goldesburgh,
          acolyte, to receive holy orders.   Cawood, 11 June 1399.

639.   [f.100v] Profession of obedience by br. Richard Gower, abbot
          of Jervaulx.   n.d.

640.   Note that the above oath was administered, and archiepiscopal
          benediction conferred, in the presence of Robert Wlfeden,
          precentor of Lichfield cathedral, Thomas Hilton, canon of
          Lincoln, M. Thomas Brustall, rector of Holy Trinity,

640.   Goodramgate, York, and M. John Stanton, notary public.   Chapel
        of the manor of Rest, 24 August 1399.

641.   Commission to the abbot and three qualified canons of Egglestone
        abbey to grant indulgences of three years and as many of 40 days
        to visitors at the altar of St John the Evangelist within the
        monastery at certain feasts throughout the year, and of 100 days
        to similar visitors within the octaves of those feasts and in
        the six days after Whitsun, as granted by papal letters (1), for
        three years.   This shall not apply to those who injure or
        attack the archbishop or the minsters at York, Beverley,
        Southwell or Ripon, to invasions of the archbishop's parks and
        manors, or the removal of notable goods therefrom without the
        consent of the archbishop or his wardens, or to assaults on
        priests and clerks which cause major injury or maiming, or to
        murderers, corruptors of nuns, deflowerers of virgins and those
        laity who seize ecclesiastical benefices or the revenues thereof,
        all such cases being reserved to the archbishop.   Bishopthorpe,
        23 January 1399/1400.

642.   [ff.100v-101] Dispensation to John Laurence [Laurance], layman,
        and Marjorie [de] Barbrun, his wife, in accordance with a
        commission from Francis [Carboni], cardinal priest of St Susanna
        and papal penitentiary (recited in full, and dated at St Peter's,
        Rome, 19 September 1398), declaring them to be divorced, but
        allowing them to remarry after a period of separation, their
        original marriage having been performed even though they were
        aware of the impediment of John's relationship in the fourth
        degree of consanguinity to Gilbert, the deceased first husband
        of Marjorie.   The parties had appeared in person before the
        archbishop on 11 June 1400, in the chapel of the manor of
        Bishop Burton.   Bishop Burton, 11 June 1400.(2)

643.   [f.101] Dispensation to William Schroude [Schrowde], deacon,
        in accordance with a commission from Francis [Carboni], cardinal
        priest of St Susanna and papal penitentiary (recited in full,
        and dated at St Peter's, Rome, 7 April 1400), to receive
        priest's orders and acquire a benefice, notwithstanding that he
        was the son of a single man and a single woman, and had
        concealed the fact when taking minor orders and those of
        subdeacon and deacon.   Bishopthorpe, 1 July 1400.

644.   [ff.101-101v] Dispensation to John Nelson, layman, and Alice
        Ward, his wife, in accordance with a commission from Francis
        [Carboni], cardinal priest of St Susanna and papal penitentiary
        (recited in full, and dated at St Peter's, Rome, 19 September
        1398), declaring them to be divorced, but allowing them to
        remarry after a period of separation, their original marriage
        having been performed even though they were aware of the
        impediment of their relationship in the fourth degree of
        consanguinity on both sides.   Cawood Castle, 30 July 1400.(2)

---

1.   See CPL, v, 175.
2.   See Testamenta Eboracensia, iii, 317.

645.   [ff.101v-102] Dispensation to John Bland, junior, layman, and Margaret, daughter of John Haw, in accordance with a commission from Francis [Carboni], cardinal priest of St Susanna and papal penitentiary (recited in full, and dated at St Peter's, Rome, 17 December 1400) allowing them to marry, notwithstanding Margaret's relationship in the fourth degree of consanguinity on both sides to Helen, daughter of Ralph Wryght, who had been John's first wife.   Bishop Burton, 19 April 1401. (1)

646.   [f.102] Dispensation to William de Holgyll, layman, and Margaret, widow of Thomas Adson, in accordance with a commission from Francis [Carboni], cardinal priest of St Susanna and papal penitentiary (recited in full, and dated at St Peter's, Rome, 15 July 1401), to confirm their marriage, which had been contracted in ignorance of the impediment of William's relationship in the fourth degree of consanguinity on both sides to Thomas, which had been brought to their attention prior to the solemnisation of the marriage. Bishopthorpe, 2 January 1401/2. (1)

[f.102v: BLANK]

[ff.103-104v: MISSING]

[ff.105-105v: BLANK]

---

1.   See _Testamenta Eboracensia_, iii, 317.

[f.106] Hexham and Hexhamshire, Howden and Howdenshire, Allerton and Allertonshire, with the jurisdiction of Gloucester, the provostship of Beverley, and the jurisdictions of Snaith and Selby.

647.   Collation of the wardenship of the hospital of St Giles, Hexham, to John Martyn, clerk, member of the archbishop's household, according to the constitution Quia contingit.   Ind: Prior of Hexham.   Rest, 18 July 1398.

648.   Deputation of the custody of the archbishop's spirituality within the county of Gloucester to br. Thomas Duk, prior of St Oswald, Gloucester.   Rest, 9 August 1398.

649.   Deputation of the Officiality of the archbishop's jurisdiction within the county of Gloucester to M. William Milton, LL.B., during pleasure.   Rest, 9 August 1398.

650.   Appointment of John Bisseley, domicellus, as the archbishop's steward and receiver within Churchdown and all other domains in Gloucestershire, during pleasure.   Rest, 9 August 1398.

651.   Appointment, during pleasure, of br. John Pleyer, subprior of St Oswald, Gloucester, as penitentiary of the archbishop's subjects in Gloucestershire, even in reserved cases, (other than invasions of the archbishop's parks and poaching of game, violation of nuns, perjury in assizes or indictments, matrimonial and divorce cases, or cases involving disinheritance, loss of life or limb, or the greater part of goods which, except for cases in mortis articulo, are reserved to the archbishop).   Rest, 9 August 1398.

652.   [ff.106–106v] Inspeximus and confirmation of the grant of a corrody (recited in full, and dated in the chapter house of the priory of St Oswald, Gloucester, Saturday, the feast of St Michael the Archangel, 21 Richard II [29 September, 1397]) by prior Thomas Duk and the convent of St Oswald, Gloucester, to Henry Hannys and Isabella his first wife, for their joint and several lives.   It shall consist of free access to the conventual fishpond and brewhouse, a loaf called a myche and a gallon of best ale every day, 26s. 8d. a year payable at the customary quarters, and a dwelling within the priory, which Walter Haldeyn formerly held, for the life of Henry and with free access thereto; in return for a tenement without Aylesgate in the suburbs of Gloucester granted by Hannys to Richard Burton and John Wotton, chaplains, their heirs and assigns.   If the landgavel for the tenement exceeds 3d., they shall be compensated at the rate of 12d. for each 1d. of excess. Hannys is to be responsible for the upkeep of the mansion within the priory.   Rest, 12 August 1398.

653.   [f.106v] Licence to the subprior and convent of Hexham to
        elect a new prior, in succession to br. Alexander de Marton,
        whose resignation had been conveyed to the archbishop by brs.
        William Wodhorn and Richard Hemeswell, canons of Hexham, his
        proctors.   Cawood Castle, 5 November 1398.

654.   Memorandum of letters dimissory granted to brs. Robert Cuter,
        Thomas Aspur, T. Goswyk, and Robert Doram, canons of Hexham,
        Cawood Castle, 9 December 1398.

655.   Confirmation of the election of br. John de Hexham as prior
        of Hexham, following the resignation of br. Alexander de
        Marton, and release to him of the spiritualities and
        temporalities of the house.   n.d.

656.   Profession of obedience by br. John de Hexham, prior of
        Hexham. n.d.

657.   Letters testimonial to br. John de Hexham, confirming his
        election as prior of Hexham, and releasing to him the
        spiritualities and temporalities of the house.   Cawood
        Castle, 9 December 1398.

658.   Mandate to the subprior and convent of Hexham, to receive
        and obey br. John de Hexham as their prior.   Cawood Castle,
        9 December 1398.

659.   [f.107] Mandate to the subprior of Hexham, to install br.
        John de Hexham as prior.   Cawood Castle, 9 December 1398.

660.   Mandate to the chapter of York (the dean being absent), to
        induct br. John de Hexham, priest, to the prebend of Salton,
        annexed to the priory of Hexham.   Cawood Castle,
        10 December 1398.

661.   Note of the appointment of William Aghton, vicar of a prebend
        in the collegiate church of Howden, as penitentiary for one
        year even in reserved cases (other than those specially
        reserved).   Cawood, 4 January 1398/9.

662.   Note of similar appointments of John Cawode, prior of Snaith,
        and Robert Lonesdale, parochial chaplain of Snaith, as
        penitentiaries for one year, except in cases specially
        reserved as in no. 651.   Cawood, 6 February 1398/9.

663.   [ff.107-107v] Certificate of M. William [de] Asshton, LL.D.,
        dean of the royal free chapel of St Martin le Grand, London,
        reciting an archiepiscopal commission (dated at Cawood Castle,
        3 January 1398/9) for an exchange of prebends between
        M. Richard [de] Wynewyk, prebendary of Christshall in the said
        chapel, and M. Robert [de] Manfeld, prebendary of Skelton in
        the collegiate church of Howden.   He had examined both parties
        on the proposed exchange, Wynewyk being represented by Thomas
        de Asshton, esq., his proctor, as was attested by letters

663.   notarised by M. Robert de Halton iuxta Burton Stather, clerk,
        dioc. Lincoln, and had received their resignations. He had
        instituted Wynewyk, in the person of Asshton, to the prebend
        of Skelton, on the presentation of the prior and convent of
        Durham.   Chapter House, St Martin le Grand [London],
        1 February 1398/9.

664.   Note that, following the receipt of the above certificate, a
        mandate was issued to the custodian of the spiritualities of
        Howden and Howdenshire to induct and install Wynewyk [Wynwyk]
        to the prebend of Skelton, Robert Hankese, domicellus, having
        first offered obedience as his proctor.   Cawood, 22 February
        1398/9.

665.   Certificate of br. John Hexham, prior of Hexham, reciting an
        archiepiscopal mandate (dated at Cawood Castle, 12 December
        1398), nominating Roger Halward, chaplain (the bearer of the
        commission), to a pension from the priory, according to the
        custom within the diocese of York on the election of a new
        prior.   The certificate confirms that an annual pension of
        five marks will be awarded, until such time as the priory can
        provide Halward with a suitable benefice.   Hexham, 16 December
        1398.

666.   Institution of William de Thurstanton, deacon, to the vicarage
        of Eastrington, on the presentation of the prior and convent of
        Durham.   Ind: Custodian of the spiritualities of Howden and
        Howdenshire.   Cawood Castle, 28 February 1398/9.

667.   Institution of William Darell, priest, to the free chantry of
        Linton, vacant by the resignation of John Martyn, on the
        presentation of Henry Percy, earl of Northumberland.   Ind:
        as above.   Cawood Castle, 4 March 1398/9.

668.   [f.108] Institution of John Byry, priest, in the person of
        William Grandesden, his proctor, to the vicarage of Leake,
        vacant by the death of German de Holme, on the presentation of
        Walter [Skirlaw], bishop of Durham.   Ind: John Luth, priest.
        Cawood Castle, 24 March 1398/9.

669.   Certificate of the custodian of the spiritualities of
        Hemingbrough, reciting an archiepiscopal commission (addressed
        to both the custodian and the parochial chaplain of Hemingbrough,
        and dated at Cawood Castle, 6 March 1398/9), setting out the
        form of public retraction to be made by Robert Babthorp and
        Thomas Hagthorp, parishioners of Hemingbrough, during mass on
        the Sunday next following [9 March].   They had enjoined their
        co-parishioners not to offer more than 1d. for mortuaries,
        marriages, and purifications, and had thereby incurred specific
        excommunication for themselves, and general excommunication for
        their adherents; and on submission and appearance before the
        archbishop had incurred penances.   The public declaration was
        to form part of their absolution, they advising their
        followers to revert to the former system of payments.   The

669.   recipients of the commission are to report on the
         proceedings before Easter next [30 March].   The commission
         had been fulfilled, Babthorp making the declaration on behalf
         of himself and Hagthorp; but he had added that neither of
         them intended personally to increase their payments, and that
         for his part he did not wish to pay anything.   Thereafter the
         custodian had read out the archbishop's commission in English
         (in vulgari).   Hemingbrough, 11 March 1398/9.

670.   [ff.108-108v] Notarial instrument, recording that John
         Poleyn, parochial priest of Hemingbrough, had appeared before
         the archbishop and had admitted ignoring a mandate from the
         commissary general of the Court of York, ordering him to
         admonish Edmund de Meetham, parishioner of Hemingbrough, to
         pay to M. Thomas Walworth, the rector, the four years' arrears
         of tithes of pasture which had been farmed out to him, and
         also the £4 costs which had been awarded against him in the
         commissary general's court as sentence in the resulting
         cause. (1)   He was granted absolution, and was ordered to
         stand at the font of Hemingbrough church on two Sundays,
         bareheaded and barefooted, wearing a surplice, and carrying a
         lighted candle weighing one pound, and during the saying of
         the mass to chant as much of the psalter as possible, and at
         the end of the second penance to offer the burning candle at
         the altar of the church.   In the presence of William
         [Northbrugge], bishop Pharensis and suffragan of York, Robert
         Wolfeden, precentor of Lichfield cathedral, M. John Garton and
         M. Thomas Burstall (rectors of Leigh, dioc. Lichfield, and Holy
         Trinity [Goodramgate], York) and John Welton, notaries public.
         The principal chapel, Cawood, 6 March 1398/9.

671.   [f.108v] Appointment of John de Mitteford, clerk, as
         receiver within the liberty of Hexham.   Bishopthorpe,
         1 December 1399.

672.   Appointment of William de Mitteford, domicellus, as steward
         within the lordships, manors, and liberties of Hexhamshire.
         Bishopthorpe, 1 December 1399.

673.   Institution of Richard de Alta Ripa [Dautry], priest, to the
         perpetual chantry founded for the soul of William de Hamelton,
         sometime dean of York, in the chapel of St Mary at Hambleton,
         vacant by the death of Robert de Catton, on the presentation
         of the chapter of York, the dean being absent.   Ind:
         Custodian of the spiritualities of Selby.   Bishop Burton,
         19 April 1400.

674.   [ff.108v-109] Appointment of the prior of Hexham as
         chancellor within the liberty of Hexham and Hexhamshire.
         Bishop Burton, 2 June 1400.

---

1.   For some of the papers relating to this case, see B.I.,
         CP.E.231.

675. [f.109] Dispensation to John Selby, clerk, dioc. York, in accordance with a commission from Bartholomew (1) [Aprano], bishop of Lucera, acting chief papal penitentiary in the absence of Francis [Carboni], cardinal priest of St Susanna (recited in full, dated at St Peter's, Rome, 25 July 1400, and sealed with the seal of the chief penitentiary), to receive orders and acquire a benefice, notwithstanding that he was the son of a priest and a single woman, and had concealed the fact when acquiring clerical status. Cawood Castle, 10 June 1401.

676. Institution of John de Hemyngburgh, priest, to the vicarage of the prebend of Thorpe in the collegiate church of Howden, on the presentation of the prior and convent of Durham. Ind: Custodian of the spiritualities of Howden. Cawood Castle, 4 July 1401.

677. [ff.109-109v] Certificate of the chapter of York Minster (the dean being absent) reciting [incompletely] an archiepiscopal commission (dated at Rest, 6 April 1402) for an exchange of benefices between John Grene, prebendal vicar of Wistow, and Thomas Litster, prebendal vicar of Skelton in the collegiate church of Howden. They had received Litster's resignation and had instituted Grene to the vicarage of Skelton, on the presentation of the prior and convent of Durham. Chapter House, York, 10 May 1402.

678. [f.109v] Institution of William Grandesden, priest, to the vicarage of Osmotherley, vacant by the death of Cuthbert de Syggeston, on the presentation of Walter [Skirlaw], bishop of Durham. Ind: Custodian of the spiritualities of Allerton and Allertonshire. York, 9 January 1402/3.

679. [ff.109v-110] Certificate of William de Norton, vicar-general of the archdeacon of Richmond, reciting an archiepiscopal commission (addressed to the archdeacon or his vicar-general and dated at Scrooby, 20 March 1402/3) for an exchange of benefices between John [de] Staynefelde [Staynefeld], rector of Barningham within the archdeaconry of Richmond, and Robert [de] Ridmershill [Redmershill], vicar of Northallerton. He had received Ridmershill's resignation, and had instituted Staynefelde to Northallerton on the presentation of the prior and convent of Durham. Croft, 23 March 1402/3.

[f.110] Ind: Custodian of the spiritualities of Allerton and Allertonshire; for Staynfeld to Northallerton. 31 March 1403.

680. Institution of Thomas de la Hay, clerk, to the prebend or portion in Osmotherley church vacant by the death of William Clay, on the presentation of Walter [Skirlaw], bishop of Durham. Ind: as above. Scrooby, 4 April 1403.

---

1. The MS. gives the name as 'Bassusseachius'.

681. Institution of William Ingilby, priest, to the vicarage of
Osmotherley, on the presentation of Walter [Skirlaw], bishop
of Durham. Ind: as above. Cawood, 24 November 1404.

682. [ff.110-110v] Certificate of the custodian of the
spiritualities of Allerton and Allertonshire, reciting an
archiepiscopal commission (dated at Cawood Castle,
8 December 1404) to inquire into the vacancy and patronage of
the rectory of Cowesby, to which Henry Vavasour [Vavasur] and
Robert [de] Lamplogh, knts., together with Richard de Burgh (1)
and Robert de Rowdon, had presented John Ottryngton, priest.
At an inquisition, the rectors of Birkby, Kirby Sigston and
Brotton, and the vicars of Northallerton, Leake, Osmotherley,
North Otterington and Thornton le Street, with Robert de
Poklyngton, John Kilpyn, Thomas Tode, John de Causeby and
William de Leek, chaplains, had declared that the church was
vacant by the death of William Ottewy, which had occurred on
1 December last; that Vavasour, Lamplogh, Burgh and Rowdon
were the rightful patrons, having acquired the lordship of
Cowesby with the advowson of the church from Elizabeth
[Hastings], lady of Elmham; and that Walter de Lee, knt.,
acting in right of his wife Joan, mother of the said Elizabeth,
had presented Ottewy (2) to the rectory, which he had held for
34 years and more and that Ottryngton was a suitable person to
hold the benefice. Sealed with the custodian's official seal,
and the seals of the inquisitors. Northallerton, 11 December
1404.

683. [f.110v] Institution of John Ottryngton, priest, to the
rectory of Cowesby, on the presentation of Henry Vavasur and
Robert de Lamplogh, knts., and Richard Burgh and Robert
Rowdon. Ind: Custodian of the spiritualities of Allerton
and Allertonshire. Cawood Castle, 13 December 1404.

684. Appointment of br. John Player, canon and subprior of
St Oswald, Gloucester, as prior or warden of the priory,
following the resignation of br. John de Shipton, and committal
to him of the spiritualities and temporalities of the house.
Cawood Castle, 17 March 1404/5.

685. Note of letters sent to the canons and convent of St Oswald,
Gloucester, ordering them to obey br. John Player as their
prior. 17 March 1404/5.

686. Memorandum of the appointment of br. John Player, prior of
St Oswald, Gloucester, as penitentiary of the archbishop's
subjects in Gloucestershire, during pleasure, and with the
customary exceptions. Cawood Castle, 17 March 1404/5.

---

1. On the first appearance of his name, the Christian name is
omitted, and the surname given as 'de Aurgh'.
2. Here called 'John'.

687.   Note of the appointment of br. Robert Horne, canon of St
        Oswald, Gloucester, and John Wotton, priest, as custodians of
        the jurisdiction of Gloucestershire, during pleasure.   Cawood
        Castle, 17 March 1404/5.

688.   Institution of M. Thomas de Weston, archdeacon of Durham, to
        the prebend of Barmby on the Marsh, in the collegiate church of
        Howden, on the presentation of the prior and convent of Durham.
        Ind: Custodian of the spiritualities of Howden and Howdenshire.
        Bishopthorpe, 28 November 1401.

        [ff.111-113v: BLANK]

Personal names appear in the form in which they occur in the text, with cross-references from variant spellings. Counties have been given in round brackets only for places outside Yorkshire.

abbeys see under names of individual
   religious houses
Aberford 34
absolution 12, 27, 51, 105-6
Acastre, John de, son of Richard de,
   of York 12
   guardian of see Sallay, William de
Acclom (Acclum), Henry 52
   Henry 89
Accres, John de 96
Acklam, West 51
Ackworth 35
   rector of see Whiston, Thomas de
acquittal 50
Adam, John 91
Addestoke, John 30, 82
Adel 34
Aderley, Thomas 75
Adewyk, John 20
administration, letters of 18
Adson, Margaret, widow of Thomas 102
Aghton, William 104
Ake, Roger 63
Alas, John 87
Aldbrough
   church of 30, 33
   vicarage of 7
   vicars of see Bardesay, Robert de;
   Cochon, Alan; Wayte, Nicholas
Alferton, William 87
Algerkyrk (Algarkyrk), Thomas de 8
Aliotti, Lewis 30
Allerthorp, Laurence 3
Allerton, fee of 94
Allerton and Allertonshire, peculiar
   jurisdiction of iii
   custodian of the spirituality of
   107-8
Alman, Robert 96
Almondbury, rector of see Elvet,
   Richard
Alne, Richard de 20
   William de 20
Alta Ripa (Dautry, Dawtre), Agnes de 8
   Laurence de 20
   Richard de 106
Alton, John de 100

Alvechurch (Worcs.) 96
Alwarthorp, Isabel de see York, All Saints,
   Pavement, chantry founded by Thomas de
   Alwarthorp
   Thomas de see York, All Saints,
   Pavement, chantry founded by Thomas de
   Alwarthorp
anchorites 34, 73
Anglia, Nicholas de 94
Anlaby, Thomas de 44
Annesley, Hugh de, knt. 39
   Hugh son of above 38-9
   John de, knt. 38
   Thomas de, of Kinoulton (Notts.) 38-9
   Thomas son of above 39
Apesthorpe, prebend in York Minster 7
   prebendaries of see Feriby, Thomas;
   Wardrober, Thomas
Appilgarth see Appylgarth
Appilton (Apilton, Appelton, Apulton),
   M. John 41
   M. Robert de, rector of Huggate, rector
   of Sturton le Steeple 57, 64, 82
   M. Robert de, rector of St Wilfrid, York
   13, 37
appropriations of churches, to dean and
   chapter of York 21-2
appropriations of churches, confirmation of
   to religious houses 33-4, 51-2, 61,
   65-7, 70, 87-8
Appylgarth (Appilgarth), M. Robert 44, 53
Aprano, Bartholomew ('Bassusseachius'),
   bishop of Lucera 107
Apulton see Appilton
Aquitaine, duke of see John of Gaunt
archdeaconries see Cleveland, East Riding,
   Nottingham, Richmond, York
Ardesley, br. William de 42
Areshom, Walter 20
Argam 60
   priests at see Gresacre, John; Raper,
   Richard
Armthorpe 43-4
   rectors of see Rouclyff, Richard;
   Sandall, John
Arnald (Arnall), M. Richard 70-1, 73, 95
   Thomas 88

Arncliffe 15
    rector of see Wyndhill, John de
Arnold (Notts.), rector of see John
Arthington priory 11
    prioress of 34
Arundel, Thomas, archbishop of York,
    archbishop of Canterbury v-vi
    suffragan bishop of see Oswald
Aschburn (Asshburn), Patrick de 42
    Robert de 5
Ask, John de, and Joan his wife 55, 60
Askam, Richard 55
Askeby (Askby), William 75
Askham Richard 30
    vicars of see Bramham, William;
    Smyth, William
Asmunderby, Richard 2
Aspur, br. Thomas 104
Asshburn see Aschburn
Asshebury (Asshbury, Asshebery), William
    de 24-5, 30
Asshefeld, Robert 38
Asshton, Thomas de 104-5
    M. William de 104
Aston 17
    rector of see Santon, Robert de
Attekirk see Kyrk
Attenborough (Notts.) 71
Attynwyk, William de 62
Atwick 67
Aughton 66
Augustinians see Clonne, William de;
    Roby, Richard
Aylif, Thomas 86
Ayndyrgate, William 100
Ayton, Great 52
Babthorp, Robert 105-6
Bacford, M. John 97
Bagby, Robert de 8
Bakster (Baxter), Elias, of Newark
    (Notts.) 94, 98
Balderby, Ralph de 19-20
Balderston, Edmund de 18
Banen, John 37
Bank, Adam del 20
Barbour, Robert 37
Barbrun, Marjorie de 101
    Gilbert, first husband of 101
Bardesay (Berdesay), Robert de 7, 58
Bardney abbey (Lincs.) 67
Barker, Peter 60
    William, of Tadcaster 22-3, 27
        Agnes, wife of 22-3
        chantry founded by William and

Agnes see Tadcaster, chantry at the
    altar of St Nicholas in the chapel of
    St Nicholas
Barking (Essex), All Saints, chantry for
    the soul of Thomas Pilk 85
    priests of see Holme, John; Tyllyng,
    William
Barmby on the Marsh, prebend in Howden
    Minster 109
    prebendary of see Weston, Thomas de
Barnard (Bernard), M. John 49, 53
Barnby, prebend in York Minster 3, 10
    prebendaries of see Haxey, Thomas;
    Hilton, Thomas de
Barnby Dun 19
    vicar of see Thomasson, John
Barneby, Robert 92
    William de 67
Barnet, M. John, Official of the Court of
    Canterbury 53
    John, canon of York 36
Barningham 107
    rector of see Ridmershill, Robert de;
    Staynefeld, John de
Barnoldswick 33
Baron, Richard 35, 87
Barre, Robert 85
Barston, John 97
Barton, Edmund de 50
    Henry de 23
    br. John de 62
    Roger de 34
Barton in Fabis (Notts.)
    rectory of 71
        rectors of see Arnald, Richard;
        Conyngton, William
Barton le Street 34, 50
    rector of see Barton, Edmund de
Barwick in Elmet 35, 41
    rector of see Canonum, William;
    Marunhull, William; Popilton, Thomas
Basage, John 85
Basefford, Henry de 12
Basely (Basele), William 31, 38
Basford (Notts.), lordship of 71
    vicarage of 98
    vicar of see Broun, John
Basset (Bassett), John 40
    Margaret 73
Bassyngham, Robert (once John) 82
bastardy, dispensations for 24, 26-7, 32,
    55-7, 60-1, 65, 73, 79-80, 93, 100-1,
    107
Basy, Elizabeth, widow of Richard 36

111

Bathley (Notts.) 88
Batley v, 19-20
    vicars of see Balderby, Ralph de;
    Esseholt, John
Bawdewyn, William 83
Baxter see Bakster
Beaufort, Henry, bishop of Lincoln 1,
    24-5, 30-1, 52-3, 61, 71-2, 74, 80,
    82, 84-5, 91-2, 95, 98
    lodgings of, at the Old Temple,
    London 1
    vicar-general of see Burbache, John
            John, earl of Somerset 66
Beauvale priory (Notts.) 71, 82
Beby, John de 89
Becket, St Thomas see St Thomas Becket
Beckingham, prebend in Southwell
    Minster 4, 9
    prebendaries of see Martyn, John;
    Merston, Henry de; Ronhall, Richard
Bedeman, William 72
Beechill with Knaresborough, prebend
    in York Minster 2, 4
    prebendaries of see Scrope,
    Stephen le; Wolvenden, Robert
Beeford 57, 67-8
    vicars of see Kylburne, John;
    Stapilton, Peter de
Beeston (Notts.) 70-1, 84
    vicars of see Mason, Richard; Serle,
    Henry
Belewe, John the father 38
            John the son 38
Belton, John de 81
Bekyngham, John de, of Newark (Notts.)
    80, 83, 86, 90, 93
benefices, unions of vii, 52, 61, 75,
    94-5
Benet, John 95
    William 81-2
Beng, John, chantry for see York, All
    Saints, North Street, chantry at the
    altar of St Mary
Bentworth (Hants.) 91
    rectors of see Cook, John;
    Wikireslay, Thomas de
Berdesay see Bardesay
Berford, John de 96
Bergh (Burgh), Richard de 108
    William 34
Bernard see Barnard
Beroby, William de 33
Bertham, William 92
Beswyk, Robert de 11

Beverlaco (Beverley), br. William de 91
Beverley 35, 64, 66, 81
    dean of 57-8, 65; see also Drax, John
    Minster iii, 16, 48, 56, 72, 100-1
        chapter of 2, 5, 10, 58, 65
        prebend at altar of St Leonard,
        vicarage of 5
            vicars of see Bradeley, John;
            Louthorp, Robert
        prebend at the altar of St Peter 10
            prebendaries of see Chesterfeld,
            Richard de; Conyngeston, Richard
        prebend at the altar of St Stephen 2
            prebendary of see Wolvenden,
            Robert
        provost of see Manfeld, Robert
            peculiar jurisdiction of iii
            Officiality of the spirituality
            of 64
    St Martin in the Charnel, parochial
    chaplain of see Ryell, William
Beyekirke, Thomas 93
Biddenden (Kent) 54
    rectors of see Hamerton, Henry;
    Morewyk, William
Bilborough (Notts.) 80
Bilbrough 34
Billesthorp (Bildesthorp), John de 83, 90,
    93
Bilton, prebend in York Minster 4
    prebendaries of see Burstall, Thomas;
    Carppe, John
Bilton, John de 18
    Robert 34
    Thomas de 17
Bingham (Notts.) 99
    chantry of St Helen 70
        priest of see Geffray, William
    vicarage of 72
        vicars of see Bedeman, William
Bingley 20
    vicars of see Alta Ripa, Laurence de;
    Emesay, Robert de
Bird, Peter 31
Birdesall see Bridsall
Birkby, rector of 108
Birkin
    chantry of the Holy Trinity 19
        priests of see Cheworth, Thomas de;
        Toneton, Thomas de
    lord of see Everyngham, John
    rectory of 39, 44, 53, 92
        rectors of see Clifton, John de;
        Seggefeld, John de; Wikireslay,
        Thomas de

Birstall, church of 30, 33
    vicar of see Lyversege, Richard de
Bishop Burton vi
    chapel of the manor of 101
    documents dated at 2-5, 23-4, 27, 31,
        50, 59-61, 63-4, 75-6, 80-2, 101-2, 106
Bishopthorpe v
    chapel at 21
    documents dated at 2, 5, 19-24, 49-50,
        58-61, 65, 74-5, 84, 87, 101-2, 106, 109
    vicarage of 31, 38
        vicars of see Basely, William;
        Bryg, John del; Nafferton, John de
Bishops Waltham (Hants.) 91, 95
Bisseley, John 103
Bitchfield (Lincs.) 82
    rector of see Bassyngham, Robert;
    Gateles, John
Blakwell, Peter 72-3
Bland, John, jr. 102
    Helen, wife of 102
    Margaret, wife of 102
Bliburgh, M. John 37
Blofield (Norf.) 74
Blyth (Notts.)
    priory at 88, 94, 99
        prior of see Anglia, Nicholas de
    vicarage of 88
        vicars of see Cumberton, Robert;
        Thorp, Thomas de
Bole, prebend in York Minster 3, 6
    prebendaries of see Conyngeston,
    Richard; Gaunstede, Simon
Bolleron, John 18
Bollesore, John 53
Bollesovere, Helen de 88
Bolton, Henry de 20
    John 34
Bolton by Bowland 41
    vicar of see Hogeson, John
Bolton (in Craven) priory 33, 35-6
    canon of see Ferrour, Thomas
    prior of see Grene, Robert
Bolton Percy 16
    rector of see Degyll, Richard
Bolton upon Dearne 38
    chantry at altar of St Mary,
    ordination of 38-9
        priest of see Ward, Thomas
    lands in (detailed) 38
Bondegate, John 7
Boniface IX, pope i, 1, 11, 55, 64,
    73-4, 86, 93, 101
Boresworth, Robert 23

Bosevyll, Achilles 98
Bosom, John 89
Boson, John 82
Botiler see Botyler
Botlesham (Bottlesham), M. John, bishop
    of Rochester 2, 86
Bottelom, Ralph de 57
Bottlesham see Botlesham
Botyler (Botiler), John 40
Boughton.(Notts.) 94
    vicar of see Vemelby, Thomas
    union of, with Kneesall 94-5
Bowdon, John 83
Bowes (Bows), Thomas 49
    William 34
Bowet, Henry, archbishop of York ii, 11
Bows see Bowes
Boynton 57, 67
    vicars of see Bottelom, Ralph de;
    Ryse, Stephen de
Bracebryg, Thomas de 34
Bracewell 33
Bradeley, John 5
Bradford 30
    rector of see Wynceby, William de
    vicar of see William; Rodes,
    William de
Bradforth, John de 32
Bradmore (Notts.) 71
Brafferton 44, 53
    rectors of see Appylgarth, Robert;
    Watton, Thomas de
Bramcote (Notts.) 71
Bramham, William 30
Brammelay, Henry de 17
Brandsby 50
    vicar of see Middelton, John
Brant Broughton (Lincs.) 52-3
    rectors of see Fawdon, William; Peek,
    William
Brasse, John 60
Bray, John 70
Braybrooke, Robert, bishop of London 81,
    85, 88, 91
Breggeford (Bregeford, Briggeford,
    Bryggeford), John, of Hockerton
    (Notts.) 74, 91
Brerehaghe, John de 22
Breton, Henry 38
Brid (Bryd), M. John 6
    Peter 62
Bridgford, East (Notts.) 70
    rectors of see Merston, Henry de;
    Sturmy, Hugh

113

Bridgford, West (Notts.) 70
Bridlington
    church of 67
    priory at 54, 57, 63, 67
        canons of see Sleghtholme, William;
        Zereslay, John
Bridsall (Birdesall), br. Peter de 22, 42
Briggeford see Breggeford
Brind 51
Broadbusk, hospital of St Mary
    Magdalene 84
    wardens of see Elmesall, Henry de;
    Merston, Henry de
Broadholme priory (Notts.) 98
Brodsworth 30, 82
    vicars of see Addestoke, John;
    Asshebury, William; Louth, Adam de
Broghton see Broughton
Broket, Richard 69
Bromham (Wilts.) 92
    rectors of see Dalton, William;
    Haukerigg, Nicholas
Bromley, William 61
Bron see Broun
Brotton 51
    rector of 108
Broughton (Broghton), John de 33
    William de, vicar of Mirfield 36, 38
    William de, rector of Kimberley 71
Broun (Bron, Broune), John, chantry
    priest in the chapel of St Nicholas,
    Wansford 58
    John, of Newark (Notts.) 86, 98
    John, vicar of Basford 98
    John, vicar of Skeckling 58
    Richard 58
Broxtow (Notts.) 80
    rector of see Dowbrygg, John
Brunby, William, proctor for William
    Thurbache 75
    William, proctor for William, lord
    of Sandiacre 83
Brustall see Burstall
Bryan (Bryane), Robert 12, 42
    William 31
Bryd see Brid
Brydlyngton, Gregory de, and Agnes, wife
    of, chantry for; see Scarborough,
    chantry at the altar of St James the
    Apostle
    see also Bridlington
Bryg, John del 31
Bryggeford see Breggeford
Brygnall, John de 100

Brynkelowe (Brynklow), M. William 6
Brynyston, John 20
Bubwyth (Bubwith), Nicholas de 1, 8
Buckden 84
Buckenham Ferry (Norf.) 82
    rectors of see Benet, William;
    Juwell, John
Budesby, br. Roger de 52
Buggcy, Peter 34
Bugge, John 60
Bukler, Adam 34
Bukton, Peter de 14
    Robert de 57
Bulcote (Notts.) 88
Bulkote, William 74
Bull, Robert 28
    William 28
bulls, papal vii, 11, 32, 91; see also
    Boniface IX
Bulwell (Notts.) 88
    rectors of see Garton, William;
    Osmund, John
Bunny (Notts.), lordship of 71
    rectory of 73
        rector of see Ulverscoft, prior of
Burbache, John 57
Burgeys, John 44
Burgh see Bergh
Burghill, John, bishop of Coventry and
    Lichfield 9, 40, 75, 85, 87-8, 96-7
Burnby, William 75
Burne, Robert, of Kirkburn 56
Burnham, br. William 19
Burnsall, mediety of 18
    rector of see Hoede, Thomas
Burstall (Brustall), M. Thomas, clerk of the
    archbishop's household, prebendary in the
    chapel of St Mary and the Holy Angels,
    prebendary of Bilton in York Minster,
    and of Norwell (Tertia Pars) in Southwell
    Minster 3-6
    M. Thomas, notary public, rector of Holy
    Trinity, Goodramgate, York 51, 57,
    100-1, 106
Burton, Henry de 20
    Isabella de 59-60
    John de 89
    John de, knt. 38
    Richard 103
    M. Roger de 81
    William de, citizen of York 34
    William, parishioner of St Saviour,
    York 34
    William, vicar of Ganton 60

Burton Fleming, chantry of the Holy
  Trinity 64
    priests of see Clifton, Robert;
    Marton, Robert
  vicar of 63
Burton Joyce (Notts.) 85, 88
  vicar of see Oxton, Geoffrey de
Burton, West 88
Burythorpe 66
Byffyn, William 43
Bykerstaf, Richard 99
Byland abbey 69
Bylay, John 14
Byngham, John de 74
Byry, John 105
Bywell, Thomas 50
Caldecote (Warw.) 40
  rectors of see Peyntour, Robert;
  Stanley, William de
Caldecote, M. Roger 72-3
Calverley 19-20
  vicars of see Balderby, Ralph de;
  Esseholt, John
Calverley, Joan, sometime wife of
  Walter 42
Cambridge, Holy Trinity parish 62
  St Michael's College, fellow of, see
  Wykyngeston, John
  university of 72
Cameryngham, Peter 80
Campsall 26, 28
  rector of see Coryngham, Roger de
Campsall, John 43
Canon, William 15, 40
Canonum (Cononum), William 41
Canterbury (Kent), archbishop of see
  Arundel, Thomas; Walden, Roger
  Officiality of the court of 36
  see also Barnet, John
  prior of 2
Cantley 30
  vicars of see Bramham, William;
  Smyth, William
Carboni, Francis iv, 24, 26-7, 32, 56,
  60-1, 65, 73, 79, 100-2
  deputy of, as papal penitentiary
  see Aprano, Bartholomew
Car Colston (Notts.) 88
cardinals see Carboni, Francis;
  Langham, Simon
Carlisle, bishop of v
Carlton in Craven 35
  vicar of see John de Scardeburgh
Carlton le Moorland (Lincs.) 92

vicars of see Bertham, William;
  Randolf, John
Carlton with Thuleby, prebend in Lincoln
  Cathedral 9
  prebendaries of see Hilton, Thomas;
  Parker, Thomas
Carnaby 67
  priest at see Foston, William
  vicar of see Mounceux, John
Carnaby, Richard 18
  Thomas de 20
Carnica, Thomas 48
Carppe, John 4
Carton see Garton
'Castel' 49
Castleford 13, 21, 38-40
  rectors of see Botyler, John; Lacy,
  Edmund; Longley, Thomas de; Middelton,
  Geoffrey de; Prentys, John
Castleton 49
Catesby priory (Northants.) 98
Caton, William 95
Catterton 21
Catton, John de 63
  Robert de 106
Causeby, John de 108
Cauthorn, John 15
Cave, John, rector of St Cuthbert, York 33
  John de, vicar of South Muskham, chantry
  priest at Wykeham 47
  Nicholas 3
Cave, North 57
  vicars of see Dighton, Nicholas de;
  Newton, Nicholas de
Cave, South, prebend in York Minster 1
  prebendaries of see Noion, William;
  Waltham, William de
Cawode, John 104
  William de 2
Cawood iv-v
  chapel of the manor of 33, 68, 93, 97
  principal chapel of 106
  documents dated at v, 7, 15-19, 25,
  29-30, 33, 40, 48-51, 55-7, 61-2, 64-5,
  67-8, 72-3, 79, 82, 91-2, 95-6, 100,
  104-5, 108
Cawood Castle, chapel of 10, 42, 57
  documents dated at 1, 3, 7-10, 14-19,
  22, 25-6, 30-2, 37-8, 40-4, 46, 48,
  50-1, 53, 55-8, 61-2, 64, 66-9, 71-4,
  79-80, 82-4, 92-100, 100-1, 104-5, 107-9
Cerney, North (Glos.) 96
  rectors of see Claypoll, John; Dalton,
  William

Chamber (Chaumber), Roger del, of
  Newark (Notts.) 89
  Thomas del 65
chantries, establishment of vi
  see also ordinations of chantries,
  and under specific places
Chapel Haddlesey, chantry of St John
  the Baptist at 19
  priests of see Chaworth, Thomas de;
  Sprotburgh, William de
Charing Cross see London
Charterhouses see Coventry, St Anne;
  Kingston upon Hull, St Michael
chastity, vows of 19-21, 42, 93
Chaumber see Chamber
Chaworth, Thomas de 19
Chester (Ches.), St John, prebend in 10
  prebendaries of see Conyngeston,
  Richard de; Hall, John; Tydde,
  Nicholas
Chester, William 98
Chesterfeld (Chestirfeld, Chestrefeld),
  Ralph 26
  Richard de 10
Chesterfield (Derbys.), chantry in
  church of 96
  priests of see Accres, John de;
  Tewer, Thomas
Cheworth, Thomas de 19
Chilwell (Notts.) 71
Chilwell, Richard 83
Chingford, All Saints (Essex) 91
  rectors of see Fuller, Nicholas;
  Walpoole, Roger
Christshall, prebend in St Martin le
  Grand, London 104
  prebendaries of see Manfeld, Robert
  de; Wynwyk, Richard de
Churchdown (Glos.), peculiar jurisdiction
  of iii; see also Gloucestershire
citations 5, 33, 42, 93, 97
Clapham, vicar of see Sandall, John de
Clarborough (Notts.) 71-2
  vicars of see Cook, Thomas;
  Patryngton, William de
Clay, William 107
Claypoll, John 96
Clayton, John de 42
Clementhorpe priory 31, 38
Clerk (Clerc), Henry, of Tollerton
  (Notts.) 85
  John, of Hucknall Torkard (Notts.) 38
  John, rector of Catwick, penitentiary
  in the East Riding 56

John, of Sheriff Hutton, vicar of
  Sancton 55
  Richard, of Rossington 70
Cleveland, archdeaconry of iii
  archdeacon of 33, 47-53
    Official of 12, 20, 47-53
  collectors within see Rievaulx abbey
  commissary-general within see Uphall,
  William de
  penitentiaries within see Paa, John;
  Roger the parish priest of Whitby;
  Seggefeld, John de; Spaunton, Thomas
  sequestrator within see Uphall,
  William de
Cliderow see Clyderowe
Clifford, Richard, bishop of Worcester
  40, 96
Clifton (Notts.) 74
  rectors of see Normanton, John;
  Weloghby, Robert de
Clifton (Clyfton), John de, rector of
  Birkin, rector of Gamston 39, 92
  John de, knt. 38
  Robert 64
Clonne, br. William de, O.S.A. 71
Cloutherom, William de 38, 40
Clyderowe (Cliderow), Henry 27, 31, 37
Clyff, Thomas 58
Clyfton see Clifton
Clyveland, John 31
coadjutors, appointments of 19-20, 55
Cochon, Alan 7-8
Cockersand abbey (Lancs.) 31-2, 43
  chapter house of 43
  canon and cellarer of see Lancastre,
  John de
Cok, Adam 61
  Robert 37
Coke see Cook
Cokerell, Thomas 57
Cokfeld, Robert 38
Coleshill (Warw.) 85
collations of benefices 1-10, 23, 25, 28,
  30, 35, 39-40, 47, 54, 56, 59, 61-4, 66,
  72-3, 75, 77, 80, 90, 103
Colne (Collom, Collum), John de 55, 60, 61
  William de 13
Colston (Notts.) 97
  rectors of see Barston, John;
  Conyngeston, James de
Colyngham, Thomas 89
Combe, M. John, of London 36
commissions (miscellaneous) 11, 34, 68,
  70, 73-4, 94, 101, 105-6; see also
  under particular subjects

Conestabill (Constabile), Edmund son of
    Roger 61
    Robert 59
confessions, licence to hear 15, 100
Cononum see Canonum
Constabile see Conestabill
Convocation iii, 16-17
Conyngeston (Conyngston), James de 97
    M. Richard de 3-6, 10, 51, 53, 68,
    74-5
Conyngton, William 71
Cook (Coke), John 84, 91
    Thomas 71-2
Copeland (Cumb.), penitentiary within
    see Wartyll, Nicholas
Corbrygg, Robert 44
corrody 103
Coryngham, M. Roger de 26, 28, 41
Costock (Notts.) 71
Cotes, John del 35
Cotese, Thomas 59
Cotgrave (Notts.) 98
    chapel of the manor of 71
    church of 71
Cotham (Notts.) 87
Cottam (Notts.), parishioners of
    (named) 86-7
    provision of chaplain for 86-7
Cotterstock college (Northants.) 19
Cottingham (Northants.), rector of see
    Merston, Henry de
Cotum (Cotump), Richard de 86-7
Couper, William 38
Courtney, Richard 7
Coventre, John de 77, 79
Coventry (Warw.), bishop of see
    Lichfield
    charterhouse of St Anne near 31
        prior of 12
    lodgings of the bishop of
        Worcester at 96
    Parliament held at 96
Cowesby
    church of 108
        rectors of see Ottewy, William;
        Ottryngton, John
    lordship of 108
        lords of see Bergh, Richard de;
        Hastings, Elizabeth; Lamplogh,
        Robert de; Raudon, Robert de;
        Vavasour, Henry
Cowlam 59
    rectors of see Hassok, Thomas;
    Wentislaw, Simon

Cowpeland, Walter de 48
Cowthorpe 24
    rector of see Croka, Thomas
Crambe, church of 66
    pension from mediety of 34
Crase, Robert, of Bishop Burton 81
Crathorn, Robert de 49-50
Crathorne 49
    pension from church of 51
    rectory of 49-50
        rectors of see Crathorn, Robert de;
        Gretham, John
Crayk, br. William de 50
Cressingham, Great (Norf.) 70
    rectors of see Merston, Henry de;
    Sturmy, Hugh
Cressop, William 30
Cressy, Hugh, of Oldcoates (Notts.) 74
    Hugh 24
        Margaret, wife of 24
    John 24
Cressyngham, br. Hugh de 24
Crich (Derbys.) 87-8
    vicars of see Garton, William;
    Osmund, John
criminous clerks 11, 70
Crispyn (Crispin), William, of York 31, 37
Croft 107
Croft, John 62
Crofton, br. John de 42-3
Croka, Thomas 24
Crophill, prebend in Southwell Minster
    see Oxton and Crophill
Crosse, Thomas 14
Crosseby, John, of Riccall 49
Croydon (Surrey) 54
Cumberland, churches of 17
Cumberton, Robert 88
Cum ex eo dispensations 13, 24, 50, 71
Cuter, br. Robert 104
Dalby, Ralph de 84
    Thomas de 3
Dalton, John de 67
    William 92, 96
Danby 51
Darell, William 105
Darfield, rents from 28
    vicar of see Derfeld, William de
Daubeney see Dawbeney
Dauncell, Thomas, of Pocklington 56-7
Dautry see Alta Ripa
Dawbeney (Daubeney), Nicholas 79, 82-3
Dawtre see Alta Ripa

117

Deen, John, prebendary in the chapel of
St Mary and the Holy Angels, York 3
John de, chaplain 1
Degyll, Richard 16
Depeden, Elizabeth 21-2
John de 12, 21-2
Derby, earl of see John of Gaunt
Dereham, West, abbey (Norf.) 24, 35
abbot of 24
canons of see Cressyngham, Hugh de;
Foston, John de; Hengham, Thomas de
churches appropriated to in the
diocese of York 24
Derfeld, Hugh de 36
William de 17
Derham, Richard 7
Derlton, M. John de 99
Dernton, M. William, notary public 71,
75
Dernyngton, John 100
Derwent, Adam de 36
Deyncourt, Robert 70
Dighton (Dyghton), John 60
Nicholas de 57
Disford (Dissheford), John de 13
dispensations iv, 12, 19, 25-6, 58, 64,
74, 82; see also bastardy; Cum
ex eo; marriage
Dispenser, Henry, bishop of Norwich 70,
74, 81
Dissheford see Disford
Doncaster 38
chantry of St Nicholas at 26
priests of see Hexthorp, William;
Hexthorp, William de
vicars of see Couper, William;
Farndale, William
Doncaster, Mulgrave and, lord of see
Mauley, Peter VIII de
Donyngton, William de 48
Doram, Dorem see Durham
Dowbrygg, John 80
Downe, William 56
Downham (Cambs.) 66
rectors of see Humbelton, Alan de;
Robert, Thomas
Dransfeld (Drensfeld), Henry de 13
Robert 26
Drax, priory 16, 20 33
canon of see Emesay, Robert de
prior of see Usflet, John de
Drax, John 68
Drensfeld see Dransfeld
Driffeld (Dryffeld), William de 22

William de, vicar of Helmsley 48
Driffield, prebend in York Minster 4, 8
prebendaries of see Bubwyth, Nicholas
de; Ronhall, Richard; Scrope,
Stephen le
Duffeld, Nicholas de 26
Robert 12
Duggylby, John de 44
Duk, br. Thomas 103
Dunham (Notts.), prebend in Southwell
Minster, vicarage of 64
vicars of see Morpath, William;
York, John
Dunnington 47
rector of see Gysburn, Walter
Dunnington, prebend in York Minster 1
prebendaries of see Noion, William;
Waltham, William de
Durham, archdeacon of see Weston, Thomas
bishop of iii, v, 16;; see also
Skirlaw, Walter
peculiar jurisdiction of see
Howden and Howdenshire
vicar general of see Weston, Thomas
diocese of iii
prior and convent of iii, 26, 84, 92,
96, 105, 107, 109
peculiar jurisdiction of see
Allerton and Allertonshire
prior of see Melsonby, Thomas de
Durham (Doram, Dorem, Dureham), Isabella
de 88
John de 80
br. Robert, canon of Hexham 104
Robert, vicar in Ripon Minster 7
Dyghton see Dighton
Eakring (Notts.), mediety of 75, 96
rectors of see Accres, John de;
Askeby, William; Tewer, Thomas;
Thurbache, William
Easington 65
Easington in Cleveland 47, 51
rectors of see Seteryngton, Thomas;
Uphall, William
East Bridgeford see Bridgeford, East
East Harlsey see Harlsey, East
East Markham see Markham, East
East Retford see Retford, East
East Riding, archdeaconry of iii
archdeacon of 33, 54-69
Official of 8, 12, 54-69
collectors with see Warter priory
penitentiaries within see Clerk, John;
Semer, Thomas de

East Rounton see Rounton, East
East Wykeham see Wykeham, East
Eastrington 105
    vicar of see Thurstanton, William de
Ebor' see York
Ecclesfield, chapel of St Michael at 12
    rectory of 12
    vicarage of 31
        vicars of see Bryan, William;
        Wyke, Arnold
Eccleshall Castle (Staffs.) 10, 40, 88,
    96-7
Eddynglay (Edynglay), Robert 83
Edlington 15, 40
    rectors of see Canon, William;
    Elughton, Richard de
Edward III, king 28
Edwinstowe (Notts.), chantry at the altar
    of St Katherine and St Margaret at 98
        priests of see Glentham, John de;
        Umfray, William
    chantries, union of 75
    vicarage of 67, 93
        vicars of see Lund, John; Norton,
        Thomas de
Edynglay see Eddynglay
Edynstow, M. Thomas de 87
Egglestone abbey 17, 101
    altar of St John the Evangelist at 101
Egleston, Adam de 40
Egremont in Copeland (Cumb.) 84
    rectors of see Dalby, Ralph de;
    Saxton, Roger de
Eland, Isabella de see Sayvill (née de
    Eland), Isabella
    Joan de 14
    Thomas de 14
elections, confirmations of, of dean of
    York 5-6
    of heads of religious houses 42-3,
    59-60, 88, 93, 97, 104; see also
    prior, appointment of
Elis (Elys), John 36
    Ralph 35
    Roger 40
Elkesley (Notts.) 85, 88
    vicars of see Sharp, John; Sutton,
    Henry de
Elland 13
    chantry of St John the Baptist at 33
        priest of see Broughton, John de
    property at 14
    Sayvill chantry in chapel at,
    ordination of 13-14

Ellerbek, Thomas 49
Ellerton, church of 66
    priory at 66
Ellingham (Northumb.), vicar of see
    Wardell, William
Elmeden, Alan 50
Elmesall, Henry de 84
Elmeswell see Emmeswell
Elmeton, br. Walter de 97-8
Elmham, lady of see Hastings, Elizabeth
Elmham, South 70, 82
Elsham priory (Lincs.) 95
Elston (Notts.) 98
    rector of see Heth, John, son of
    Henry del
Eltham (Kent.), royal manor of 6
Elton (Notts.) 99
    rectors of see Gernell, Thomas;
    Redmyld, John
Elughton, Richard de 40
Elvet, John 4
    Richard 13
Ely, bishop of see Fordham, John
Ely, John 7
Elys see Elis
Emesay, br. Robert de 20
Emlay, Cecilia de 78
Emmeswell (Elmeswell), Robert de (once
    John) 23, 34, 41
England
    earl marshal of see Mowbray, Thomas
    high steward of see John of Gaunt
    king of 11, 12, 37; see also
    Edward III, Henry IV, Richard II
    council of v
    papal collector in see Aliotti, Lewis
    papal nuncio in see Aliotti, Lewis;
    Langham, Simon
Ermyn, Thomas 49
Esby, br. Robert de 51
escheat 61
escheator see Bukton, Peter de
Esseholt, John 19-20
Eston 51
Eston, John 34
Esyngwald, M. Roger de 51
Etton, chantry of Holy Trinity at 54, 64
    priests of see Clifton, Robert;
    Marton, Robert; William son of John
    son of Roger; Scot, Patrick
Everton, Bernard 37
Everyngham, John de 19, 39, 44
exchanges of benefices v-vi, 1, 7-12,
    24-5, 30-2, 34-6, 39-41, 44, 47, 52-4,

exchanges of benefices (cont.)
57-9, 61, 63-4, 66, 68, 70-5, 79-82,
84-8, 91-3, 95-8, 104-5, 107
exchequer, royal 17
excommunication 27, 31, 51, 105
Eynesford (Eynisford), John 81
Eynsford (Kent) 72-3
rectors of see Hayward, William;
Ruggelay, Thomas
Fairstead (Norf.) 88
rectors of see Cumberton, Robert;
Thorp, Thomas de
Farefax (Fayrefax), M. Brian 48
Gregory 76
Farndale, William 38
Faroe Islands v
Faryndon, Robert 10
Fauconeres, prebend in St Martin le
Grand, London 7
prebendaries of see Feriby, Thomas;
Wardrober, Thomas
Fawdon, William 52-3
Fayrefax see Farefax
Featherstone 35
vicars of see Cotes, John del;
Thorp, William de
Felde (de la Feld), Richard 80-1
Felkirk 36
vicars of see Derfeld, Hugh de;
Skyres, John
Feriby, Thomas 6
Ferrour (Ferrur), Beatrice, wife of
Thomas 89
Margaret, daughter of Thomas 89
Matilda, wife of Thomas 89
Thomas, of Newark (Notts.) 80, 86, 89
chantry founded by see Newark, St
Mary Magdalene, chantry at the
altar of the Holy Trinity
br. Thomas, canon of Bolton, vicar of
Skipton 35
Ferry Fryston 28
vicar of see Adewyk, John
Fery, William, of Wakefield 28-9
Filey 61, 67
FiltzWilliam, John 19
Firsby (Lincs.) 98
rectors of see Chester, William;
Kelsay, Robert de
first fruits 30
Fissewyk see Fyssewyk
Flamborough 67
chantry at 59
priests of see Cotese, Thomas;
Wryght, John

Fledborough (Notts.), lady of see
Basset, Margaret
rector of see Grene, Robert
Flemmyng (Flemyng), Alan, chantry founded
by see Newark, chantry of Corpus Christi
Richard 39-40
Thomas 13
Flintham (Notts.), church of 88
vicarage of 86, 92
vicars of see Peek, William;
Seward, Nicholas
Folketon, Robert de 31, 42
Folkton, rectory of 66
rectors of see Graystok, Ralph;
Kylburne, John de
vicarage of 63
vicars of see Catton, John de;
Whihot, Thomas
Fordham, John, bishop of Ely 66
Forest, William 41-2
Forester, Thomas 1
Forster, John 56-66
Forthington, Ralph de 81
Foston 44
vicars of see Lyndesay, William de;
Wakefeld, Richard de
Foston (in Cleveland) 51
rectors of see Esyngwald, Roger de;
Nundy, Henry
Foston (Fosseton), br. John de, canon of
West Dereham, vicar of Kirkby Malham 35
John de 42
William 60
Foughler, M. John 37
Fountains abbey 17
Fox, Henry 87
John, son and heir of William 29
Thomas 79
Foxholes 52
Frakys, Robert 68
Franceys see Fraunces
Frankys, William 68
Fraunces (Franceys, Frauncyss), M. John
50, 53
Robert 58
Freston, Robert 15
friars see Fyssewyk, Adam de; Northbrugge,
William
Friesthorpe (Lincs.) 80
rectors of see Langham, Henry; Tantot,
John
Frodingham, North 68
vicars of see Frakys, Robert; Frankys,
William
Frost, William 34

Fryston, John 65
  John de, vicar of Walesby, chantry priest
  at the altar of the Holy Trinity in East
  Retford 80
Fuller, Nicholas of Fullbourne (Cambs.)
  74, 91
Full Sutton 8
  rectors of see Bagby, Robert de;
  Malton, Roger de
Fulman, William 55
Furnivall, lord see Nevill, Thomas de
Futtyng, John 84
Fyfhide, M. John 62
Fyschlake, Robert 94
Fyssewyk (Fissewyk), br. Adam de, O.P. 100
Galander (Gallander), William 28
Galon, Robert, and Alice his wife, chantry
  founded for see Scarborough, St Mary,
  chantry at the altar of St James
Gamston (Notts.) 39, 84, 91-2
  vicars of see Clifton, John de; Cook,
  John; Thoresby, John; Wikireslay,
  Thomas de
Ganton, church of 67
  vicarage of 63
    vicars of see Ake, Roger, Burton,
    William; Raygate, Richard
Garforth 33
  rector of see Beroby, William de
Garton (Carton), M. John, notary public,
  rector of Leigh 106
  John de 74
  Richard de 57-8
  Thomas 17-18
  William, of Driffield 88
Garton in Holdernes, John de 56
Garton in Holderness 62
  vicars of see Croft, John; Smyth,
  Richard
Garton on the Wolds, church of 66
  vicarage of 62
    vicars of see Attynwyk, William de;
    Wynteryngham, Walter de
Gateles, John 82
Gaunstede, Simon, prebendary of Bole 6
  Simon, rector of Sutton Bonington 80
Gaunt, John of see John of Gaunt
  Thomas 18
Gaynesburgh, Robert de 11
Gaytford, John de 74
Gayton (Northants.) 95
  rectors of see Benet, John; Porter,
  John

Gedling (Notts.) 87
  medieties of 88
  rectory of mediety of 87
    rector of see Kelum, Richard
  vicar of mediety of see Landford,
    John de
Geffray, William 70
Gerard, John 34
Gerberg, Thomas 28
German, John 59
Gernell (Gernelle), Thomas 99
Giggleswick, rector of see Stalmyn,
  William
Gilby (Gylby), M. John 91
  M. John, registrar to the archbishop 53
Gilling in Ryedale 48
  rector of see Farefax, Brian
Giloth see Gyloth
Gislay, Hugh 34
Givendale and Skelton, prebend of, in
  Ripon Minster 1
  prebendaries of see Bubwyth, Nicholas
  de; Forester, Thomas
glebe 32
Glentham, John de 98
Gloucester (Glos.) property within the
  suburbs of 103
  St Oswald's priory at 103, 108
    canon of see Horne, Robert
    chapter house of 103
    priors of see Duk, Thomas; Pleyer,
    John; Shipton, John de
    sub-prior of see Pleyer, John
Gloucestershire, spirituality within,
  custodian of see Duk, Thomas; Horne,
  Robert; Wotton, John
  Official within see Milton, William
  penitentiary within see Pleyer, John
  steward and receiver in see Bisseley,
  John
Goldale, Robert 63
Golde, William 18
Goldesburgh, Anthony de 100
Goldthorpe, lands at (detailed) 38-9
Goodmanham 58
  rectors of see Clyff, Thomas; Lewys,
  Robert
Gosse, Richard 94
Goswyk, br. T. 104
Gote, John 86
Gower, lord see Mowbray, Thomas
Gower, br. Richard 100
Gra, John, of York 27,31
  Richard 31

Gra, Thomas 27, 31, 37
    William, citizen of York 27, 31, 37
        chantry for see York, St Mary
        Castlegate, chantry in the chapel
        of St John the Baptist and St John
        the Evangelist
    William, citizen and merchant of York,
    and Matilda his wife, chantry for
    see York, St Helen, Stonegate, chantry
    at the altar of St John the Baptist
Granby (Notts.) 87
Grandesden, William 105, 107
Gray, Walter de, archbishop of York 26
Graystok (Graystoke), Joan de 63, 66
    Ralph 66
Greatham (Durh.) 63
Great Ayton, see Ayton, Great
Great Schism vi
Grene, John 107
    br. Robert, prior of Bolton 12
    Robert, rector of Fledborough 73
Gresacre, John 60
Gretham, John 49
Gringley (Notts.) 73, 88
    vicar of see Thorp, John
Grome, Robert 59
Grove (Notts.) 72
    rector of see 3ong, William
Grymeston (Grymston), John de 67
    William de, of Holderness 58-9
Guisborough 68
    church of 51
    parish priest of see Seggefeld,
    John de
    priory at 47, 49-51, 62, 67-8
        canons of see Barton, John de;
        Bywell, Thomas; Elmeden, Alan;
        Marke, Richard
Guiseley, rector of see Marass, Richard
    vicar of see Otteley, Richard de
Gunthorp, William de 3
Gylby see Gilby
Gyllyot, Richard 65
Gyloth (Giloth), William 36
Gysburn (Gyseburn), Walter 47
    William, prebendary in the chapel of
    St Mary and the Holy Angels, York
    4, 10
    William de, rector of St Helen,
    Stonegate, York 16, 19
        coadjutor of see John de Suthwell
Hackness 52
    parochial chaplain of 63
Hadham (?Herts.) 85

Hadilsay, Richard 24, 33
Haget, Robert, and Helen his wife, chantry
    for, see York, All Saints Pavement,
    chantry founded by Thomas de Alwarthorp
Hagthorp, Thomas 105-6
Hake, Hugh 86
Haldeyn, Walter 103
Halifax, vicar of 14
    see also Elland
Hall, John 10
    William 15
Hallamshire, lord of see Nevill, Thomas de
    penitentiary within see Brammelay,
    Henry de
Hallom, Robert de 2
Halloughton (Notts.), prebend in Southwell
    Minster 1
    prebendary of see Layot, John
Haltemprice priory 66
    canons of see Hessay, William
Halton, Robert, chantry priest of St Mary
    in St Peter le Willows, Walmgate,
    York 41
    Robert de, founder of above chantry 26
Halton iuxta Burton Stather, M. Robert de
    105
Halward, Roger 105
Hambleton, St Mary, chantry founded for
    William de Hamelton, dean of York, at,
    106
    priests of see Alta Ripa, Richard de;
    Catton, Robert de
Hambleton (Leics.) 31
    vicars of see Bryan, William; Wyke,
    Arnold
Hamelton, William de, chantry founded for
    see Hambleton, St Mary
Hamerton, M. Henry 54
Hamlake, lord of see Roos, William de
Hanaper, payments to 14, 21, 28
Hankese, Robert 105
Hanlay, John 33
Hannys, Henry 103
    Isabella, wife of 103
Hardewyk, Thomas de 38
Hardyng, Richard 56
Harlaxton (Lincs.) 74
    rectors of see Normanton, John;
    Weloghby, Robert de
Harlsey, East 51
Harpame (Harpham), Nicholas 58, 65
Harpham, priest at see Barker, Peter
Harthill 36
    rectors of see Gyloth, William;
    Oxeford, John de

Harwod (Harwode), John de 51, 57
Hassok, Thomas 59
Hastings (Hastynges), Edward de 25, 44
    Elizabeth 108
Hathersage (Derbys.) 85
    rectors of see Basage, John; Martill,
    Hugh
Haukerigg, Nicholas 92
Haw, Margaret, daughter of John 102
Haward, Roger 1
Hawksworth (Notts.) 80, 92
    rectors of see Taylour, John;
    Watton, Thomas
Haxey, Thomas 10, 98
Hay, Thomas de la 107
Hayton, Richard de 68
    Thomas de 68
Hayward, William 72-3
Hazelwood, chapel of St Leonard, chantry
    in 18
    priests of see Golde, William;
    Hesilwode, John
Headon (Notts.), rectory of 71, 83
    rectors of see Farefax, Gregory;
    Ker, Hugh de; Ker, Peter del
    vicarage of 76
        vicars of see Leverton, John;
        Upton, Gregory de
Healaugh, appropriation of church, to
    Healaugh Park priory 21-2
    lord of the manor of 21
    rector of see Polowe, William
    vicarage of 22, 42
        vicars of see Bridsall, Peter de;
        Kirkeby, John
Healaugh Park priory 12, 21-2, 33, 42-3
    altar of St John the Evangelist and
    St Anne in 21
    canons of see Bridsall, Peter de;
    Kirkeby, John
    prior of 21-2
Heckmondwike 28
Heighington (Durh.) 63
    vicars of see Catton, John de;
    Whihot, Thomas
Helmesale, Henry 95-6
Helmesley, John 41
    William de 42
Helmsley 66
    vicarage of 48
        vicars of see Driffeld, William de;
        Rolleston, William
Hemeswell, br. Richard 104
Hemingbrough 106
    church of 106

Hemingbrough, custodian of the
    spirituality of 105
    parishioners of (named) 105-6
    parochial chaplain of 105
    parochial priest of see Poleyn, John
    rector of see Walworth, Thomas
Hemmyng, William 18
Hemsworth 14
Hemyngburgh, John de 107
Hendeley, John de 81
Hengham, br. Thomas de 24, 35
Henry IV, king i, v, 2-3, 8, 25-6, 35,
    38-41, 61, 65, 76, 80, 88-9
    Council of, at Lichfield 96
    Joan, wife of 38
Henry of Lancaster, earl of Lancaster 14
Henryson, John, of Hazelwood 18
    son of see Hesilwode, John
Hercy, Thomas 72, 82
Herle, Alexander 66
    John 13
Hesill, Thomas 37
Hesilwode, John 18
Hessay, br. William 66
Hessle 51
    vicarage of 62
        vicars of see Barton, John de;
        Marke, Richard
Heth, John son of Henry del 98
    Robert de 28-9
Heton, John de 13
    William de 13
Hexham (Northumb.) 105
    priory at
        canons of see Aspur, Thomas; Cuter,
        Robert; Durham, Robert; Goswyk, T.;
        Hemeswell, Richard; Wodhorn, William
        prior of 103, 106; see also Hexham,
        John de; Marton, Alexander de
        sub-prior of 104
        sub-prior and convent of 104
    St Giles' hospital at 103
        warden of see Martyn, John
Hexham, br. John de 104-5
Hexham and Hexhamshire, liberty of,
    chancellor in see Hexham, prior of
    receiver in see Mitford, John de
    steward in see Mitford, William de
Hexham and Hexhamshire, peculiar
    jurisdiction of iii
Hexthorp, William, chantry priest of St
    Nicholas at Doncaster 26
    William de 26
Heynings priory (Lincs.) 36
    prioress of 89

123

High Hoyland 15, 24–5
   rectors of medieties of see Asshebury,
   William de; Cauthorn, John;
   Qwytcherche, David
Hildiard, M. John 57
Hill, Robert de 24
Hilton (Hylton), Robert de 64
   Thomas, prebendary of Carlton cum
   Thurlby in Lincoln cathedral,
   prebendary in the chapel of St Mary
   and the Holy Angels, York 9, 57, 100
   Thomas de, prebendary of Barnby in York
   Minster, clerk of the archbishop's
   household, prebendary of Weighton in
   York Minster 3, 10
Hirvyng (Hirnyng), William 28
   Alice, wife of 28
Hobyn, Thomas 59
Hoede, Thomas 18
Hogeson, John 41
Hockerton (Notts.), St Nicholas 74, 91
   rectors of see Fuller, Nicholas;
   Revell, Thomas; Walpoole, Roger
Holand, Thomas, earl of Kent 61
Holden, Thomas 6
Holderness 17
Holgyll, William de 102
   Margaret, wife of 102
Holme (Notts.) 88
Holme (Howm, Howme), German de 105
   John, chantry priest in All Saints,
   Barking, London, vicar of Walesby 85
   John de, rector of Wheldrake 47
   John de 55
   Nicholas 41
   M. Richard 6
   Robert de, son of Robert de, of York
   40
Holme on Spalding Moor 59
   rectors of see German, John; Wryght,
   John
Holme Pierrepont (Notts.) 83
   rectory of 25, 75, 79, 82–3, 86, 95–6
      rectors of see Dawbeney, Nicholas;
      Helmesale, Henry; Peek, William;
      Tewer, Thomas; Thurbache, William
Holmesfield, John 40
Holme super Trent see Holme Pierrepont
Holy Sepulchre 54
homicide 74
Hooton Pagnell 34
Hooton Roberts 33
   vicar of see Hanlay, John
Hopton, Nicholas de 77

Horbury 28
Hornby see Horneby
Horne, br. Robert 109
Horneby (Hornby), Ralph de and Joan his
   wife, chantry for see York, St Helen
   Stonegate, chantry at the altar of St
   Michael
   Richard 41
   William de 18
Hornyngese, John 70
Horslay, John 37
hospitals see under names of individual
   hospitals
Hotham 55
   rectors of see Martyn, Thomas;
   Wresill, Ralph
Hothom, John de 59
Hoton, John 27
Hoveden, John dictus de 87
Hoveringham (Notts.) 87
Hovingham, parochial chaplain of see
   Wryght, William
Howby, John de 71
Howden 35, 66, 68
   Minster, prebends in see Barmby on the
   Marsh; Skelton; Thorpe
      prebendaries of see Manfeld, Robert
      de; Weston, Thomas de; Wynewyk,
      Richard de
   vicars of prebends in see Aghton,
   William and under individual prebends
Howden and Howdenshire, peculiar
   jurisdiction of iii
   custodian of the spirituality of 105,
   107, 109
Howm, Howme see Holme
Howland, High see High Hoyland
Huddersfield, vicar of 14 see also
   Wath, John de
Huggate 64
   rectors of see Appilton, Robert;
   Parker, Thomas
Hugon, Nicholas (once Hugh) 58–9
Hull, M. William 41
Hulot, Thomas 36
Humbelton (Humbleton), Alan de 63, 66
   John 26
Humber river 17
Humbleton see Humbelton
Hunmanby 67
Hunston, William 74
Hunt, Robert 30
   Thomas, of Linby (Notts.) 38

Huntington
    pension from 52
    vicarage of 20, 49
        vicar of see Areshom, Walter
Hutton Buscel 52
Hutton Cranswick, church of 61
    vicarage of 67
        vicar of see Wissenden,
        William de
Hutton Rudby, chaplain of see Ellerbeck,
    Thomas
    rector of see Wyclyff, Robert
Hvar v
Hylton see Hilton
Ikelyngton, John 47
Ile, John del 78
inductions to benefices vi, 1-15, 18-28,
    30-42, 44, 47-55, 57-76, 79-87, 90-9,
    104-9
indulgence, grants of 12, 101
Ingelby (Ingilby, Yngelby), John de 27
    John de, vicar of Marske by the Sea 50
    William 108
Ingleby Arncliffe 51
Ingleby Greenhow 52
inquisitions 86-7, 94; see also
    patronage, inquisitions into
institutions to benefices vi, 1-2, 7-9,
    11-15, 18-28, 30-44, 47-55, 57-72, 74-5,
    79-99, 105-9
Irby, William 30
Iwelay, Richard 37
Ixworth, M. John 10
Jakelyn, William, of Etton 54, 64
Jankynson, Alice wife of John, of
    Sturton 95
Jervaulx, abbot of see Gower, Richard
John, rector of Arnold 72
John, rector of a mediety of St Helen on
    the Walls, York 18
John of Gaunt, duke of Aquitaine and
    Lancaster, earl of Derby, Lincoln, and
    Leicester 13-14, 44
Juliers, Elizabeth, countess of Kent 53
justices, royal 70
    at Westminster 68
    at York 11
Juwell, John 81-2
Kay, William 28
Kayser, Nicholas, of Newark (Notts.) 80,
    83, 86
Kedelham see Kydlambe
Keighley 12
    rector of see Duffeld, Robert

Kelburne see Kylburne
Kelham (Notts.) 82
    rector of see Normanton, Henry de
Kelk, John 53
Kellow, Thomas 48
Kelsay, Robert de 98
Kelum (Killom), M. Richard 87
    Thomas de 89
Kendale, Robert 7
Kenlay, John de 30
Kent, countess of see Juliers, Elizabeth
    earl of see Holand, Thomas
Kentisburn, prebend in Wimborne Minster 41
    prebendaries of see Canonum, William;
    Marunhull, William
Ker, Hugh de/del 71, 75-6, 79
    John del, of Stoke (Notts.) 83
    Peter del 83
Keyingham 65
Kilburne see Kylburne
Kildwick 36
    vicar of see Hulot, Thomas
Killingwoldgraves, hospital of St Mary
    Magdalene at 59
    warden of see Northbrugge, William
Killom see Kelum
Kilnsea 30, 33
Kilpyn, John 108
Kilvington (Notts.) 83
    rectors of see Eddynglay, Robert;
    Maundevyle, William
Kimberley (Notts.) 71, 82
    rectors of see Bassyngham, Robert;
    Broughton, William de; Gateles, John;
    Webster, Richard
King's Bench, court of 22
Kingston upon Hull, charterhouse of St
    Michael at 57
    Holy Trinity chapel at 62; see also
    Hessle
Kippax, rector of see Patteswyk, Walter
Kirby Grindalythe, church of 65
    vicarage of 65, 67
        vicars of see Dalton, John de;
        Whitwell, John
Kirby Sigston, vicar of 108
Kirby Underdale 60
    rector of see Newton, Robert de
Kirkburn, church of 51
    vicarage of 68
        vicars of see Hayton, Thomas de
        Melreth, John
Kirkburton, vicar of see Pelle, Robert
Kirkby in Ashfield (Notts.) 70
    rector of see Wetewang, Richard

125

Kirkby in Cleveland, church of 52
  rectory of 9, 50, 53
    rectors of see Bollesore, John;
    Fraunces, John; Salisbyry, William
Kirkby Malham 24, 35
  vicars of see Cressyngham, Hugh de;
  Foston, John de; Hengham, Thomas de
Kirkeby (Kyrkeby), br. John 42
  Richard 43
  Thomas de 38
Kirk Ella 66
Kirkham priory 41, 48, 57-8, 62, 65-7
Kirkheaton, rector of see Dransfeld,
  Henry de
Kirkleatham 49, 53
  rector of see Barnard, John; Sandon,
  John
Kirk Leavington 51
Kirklees priory 7, 36, 38, 40
Kirk Sandall, rector of see Hemmyng,
  William
Kirk Smeaton 25-6
  rectors of see Ossett, Richard;
  Stanhurst, Thomas
Kirkstall abbey 7, 30, 33, 58-9, 67
Kirton (Notts.) 30, 32, 82, 84
  rectors of see Addestoke, John;
  Louth, Adam de; Porter, Thomas
Knapton 51
Knaresborough, house of St Robert at 44
  brethren of see Lyndesay, William de;
  Wakefeld, Richard de
Knaresborough, prebend of in York Minster
  see Beechill with Knaresborough
Knayton, John de 23
Knebworth (Herts.) 98
  rector of see Thurgarton, John de
Kneesall (Notts.) rector of 95
  union of, with Boughton 94-5
Knolles, Robert 15, 24, 44-5
  Constance, wife of above 44
  hospital founded by see Pontefract,
  Holy Trinity hospital
Kyddelow, John 97
Kydlambe (Kedelham, Kydlame), William
  13, 37, 42
Kylburne (Kelburne, Kilburne, Kylburn),
  John de 63, 66, 68
Kynalton, br. William de 97
Kyng, John 86
Kyngeston, Richard 85, 99
Kyrk (Attekirke, Kyrke), M. Robert, of
  South Scarle (Notts.) 89
  Robert atte, of Thurlestone 81, 85

Kyrkeby see Kirkeby
Kyrketon iuxta Kyrkcolston see Screveton
Kyrkham, John de 42
Kyrkton, M. John de 42
Lacy, Edmund 38
Laghton, br. John de 93
  M. Robert 71, 72
Laiburn, William 100
Lake, John, of Newark (Notts.) 86
Lakenby, Margaret 34
Lamplogh, Robert de 108
Lancaster, duke of see John of Gaunt;
  Henry IV
  earl of see Henry of Lancaster
Lancastre (Loncastre), br. John de 32, 43
Landford, John de 87
landgavel 103
Laneham (Notts.), dean of 72, 81
Langar (Notts.) 71
Langham, Henry 80
  Simon 87
Langley (Derbys.) 71
Langley see Longley
Langtoft, prebend in York Minster 2, 4
  prebendaries of see Elvet, John;
  Scrope, Stephen le
Langton, Thomas 41
  William de 65
Langwath, Thomas de 87
Laschyn, John 64
Lastingham, parish priest of see Paa,
  John
Laton, John de 20
Latoner, John 37
Laughton en le Morthen, prebend in York
  Minster 10
  prebendaries of see Conyngeston,
  Richard de; Faryndon, Robert
Laurance (Laurence), John 101
  Marjorie, wife of 101
Laxton (Notts.), rector of see Haxey,
  Thomas
  vicarage of 98
    vicars of see Glentham, John de;
    Umfray, William
Layot, M. John 1
Leake 96, 105
  rector of see Berford, John de
  vicar of 108; see also Byry, John;
  Holme, German de
Leathley 43
  rectors of see Campsall, John;
  Wyghall, Richard de
Leconfield, rector of see Drax, John

Ledes, Robert de, of York 41, 57-8, 65
Ledsham 26
  vicars of see Duffeld, Nicholas de;
  Morley, William de
Lee, Walter de, knt. 108
  Joan, wife of above 108
    daughter of above see Hastings,
    Elizabeth
Leeche, William 79
Leeds, church of 34
  pension from vicarage of 34
  vicar of see Snytall, John
Leek (Leke), John de 89
  William de 108
  William, vicar of Wharram Percy 55
Leicester, earl of see John of Gaunt
Leigh (Kent) 86
  vicars of see Gote, John; Sybthorp,
  Robert
Leigh (Staffs.), rector of see Garton,
  John
Leighton Manor, prebend in Lincoln
  cathedral 1
  prebendaries of see Noion, William;
  Waltham, William de
Leke see Leek
Lekynfeld, John de 60
Lenton (Notts.) 77
  church of 70-1
  priory at 70-1, 77-9, 83-5, 87, 97
  vicar of see Thornton, Robert
Lepyngton, John de 4
  John de, notary public, scribe for
  John de Suthwell 51
Lescrop see Scrope
Lesina see Hvar
Lesingham, John de 89
letters dimissory 13, 15, 18-19, 23, 47,
  49-50, 56, 58-9, 75, 100, 104
Levari facias, writ of 68
Leverton, John 76
Leverton, South (Notts.), church of 87
  vicarage of 81, 86-7
    vicar of 86-7; see also Belton,
    John de; Gote, John; Langwath,
    Thomas de; Sybthorp, Robert
Levisham, rector of see Uphall, Richard
Lewer, Thomas 19
Lewes priory (Sussex) 36
Lewys, Robert 58
licences to farm out benefices 12, 73,
  82; see also non-residence, licences
  for
licences (miscellaneous) 27, 49, 73

Lichefeld (Lychefeld), Adam de 20, 37
  John de 74
Lichfield (Staffs.) 96
  bishop of see Burghill, John; Scrope,
  Richard le
    palace at 75
  cathedral, canons of see Brynkelowe,
  William; Parker, Thomas
    dean and chapter of 96
    precentor of see Wolvenden, Robert
  royal council at 96
Linby (Notts.) 85
  church of 71
  rectory of 85
    rectors of see Syleby, John; Vale,
    William
Lincoln 53, 98
  archdeacon of 98
  bishops of see Beaufort, Henry;
  Repingdon, Philip
    lodgings of, in London 1, 9
    vicar-general of see Burbache, John
  cathedral, dean of 93; see also Shepey,
  John
    prebends in see Carlton cum Thurlby;
    Leighton Manor
    prebendaries and canons of see
    Burbache, John; Fyfhide, John;
    Hilton, Thomas; Noion, William;
    Parker, Thomas; Waltham, William de
    subdean and chapter of 93
  earl of see John of Gaunt
  St Katherine's priory at 88
    prior of 89
Lincoln, Robert de 40
Linton in Craven 7, 16, 26
  rectors of mediety of see Polles, Henry;
  Wyles, John
Linton (nr. Howden), chantry 105
  priests of see Darell, William; Martyn,
  John
Littleborough (Notts.) 88
Litster, Thomas 107
Lockington 54, 64
  rectors of see Hamerton, Henry;
  Morewyk, William
Lofthows, Margaret, wife of Robert, of
  York 31
Lokwode, John 27
Loncastre see Lancastre
London (Middx.), iv, 1, 7, 9, 20, 30, 36,
  40, 45, 53, 87, 95
  bishop of see Braybrooke, Robert

127

London (cont.)
Official of see Storteford,
William de
palace of 81, 88
churches in see
St Martin le Grand, canons of
see Feriby, Thomas; Manfeld,
Robert de; Wardrober, Thomas;
Wynewyk, Richard de
chapter house 105
dean of see Asshton, William
de; Derham, Richard
prebends in see Christshall;
Fauconeres
St Paul's cathedral, canons of
see Martyn, John; Merston, Henry;
Storteford, William de
prebend in see Oxgate
citizens of see Knolles, Robert;
Marcheford, William; Trescour,
William
custodian of the spiritualities of
the see sede vacante see Storteford,
William de
London, M. Walter 97
Lonesdale, Robert 104
Long Marston see Marston, Long
Longley (Langley, Longeley, Longle),
Thomas de, rector of Castleford 13
Thomas, keeper of the Privy Seal,
prebendary of South Newbald in York
Minster, dean of York 4-6
Lord, John of Cottam (Notts.) 86-7
Loughton see Lughton
Louth (Luth), Adam de 30, 32, 82, 84
John 105
Louther (Lowther), Robert 37
Thomas de 36
Louthorp, Robert 15
Lower Stoke see Stoke, Lower
Lowther see Louther
Lowthorpe 60
church of 60
chantry at 62
priests of see Brid, Peter;
Skeftlyng, Stephen de
chantry founded for the dean and
chapter of York and William de Roos
and his successors 59
priests of see Grome, Robert;
Hobyn, Thomas
chantry founded for the patron 59
priests of see Grome, Robert;
Hobyn, Thomas
priest at see Brasse, John
rector of see Dighton, John

Lucera, bishop of see Aprano, Bartholomew
Lucy, lady de see Graystok, Joan de
Lughton (Loughton), John 81
Lumle, Ralph de 48
wife of 48
Lund, church of 65
chantry at the altar of St Nicholas
56, 66
priests of see Forster, John;
Tyryngton, John
vicarage of 54
vicar of see Mason, John
Lund (Lunde), John, rector of Skirpenbeck,
vicar of Edwinstowe 67, 93
M. John de, rector of All Saints,
Pavement, York 42
Luth see Louth
Lychefeld see Lichefeld
Lydd (Kent) 36
vicars of see Gyloth, William;
Oxeford, John de
Lyddington (Rut.), 25, 30, 58, 74, 80, 92,
95
Lyndby (Lyndeby), Hugh de 79
br. Robert de 96-7
Lyndesay (Lyndesey), Robert de 90
br. William de 44
Lythe 48
rector of see Kellow, Thomas
Lyversege, Richard de 13
Maidstone (Kent), master of the college at,
see Wetton, John
Malo Lacu see Mauley
Malton, church of 51
priory at 51
Malton, Richard 47, 50
Roger de 8
Maltster, John 33
mandates (various) 30, 87; see also under
individual subjects
Manfeld, M. Robert de 64, 107
Mansfield (Notts.) 92
vicars of see Bertham, William;
Randolf, John
Manthorp, John 89
Mapirley (Mapyrlay), Thomas, of Nottingham
(Notts.) 70, 72-3
William de 70
Marass, Richard 43
Marchall see Marshall
Marcheford, William 53
Marke, br. Richard 62
Markham, East (Notts.) 99
vicars of see Derlton, John de; Orchard,
Roger

128

Markham, West (Notts.) 81
    vicars of see Hendeley, John de;
    Marton, John de
Marnhull see Marunhull
marriage, dispensations for iv, 24,
    101-2
Marshall (Marchall, Marschall), John 43
    Robert 33
    William, of Durham 63
Marshland 17
Marske by the Sea, church of 51
    vicarage of 50
    vicars of see Ingelby, John de;
    Thorp, William de
Marston, Long 27
Martha, William 80
Martill, M. Hugh 74, 85
Marton, br. Alexander de 104
    John de 81
    Robert 64
Marton priory 50, 52
    canons of see Budesby, Roger de;
    Crayk, William de; York, Adam de
Marton in Cleveland 51
Marton on the Forest 51
Martyn, John, chantry priest at Linton 105
    John, warden of St Giles' hospital,
    Hexham, member of the archbishop's
    household 103
    John, clerk of the archbishop's
    household, prebendary of Beckingham
    in Southwell Minster, prebendary of
    Oxgate in St Paul's cathedral, London
    4, 9
    Thomas, vicar in York Minster 41
    Thomas, rector of Hotham 55, 60
Marunhull (Marnhull), William 35, 41
Masham, lord of see Scrope, Stephen le
Mason (Mayson), John 54
    Richard 84
Mattersey (Notts.), priory at 82, 84,
    91-2
    canon of see Retford, Thomas de
    vicarage of 80
    vicars of see Langham, Henry;
    Tantot, John
Maudesley see Mawdeslay
Mauley (Maule, Malo Lacu), Peter I de,
    chantry founded by 65
    Peter VIII de 54, 67
    grandfather of 54
Maundevyle, William 83
Mavesyn Ridware (Staffs.), lord of see
    Mawvesyn, John

Mawdeslay (Maudesley, Mawdesley), Thomas,
    of Newark (Notts.) 86, 90, 93
Mawvesyn, John 96
May, William, of Cottesmore (Rut.) 31
Mayson see Mason
Meaux abbey 17, 65
Meetham, Edmund de 106
Melreth (Milreth), John de 68
Melsonby, Thomas de 26
Melton, John 79-80
    Katherine de, of Aston 19
    William, archbishop of York 31-2
    William de, parochial chaplain of
    St Helen, Stonegate, York 18
Meppershall (Beds.) 95
    rectors of see Caton, William;
    Oxton, Robert de
Merston, Henry de 9, 70, 84
Metham, Thomas 52
Methley 25, 79
    rectors of see Dawbeney, Nicholas;
    Thurbache, William
Michell, William 38
Middelton (Midelton), Elias de 92
    Geoffrey de 21
    John 50
    Nicholas de 22
Middlesbrough 52
Middleton in Pickering Lythe 47, 52-3
    rectors of see Fawdon, William;
    Peek, William
Midelton see Middelton
Midilsburgh, John 52
Milreth see Melreth
Milton, M. William 103
Mirfeld, Adam de 13
Mirfield, church of 20
    rector of see Wylgyn, John
    vicarage of 36, 38, 40
    ordination of 7, 38
    vicars of see Basset, John;
    Broughton, William de; Cloutherom,
    William de
Misson (Notts.) 82, 84
    vicars of see Futtyng, John; Retford,
    Thomas de; Steven, William
Misterton (Notts.), poor of 8
    vicarage of 90
    ordination of 8, 92
    vicar of see Algerkyrk, Thomas
Mitford (Mitteford), John de 106
    Richard, bishop of Salisbury 92
    William de 106

Mitton, ordination of vicarage at 31-2, 43
   parishioners of 32
   vicar of 32
Molescroft, chantry in church of St Mary 57-8, 65
   priests of see Chamber, Thomas del; Cokerell, Thomas; Garton, Richard de; Harpame, Nicholas
Monk, Robert 86
Monk Bretton priory 16, 33, 36, 42-3
   chapter house of 43
   priors of see Ardesley, William de; Crofton, John de
   subprior and convent of 43
Mook, William 89
Moreby, chapel of St Anne near the manor of 52
Moreton, John son and heir of Roger de, of York 33
Morewyk, William 54, 64
Morley (Morlay), William de 26
Morpath, William 61, 64
Morpeth (Northumb.) 66, 68
   rectors of see Graystok, Ralph; Kylburne, John; Stapilton, Peter de
mortmain licences 14, 21, 22, 28, 77, 89
mortuaries 29, 71, 105
Moubray see Mowbray
Mounceux, John 60
Mowbray (Moubray), John de 21
   Thomas de [d.1399], Duke of Norfolk, heir to 80
   Thomas de [d.1405], earl of Nottingham; lord Mowbray, Segrave, and Gower, earl marshal of England 43-4, 80, 95
Moxby priory 36
Mulgrave and Doncaster, lord of see Mauley, Peter VIII de
Muskham, North (Notts.), mediety of 88
   vicarage of a mediety of 91
      vicars of see Saxendale, Thomas; Scrimschire, John
Muskham, South (Notts.), prebend in Southwell Minster, prebendary of, see Tibbay, John
   vicarage of 47
      vicars of see Cave, John de; Paule, Thomas
Muskham (Muscham, Muskcham), Thomas de 86, 89-90
Mynyers, Stephen 89
Mysne, William 82
Naburn, chapel of St Nicholas at 52
   chantry in 52

Nafferton, church of 65
   priest of see Scharpyng, William
   tithes of 52
   vicarage of 56, 61, 64
      vicars of see Morpath, William; Northbrugge, William; York, John
Nafferton, John de 38
Nelson, John 101
   Alice, wife of 101
Neuburgh see Newburgh
Neuport, Gregory 96
   M. William 10
Neuthorp, John de 45
Neuton see Newton
Nevill (Nevyll), Alexander, archbishop of York 2, 45
   Thomas de 25, 36
   Joan, wife of 36
Newall, William 43
Newark (Notts.) 89
   castle at 75
   church of St Mary Magdalene 88-9
      altar of the Holy Trinity 89
         custodian of see Muskham, Thomas de
      chantry at the altar of Corpus Christi 80
         priests of see Durham, John de; Martha, William
      chantry of Corpus Christi 83
         priest of see Bowdon, John
      chantry at the altar of Holy Trinity 86
         ordination of 89-90
         priest of see Muskham, Thomas de
      chantry of Holy Trinity 94
         priests of see Gosse, Richard; Thurleby, John de
      chantry at the altar of St James 90, 93
         priests of see Beyekyrke, Thomas; Lyndesay, Robert de; Swafeld, John de
      chantry at the altar of St Katherine the Virgin 86
         priest of see Aylif, Thomas
      chantry of St Mary at the altar of All Saints 83, 98
         priests of see Bawdewyn, William; Chester, William; Kelsay, Robert de
   dean of see Trowell, Robert
   fraternity of the Holy Trinity 89-90
      provost or keeper of 89-90; see also Bakster, Elias

Newark, (cont.)
fraternity of St Mary, chantry of see
Newark, church of St Mary Magdalene,
chantry of St Mary at the altar of All
Saints
    members of (named) 83, 98
    warden of see Sayvill, Richard
parishioners and inhabitants of (named)
80, 83, 86, 89, 93
property in (defined) 89
vicar of 90; see also Sharp, John
see also Newerk
Newbald, North, prebend in York Minster
5, 7
prebendaries of see Courtney, Richard;
Scrope, Geoffrey le
Newbald, South, prebend in York Minster 4
prebendaries of see Elvet, John;
Longley, Thomas; Wolvenden, Robert
Newburgh priory 53
Newburgh (Neuburgh), John de 55, 58
Neweby, Robert de 65
Newerk (Newark), M. Alan de 40, 42, 44
John 4
Newerk alias Shepeley, William de 40
Newstead, chapel of the manor of 20
Newstead priory (Notts.) 75, 98
Newton (Notts.) 88
Newton (Neuton), John de, chantry priest
of St Stephen in St Mary, Scarborough
62-3
M. John de, treasurer of York, Official
of the Court of York, canon of York,
vicar-general of York 5, 11, 54, 57,
85, 94
Nicholas de 57
Robert de 60
William de 13
Newton Kyme, rector of see Lincoln,
Robert de
Newton Longville (Bucks.), rector of
see Wysebech, John
Newton upon Ouse 34
Noion, William 1
non-residence, licences for vii, 12-13,
15-18, 21, 24-6, 28, 33, 40, 47-50, 52,
54-5, 57, 60, 62-4, 67, 70, 72-3, 79,
81, 85, 87
Norfolk, duke of see Mowbray, Thomas de
Norham, William de 63
Normanton (Notts.), church of 88
rectory of 13, 25-6
    rector of see Spygurnell, William

Normanton, Henry de, burgess of
Nottingham 79
Henry de, rector of Kelham 82
John 74
br. Robert 68
Thomas 91
Normanton on Soar (Notts.) 92, 96
rectors of see Claypoll, John;
Dalton, William; Haukerigg, Nicholas
Normanvill, John de 22
North Cave see Cave, North
North Cerney see Cerney, North
North Muskham see Muskham, North
North Newbald see Newbald, North
North Otterington see Otterington, North
Northallerton 108
vicarage of 107
    vicar of 108; see also Ridmershill,
    Robert de; Staynefeld, John de
Northbrugge, William, bishop Pharensis
v-vi, 20, 25, 42, 55-6, 59, 88, 106
Northumberland, churches of 17
earl of 23; see also Percy, Henry
Norton, church of 51
free chapel at 44
    wardens of see Burgeys, John;
    Newerk, Alan de
Norton, Richard de 40
Thomas de 67, 93
William de 84, 107
Norton Cuckney (Notts.) 88
Norton iuxta Twycross (Leics.) 58
rectors of see Newburgh, John; Pigot,
John
Norwell (Notts.), vicarage of the south
part of 11
    vicars of see Beswyk, Robert de;
    Gaynesburgh, Robert de
Norwell Overhall, prebend in Southwell
Minster 10
    prebendaries of Chesterfield,
    Richard de; Wolvenden, Robert
Norwell Palishall, prebend in Southwell
Minster 3
    prebendaries of see Conyngeston,
    Richard de; Gunthorp, William de
Norwell (Tertia Pars), prebend in Southwell
Minster 6
    prebendaries of see Brid, John;
    Burstall, Thomas
Norwich, bishop of see Dispenser, Henry
Nostell, priory of St Oswald at ii, 14,
19, 20, 33, 35-6, 45
canon of see Burnham, William
prior of 45-6

notarial instruments 6, 51, 57, 62, 75, 86-7, 106
notaries public 14, 29, 45; see also Burstall, Thomas; Combe, John; Dernton, William; Garton, John; Halton iuxta Burton Stather, Robert de; Hoveden, John dictus de; Kyrk, Robert; Lepyngton, John de; Rippeley, John; Selowe, John; Staynton, John; Sutton, William de; Topcliff, William; Welton, John de
Nottingham (Notts.) 77, 79
   archdeaconry of iii
      archdeacon of 33, 70-99
         Official of 12, 70-99
      collectors within see Welbeck abbey
      penitentiary within see John, rector of Arnold
      sequestrator within see Arnald, Richard
   dean of 70, 79, 97; see also Burnby, William
   town, bailiffs of see Fox, Thomas; Stookys, William de
      burgesses of (named) 74, 79
      community of 76
      churches of
         St Mary 70
            property of 78
            support for priest in 74
            vicarage of 83
               vicars of see Chilwell, Richard; Retford, Robert de
         St Nicholas, pension from 71
         St Peter 77
            pension from 71
            rectory of 73
               rector of see Rodyngton, William
      friars minor at 77
      hospital of the Annunciation, ordination of chantry of the Annunciation in the chapel 76-9
         priests of see Coventre, John de Tawburn, Thomas
      inhabitants of (named) 77-8
      mayor of see Tannesley, John de
      property in (defined) 77-8
Nottingham, earl of see Mowbray, Thomas de
Nunburnholme 62-3, 66
   rectors of see Humbelton, Alan de; Robert, Thomas; Syxendale, William
Nundy, Henry 51
Nunkeeling priory 59
   prioress of see Burton, Isabella de

Nun Monkton priory 30
nunneries 16
Nutebroun, Gilbert 71
Nuthall 56
   rector of see Sawer, William
Nutteman, John 36
Oakenshaw see Wyke
obedience, professions of 6, 43, 58-9, 88, 91, 93, 97, 100, 104-5
obits see ordinations of chantries; appropriations of churches
Ockendon, South (Essex) 81
   rectors of see Forthington, Ralph de; Lughton, John
Octon and Swaythorpe, chapelries 61
   chaplains of see Bromley, William; Cok, Adam; Stanell, Marmaduke
   lord of see Thweng, Thomas
Orchard, Roger 99
ordinations vi
   register of ii-iv
ordinations of chantries vii, 13-14, 22-3, 28-9, 38-9, 52, 76-9, 89-90
ordinations of vicarages 7-8, 31-2, 38
Ormesby 51
Osbaldwick prebend in York Minster 2
   prebendaries of see Botlesham, John; Hallom, Robert de
Osberton (Notts.) 88
Osmotherley, prebend in 107
   prebendaries of see Clay, William; Hay, Thomas de la
   vicarage of 107-8
      vicar of 108; see also Grandesden, William; Ingelby, William; Syggeston, Cuthbert de
Osmund (Osmud, Osnund), John 87-8
Osmundthorp, Hugh 89
   William 89
Osnund see Osmund
Ossett 28
Ossett, Richard 25
Oswald, bishop of Whithorn v-vi
Oter, Thomas 39
Otford (Kent) 72
Otley 43
   dean of 26, 43
Otringham, Richard de, chantry founded by 65
Otteley, Richard de 43
Otterington, North, vicar of 108
Otterington, South, mediety of 50
   rector of mediety of see Thornton, Richard de
Ottewy, William (once John) 108

Ottringham 67
Ottryngton, John 108
Ouston, Thomas de 86-7
Owthorne 30, 33
Owthorpe (Notts.) 87
Owytcherche see Qwytcherche
Oxeford, John de 36
Oxford 31
  university of 12, 50, 79
    Queen's College 41
Oxgate, prebend in St Paul's cathedral,
  London 9
      prebendaries of see Martyn,
      John; Merston, Henry de
Oxton, Geoffrey de 85
  Robert de, prebendary of Tockerington
  in York Minster 4, 51
  M. Robert de, rector of Meppershall,
  rector of Sutton Bonington 95
Oxton and Crophill (Prima Pars), prebend
  in Southwell Minster 10
      prebendaries of see Ixworth,
      John; Wolvenden, Robert
Paa, John 48
Paddelay, Richard de 71
Parker (Parcour), Thomas, rector of
  Huggate 64
  Thomas, canon of Lichfield 3, 10
  Thomas, prebendary in the chapel
  of St Mary and the Holy Angels, York,
  prebendary of Carlton cum Thurleby in
  Lincoln cathedral 9
Parliament v, 96
Patrick Brompton, rector of see
  Popilton, John de
patronage, grant of 26-7
patronage, inquisition into 2, 7, 9,
  18-19, 30, 37, 41-3, 49, 53-4, 60-3,
  76, 83, 85, 97-9, 108
Patryngton, William de, rector of
  Spridlington, vicar of Clarborough
  71-2
  William de, chantry priest at the
  altar of the Holy Innocents in York
  Minster, chantry priest at the altar
  of St John the Evangelist in York
  Minster 9
Patteswyk (Patyswyk), Walter, rector of
  Kippax 68
  Walter, clerk of the archbishop's
  household, prebendary in the chapel
  of St Mary and the Holy Angels, York
  5, 10
Paule, Thomas 47, 49

Paull, church of 30, 33
  vicarage of 7-8, 58
    vicars of see Bardesay, Robert de
    Cochon, Alan
peculiar jurisdictions iii, 17; see also
  Allerton and Allertonshire; Beverley,
  provostship of; Churchdown;
  Gloucestershire; Hexham and Hexhamshire; Howden and Howdenshire; Selby;
  Snaith
Peek (Pek), William, rector of Middleton
  in Pickering Lythe, rector of Brant
  Broughton 47, 53
  William, rector of Holme Pierrepont,
  vicar of Flintham, warden of St Mary's
  chantry, Sibthorpe, rector of Weyhill
  83, 86, 92, 95
Pelle, Robert 24
penances 51, 105-6
penitentiaries, appointments of 16-17,
  20, 48, 54-6, 71-2, 100, 103-4, 108
penitentiaries, papal see Aprano,
  Bartholomew; Carboni, Francis
Pensax, Margaret, of Hawton (Notts.) 73
pensions, confirmations of, to religious
  houses 34, 51-2, 66-7, 71, 88
pensions, grants of, from benefices
  68, 83
pensions, grants of, from religious
  houses 18, 43, 57, 105
Pepircorn (Pepurcorne), Henry 71, 92
Percy, Henry, earl of Northumberland 15,
  22, 44, 47-8, 105
  John 34
perjury 12
Perpount (Perpond, Perpaund, Pierpount),
  Edmund, knt. 75, 79, 83, 89, 95
Person, William 86
pestilence 12
Pety, Robert 48
Peyntour, Robert 40
Pharensis, bishop see Northbrugge, William
Pierpount see Perpount
Pigot (Pygot, Pygote), John, jr. 18
  John, sr. 58, 62
  Thomas 18
pilgrimage ii, 54-5
Pilk, Thomas, chantry founded for see
  London, All Saints, Barking
Player see Pleyer
Playford, Thomas, of 'Banburgh' 74
Pleyer (Player), br. John 103, 108
Plumptre, Henry de 77, 79
  John de, of Nottingham 76-9
    Emma, wife of 76

Plumptre, John de (cont.)
  chantry founded by see Nottingham,
  hospital of the Annunciation, chantry
  of the Annunciation
pluralism, licences for 64, 86
Pokley, John 66
Poklyngton, Robert de 108
Poleyn, John, of Sherburn in Elmet 43
  John, parochial priest at
  Hemingbrough 106
Polles (Pollys), Henry 2, 7
Polowe, William 21
Pontefract
  anchorite at 34
  castle at 53
  hospital of Holy Trinity, parish of
  All Saints, chaplaincies in 15, 24
    ordination of 44-6
    priests of see Freston, Robert;
    Hall, William; Hill, Robert de;
    Raudon, Alexander
  Knollesalmshouses see hospital of
  Holy Trinity above
  priory at 26, 33, 39-40
    document dated at 58
    prior of 34
  rents from 28
  St Mary, vicar of see Thornton,
  John de
Popilton, John de, proctor for William
  Noion 1
  John de, rector of Patrick Brompton,
  prebendary in the chapel of St Mary
  and the Holy Angels, York 2
  John (or Thomas) de, prebendary in
  the chapel of St Mary and the Holy
  Angels, York 2
  Thomas 35
Porter, John 95
  Thomas 32, 84
Powger, William 96
Poynton, Thomas de 67
prebends see under Beverley Minster;
  Chester, St John; Howden Minster;
  Lincoln cathedral; London, St Martin
  le Grand; London, St Paul's
  cathedral; Osmotherley; Ripon
  Minster; Shrewsbury, St Chad;
  Southwell Minster; Wimborne Minster;
  York Minster
Prentys, John 39-40
presentation, letters of 62, 68, 75, 83
Preston, John 37
prior, appointment of 108

priories see under individual
  religious houses
private masses, licence for celebration
  of vii, 15, 56, 58
Privy Seal, keeper of see Longley,
  Thomas
probate jurisdiction iii
probate register i
processions, mandate to order 12
procuration 5, 43
Pudsay, John de 41
Purston Jaglin 28
Py (Pye), Roger 55 69
  coadjutor to see Fulman, William
Pygot(e) see Pigot
Pypyne, William 64
Pyry, John 10
Quia contingit 1, 103
Qwhixlay, Thomas 37
Qwytcherche (Owytcherche, Qwhitcherche),
  David 24-5
Radcliffe on Trent (Notts.), church of 87
  pension from 88
  vicarage of 97-8
    vicars of see Elmeton, Walter de;
    Thurgarton, John de
Radclyff, John de 4
Radford (Notts.), church of 70
  pension from 71
  vicarage of 35, 87
    vicars of see Alferton, William;
    Baron, Richard
Ragenhill (Ragnehill), M. Robert, parson
  in York Minster, rector of Whiston 25
  M. Robert, advocate of the court of
  York 37
Raithby (Lincs.) v
Randolf, John 92
Randson, John 67
Raper, Richard 60
Rasyn, M. Richard, sequestrator in the
  archdeaconry of York 13, 20
  Richard, proctor 38
Raudon (Rowdon), Alexander 15
  Robert de 108
Raveneswath, Henry de 21, 31
Raygate, Richard 63
Redmershill see Ridmershill
Redmyld, John 99
Reighton, vicar of 63
Remay, Agnes 77
Rempstone (Notts.), church of 71
  rectory of 97
    rectors of see Barston, John;
    Conyngeston, James de

Repingdon, Philip, bishop of Lincoln v, 9
resignation, commissions to receive 2, 51, 88
resignation, letters of 62, 75, 81
Rest v
    chancery of the manor of 3
    chapel of the manor of 86, 101
    documents dated at 1, 11-13, 15, 18-20,
    31, 33-5, 47, 51-2, 54-5, 58, 65-7,
    70-1, 83-6, 94, 100-103
Retford (Notts.) 76, 83
    dean of 87, 93; see also Fyschlake,
    Robert de; Ouston, Thomas de
Retford, Robert de 83
    br. Thomas de 82
Retford, East (Notts.), bailiffs and
    commonalty of 81
    St Swithin, chantry at the altar of
    Holy Trinity 80-1
        priests of see Fryston, John;
        Tyllyng, William
Retford, West (Notts.) 82
    rector of see Mysne, William
Revell, Thomas 74
Ribstane, William 36
Richard II, king i, v, 1, 14, 16, 21-2,
    28, 44, 54, 80
Richmond, archdeaconry iii-iv, 3, 8
    archdeacon of 107; see also
    Bubwyth, Nicholas de; Dalby, Thomas
    de; Scrope, Stephen le
        Official of 12
        vicar-general of see Norton,
        William de
    collectors within see Fountains abbey
    licence to hear confessions in 100
    penitentiaries within see Brygnall,
    John de; Dernyngton, John
    suffragan bishop within see Oswald
Richmund, John de 18
Ridmershill (Redmershill), Robert de 107
Rievall, Richard de 12
Rievaulx abbey 17
    monk of see Esby, Robert de
Rillington 69
    vicars of see Broket, Richard;
    Py, Roger
Ripon 2, 7
    dean of 1, 7
    hospital of St John at 1
        wardens of see Haward, Roger;
        Tanfield, Robert
    Minster iii, 2, 7, 16, 48, 56, 72,
    100-1
        chapter of 1-2, 5

Ripon (cont.)
    chantry at the altar of St John the
    Evangelist 2, 7
        priests of see Asmunderby,
        Richard; Kendale, Robert;
        Polles, Henry
    prebends in see Givendale and
    Skelton; Studley
        prebendaries of see Bubwyth,
        Nicholas de; Forester, Thomas;
        Scrope, Stephen le
    vicars of see Bondegate, John;
    Durham, Robert; Ely, John
Ripon, Arnold de, chantry for see York,
    St Helen Stonegate, chantry at the
    altar of St John the Baptist
    John son of Arnold de 44
Rippeley, John 6
Risley (Derbys.), lord of see Weloghby,
    Hugh de
Rither, William de, knt. 32
Robert son of John 28-9
Robert, Thomas 66
Roby, br. Richard (once Robert), O.S.A. 12
Roche abbey 33
Rochester, bishop of see Botlesham, John
Rodes, William de 30
Rodyngton, William 73
Roger, parish priest of Whitby 48
Rolleston, William 48
Romaldkirk, vicar of see Laton, John de
Rome, Curia at 51
    payment of first fruits to 30
    St Peter's 11, 24, 26-7, 32, 56, 60-1,
    64-5, 73-4, 80, 93, 100-2, 107
Ronhall (Rownale), M. Richard 4
Roos, pension from 66
    rectory of 55, 58, 64
        rectors of see Newburgh, John de;
        Pigot, John
Roos (Ros), Robert 24
    William de, chantry for see Lowthorpe,
    chantry founded for the dean and canons
    of York and William de Roos and his
    successors
    William de, lord of Hamlake 70, 75, 96
Rossedale (Rosdall), Robert 25
Rosselynne, Cecilia 38
Rothwell, chantry of Holy Trinity at 30
    priests of see Hunt, Robert; Irby,
    William
Rouclyff, Richard 43
Rouley, Richard de 68
Rounton, East 49

Rounton, West, rector of see Bowes, Thomas
Routh, Richard 91
Row, John 87
Rowdon see Raudon
Rowley 55, 61
    rectors of see Colne, John de;
    Walkington, John de
Rownale see Ronhall
Rozer, John de 17
Ruddington (Notts.), lordship of 71
    vicarage of 84
        vicars of see Dalby, Ralph de;
        Saxton, Roger de
Rudston, priest at see Bugge, John
    vicar of see Ward, John
Rufford priory (Notts.) 17
Ruggelay (Ruggeley, Ryggelay), M. Thomas
    70, 72-3
Russell, John
Ruston, Thomas 41
Rutland, Edward, earl of 28-9
Ryell, William 54
Ryggelay see Ruggelay
Ryse, Stephen de 57
Ryther 32, 84
    rectors of see Louth, Adam de;
    Porter, Thomas
St Bees priory (Cumb.), prior of see
    Wartyll, Nicholas
St Gregory, Trentale of 90
St James, shrine of 54
St John of Jerusalem, Order of, locum
    tenens of the prior of in England
    see Normanton, Robert
St Paul, shrine of 54-5
St Peter, shrine of 54-5
St Sixtus, cardinal priest of see
    Langham, Simon
St Susanna, cardinal priest of see
    Carboni, Francis
St Thomas Becket i
St William of York i
    tomb of 51
Salisbury, bishop of see Mitford,
    Richard
Salisbyry (Salysberi), William de 49-50
Sallay, William de 12-13
Salton, prebend of in York Minster 104
    prebendary of see Hexham, John de
Salysberi see Salisbyry
Samon, John 78-9
Sancton 55
    vicar of see Clerk, John
Sandall, John de, vicar of Clapham 100
    John, rector of Armthorpe 43

Sandall Magna, vicar of see Rozer,
    John de
Sandiacre (Derbys.), lord of see William
Sandon, John 53
Santon, Richard, of North Cave 68
    Robert de 17
    William son of Richard de, chantry for
    see York, St Helen Stonegate, chantry
    at the altar of St John the Baptist
Sarle, William 54
Sausthorpe (Lincs.) 25
    rectors of see Ossett, Richard;
    Stanhurst, Thomas
Savage, John 53
Savill, Savull see Sayvill
Sawer, William 56
Sawley abbey 33
Saxendale, Thomas 91
Saxondale (Notts.) 88
Saxton, Roger de 84
    Thomas 15
Sayvill (Savill, Savull, Sayvell, Sayvyll,
    Seyvell), Henry 13, 35
    (née de Eland), Isabella 14, 20, 33
    John 14
    John, knt., the elder 14, 20, 33
        children of 14
        wife of see Sayvill, Isabella
    Margery 14
    Richard, of Newark (Notts.) 80, 83,
    89, 98
        chantry founded by see Newark, St
        Mary Magdalene, chantry of the
        Holy Trinity
Scalby 67
Scarborough 55, 62-3
    bailiffs of 58, 62-3; see also
    Shilbotell, Robert; Waldife, Alan
    burgesses of 58, 62-3
    churches of:
        St Mary 63
            chantry at the altar of St James
            the Apostle 57
                priests of see Bukton, Robert
                de; Sherburn, William de
            chantry of St Stephen 58, 62-3
                priests of see Newton, John
                de; Shropham, Richard;
                Sylesthorn, John
        The Charnel, chantry in 65
            wardens of see Gyllyot, Richard;
            Neweby, Robert de
    commonalty of 57
    parochial chaplain of 63

Scarborough (cont.)
  penitentiary within see Askam, Richard
  rector of 63
  vicar of 63; see also Askam, Richard
Scardeburgh, John de 35
  Thomas de 42
Scarle, John 3, 6
Scauceby, William 41
Scharp see Sharp
Scharpyng, William 60
Schefeld (Scheffeld), John de, of
  Misterton (Notts.) 8
  John de, of York 42
Schepard, Richard, of Elland 14
Schirwynd, Thomas 44
Schroude (Schrowde), William 101
Scot (Scott), John 13, 25
  Patrick 54
Scotland vi
Scots, attacks by 17
Screveton (Notts.) 81-2
  rectors of see Benet, William;
  Juwell, John
Scrimschire, John 91
Scrooby (Notts.) v
  archbishop's chapel at 95
  chapel of the manor at 6, 91
  documents dated at 4-8, 26-7, 30,
  35-7, 39-40, 52-3, 62-3, 67, 80, 84,
  87-8, 90-3, 107
Scrope (Lescrop), Geoffrey le 5
  Richard le, archbishop of York i, vi,
  14, 28-9
    bishop of Lichfield and Coventry 11
    brother of see Scrope, knt.,
    Stephen le
    chancellor of see Conyngeston,
    Richard de
    commissary of 23
    commissary general of, in the
    archdeaconry of Cleveland see
    Uphall, William de
    cult of ii
    household clerks of see Burstall,
    Thomas; Hilton, Thomas de;
    Humbelton, Alan de; Scrope,
    Geoffrey le; Martyn, John; Newerk,
    John; Parker, Thomas; Patteswyk,
    Walter; Tydde, Nicholas; Wolvenden,
    Robert
    household priest of see Bradeley,
    John
    prayers for 89
    receiver general of, at York 3-5;
    see also Suthwell, John de

Scrope (Lescrop), Richard le (cont.)
  register of ii-viii, 29
  registrar of see Gilby, John;
  Thurbache, William
  scribe of see Welton, John de
  suffragan bishops to v-vi; see also
  Oswald; Northbrugge, William
  tomb of ii
  vicars-general of i, vi, 54; see
  also Newton, John de
    register of ii-iv
  M. Stephen le, jr., prebendary of
  Langtoft, of Beechill with
  Knaresborough, and of Driffield in
  York Minster, archdeacon of Richmond,
  prebendary of Studley in Ripon Minster
  2-5, 8
    vicar-general of in archdeaconry of
    Richmond see Norton, William de;
  Stephen le, knt., lord of Masham 60
Sculthorpe (Norf.) 45
Scurveton, M. Robert 44
seals (mentioned) 2, 7, 19, 29, 32, 36,
  37, 41, 42, 51, 53, 63, 79, 85, 87,
  94, 95, 96, 108
Seamer, church of 52
  vicar of 63
Seaton Ross, mediety of 65
secular priests, approval of use of in
  place of perpetual vicars 51
Sedgebrook (Lincs.) 61
  rectors of see Colne, John de;
  Walkington, John de
Seggefeld (Seggesfeld), John de, rector
  of Birkin, rector of Stokesley 44,
  52-3
  John de, parish priest of Guisborough,
  penitentiary in the archdeaconry for
  Cleveland 48
Segrave, lord see Mowbray, Thomas de
  M. William 79
Selby abbey 17, 33
Selby, peculiar jurisdiction of iii
  custodian of the spirituality of 106
Selby, John 107
  Robert de 71
Selowe, John 41
Seme, William 83, 89
Semer, Thomas de 56
Sempringham, Order of, appropriated
  churches and houses of, in diocese of
  York 91
  Master of see Beverlaco, William de
sequestration 8, 30, 32

sequestrators, appointments of 13, 20, 47, 70
Serle, Henry 84
Sessay 15
  rector of see York, John de
Seteryngton (Setryngton), M. Richard de 37
  Thomas 47
Settrington 48
  rector of see Carnica, Thomas
Seward, Nicholas 92
Seyvell see Sayvill
Shafton 28
Sharp (Scharp, Sharpe), John, vicar of East Wykeham, vicar of Elkesley 85
  br. John, vicar of Newark 75, 80, 83, 86, 89-90, 93
Shcefford see Shefford
Sheepe, John 77
Sheffield, church of, a third of the 88
  vicar of see Brammelay, Henry de
Shefford (Shcefford), M. John 11
Shelford (Notts.) 97
  church of 88
  priory at 85, 88, 91, 96-7
    prior of see Kynalton, William de; Lyndby, Robert de
    sub-prior and convent of 97
Shelford, William 49
Shepeley see Newerk alias Shepeley
Shepey (Shepeye), M. John de 81, 86, 92
Sherburn (Shirburn), John 42
  William de 57
Sherburn in Elmet 83
Sherburn in Harford Lythe, church of 51
  vicarage of 67
    vicars of see Grymeston, John de; Randson, John
Sheriff Hutton 50, 52
  vicars of see Budesby, Roger de; York, Adam de
Sherman, Emmota 34
Shilbotell, Robert 57
Shipton, br. John de 108
Shirburn see Sherburn
Shrewsbury (Salop.), St Chad, dean of 75
  prebendaries of see Aderley, Thomas; Tewer, Thomas; Thurbache, William
Shropham (Shroppam), M. Richard 58, 62-3
Sibthorp see Sybthorp
Sibthorpe (Notts.), chantry of St Mary at 71, 91-2
  chaplains of see Adam, John; Barneby, Robert; Nutebroun, Gilbert; Paddelay, Richard de; Pepircorn, Henry;

Sibthorpe (cont.)
  Routh, Richard
  wardens of see Howby, John de; Peek, William; Normanton, Thomas; Selby, Robert de; Seward, Nicholas; Thorp, Thomas
Silkstone 35
  vicars of see Elis, Ralph; Ullerston, Richard
Sissotson, Roger 51
Sixindale see Syxendale
Skeckling, church of 30, 33
  vicarage of 59
    vicars of see Broun, John; Hugon, Nicholas
Skeftlyng, Stephen de 62
Skelbrooke, chantry at the altar of St John the Evangelist 36
  priests of see Derwent, Adam de; Well, William atte
Skellow, chantry at 40
  priest of see Elis, Roger
Skelton (near York), rector of see Louther, Robert
Skelton, prebend in Howden Minster 104-5
  prebendaries of see Manfeld, Richard de; Wynewyk, Richard de
  vicarage of 107
    vicars of see Grene, John; Litster, Thomas
Skelton, prebend in Ripon Minster see Givendale and Skelton
Skelton, Geoffrey de 78
  John 37
  Thomas 37
  William 37
Skelton in Cleveland 51
Skidbrook (Lincs.) 84
  rectors of see Cook, John; Thoresby, John
Skipse see Skypse
Skipsea 65
Skipton 35
  vicar of see Ferrour, Thomas
Skirlaw, Walter, bishop of Durham i, 35, 66, 68, 105, 107-8
Skirlington, John 89
Skirpenbeck, pension from 52
  rectory of 67, 93
    rectors of see Lund, John; Norton, Thomas de
Skypse (Skipse), M. Richard de 12, 39
Skypwith, Margaret 24
Skyres, John 36

138

Slaidburn, rectory of 39-40
  rectors of see Flemmyng, Richard;
  Newerk alias Shepeley, William de;
  Skypse, Richard de
Sledmer, William 36, 42
Sleghtholme, br. William 55
Slingsby 52
Slyngesby, Margaret of 21
Smyth, Richard, of Garton 62
  Robert 98
  William, vicar of Askham Richard,
  vicar of Cantley 30
  William, of Welton, chantry priest
  at the altar of St Michael in St Helen,
  Stonegate, York 18-19
Smytheman, John, of Ruddington (Notts.) 74
Snaith, parochial chaplain of see
  Lonesdale, Robert
  peculiar jurisdiction of iii
  prior of see Cawode, John
Snytall, John 15
Somerby near Grantham (Lincs.) 91
  rector of see Normanton, Thomas;
  Thorp, Thomas
Somerset, earl of see Beaufort, John
Somersham (Hunts.) 66
South Cave see Cave, South
South Elmham see Elmham, South
South Leverton see Leverton, South
South Muskham see Muskham, South
South Newbald see Newbald, South
South Ockendon see Ockendon, South
South Otterington see Otterington,
  South
Southwell (Notts.) 47, 70, 93
  Minster iii, 16, 48, 56, 72, 100-1
  canons of see Brid, John;
  Burstall, Thomas; Cawode,
  William de; Chesterfield, Richard
  de; Conyngeston, Richard de;
  Gunthorp, William de; Ixworth,
  John; Layot, John; Martyn, John;
  Merston, Henry de; Ronhall,
  Richard; Tibbay, John de;
  Wolvenden, Robert
  chapter of 1, 3-4, 6, 9-11, 47,
  64
  chapter house of 11, 47, 64
  prebends in see Beckingham;
  Dunham; Halloughton; Muskham,
  South; Norwell Overhall; Norwell
  Palishall; Norwell (Tertia Pars);
  Oxton and Crophill (Prima Pars)
Sparowe, William 33
Spaunton, Thomas, of Guisborough 48

Spede, William 34
Spenne, John 29
Spenser, John 42
Spigurnell see Spygurnell
Spital 84; see also Broadbusk
Spofforth 22
  rectory of 44
  rector of see Anlaby, Thomas de
Spridlington (Lincs.) 71
  rectors of see Cook, Thomas;
  Patryngton, William de
Sproatley 54
  rector of see Ulverston, Richard
Sprotburgh, William de 19
Spygurnell (Spigurnell), William 13,
  25-6
Stainton 51
Stalmyn, William 16
Stamford (Lincs.) 85
Staneley see Stanley
Stanell, Marmaduke 61
Stanford on Soar (Notts.) 87
  rector of see Fox, Henry
Stanhurst (Stanyhurst), Thomas 25-6
Stanley 28
Stanley (Staneley), M. William de 40
Stanton see Staynton
Stanyhurst see Stanhurst
Stapilton, M. Peter de 57, 68
Stapleford (Notts.) 71
Starfeld see Staynefeld
Staunton in the Vale (Notts.) 70, 72-3
  rectors of see Hayward, William;
  Mapirley, William de; Ruggelay,
  Thomas
Staynefeld (Starfeld, Staynefelde,
  Staynfeld), John de 37, 107
Staynton (Stanton), M. John 6, 37, 94,
  101
Steven, William 82
Stillingfleet, church of 52
  chantry at 52
  vicarage of 48
  vicars of see Cowpeland, Walter de;
  Pety, Robert
stipendiary priests, approval of use of
  in place of vicars 51, 66
Stitenham, John 23
Stoke, Lower (Kent) 91
Stoke Bardolph (Notts.) 88
Stokes, Robert de 20
Stokesley 44, 52-3
  rector of see Seggefeld, John de;
  Wikireslay, Thomas
Stookys, William de 79

Storteford, William de 9
Stow Park (Lincs.) 61, 72
Stratton, William de 86
Straunges, Hugh 34
Strelley (Strilley, Strylley), Nicholas
   de 38, 40
   Thomas, of Woodborough (Notts.) 74
Strensall, prebend of in York Minster,
   vicarage of 34, 41
     vicars of see Bukler, Adam;
     Emmeswell, Robert de; Wace, John
Strilley, Strylley see Strelley
Studley, prebend of, in Ripon Minster 5
   prebendary of see Scrope, Stephen le
Sturmy, Hugh 70
Sturton le Steeple (Notts.) 82
   rector of see Appilton, Robert
subsidy, grants of to king iii, 16-17
Suthwell, M. John de 18-19, 21, 41,
   51, 94
     scribe of see Lepyngton, John de
Sutton, Henry de 85
   Thomas de 42
   Walter de 62
   William de 61
Sutton Bonington (Notts.) 79-80, 95
   rectors of see Caton, William;
   Gaunstede, Simon; Oxton, Robert de;
   Segrave, William
Sutton in Ashfield (Notts.) 87
Sutton in Holderness, College of St James
   64, 67
   chantry priests of see Laschyn, John;
   Pypyne, William
   chaplains of see Poynton, Thomas de;
   York, Richard
   masters of see Barneby, William de;
   Poynton, Thomas de
Sutton on Derwent 52
Sutton on the Forest 50
   rector of see Crayk, William de
Sutton on Trent (Notts.), church of 77
   vicar of see Trowell, Robert
Swafeld, John de 90, 93
   Thomas see Beyekirke, Thomas
Swaythorpe see Octon and Swaythorpe
Swerde, William 19
Swylyngton, Robert de 84
Swynton, John de 42
Sybthorp (Sibthorp), Robert 81, 86
   Simon de, of Newark (Notts.) 83
Syggeston, Cuthbert de 107
Syleby, John 85
Sylesthorn, John 58
Symson, John 49

Syxendale (Sixindale), William de 62-3
Tadcaster 22
   chantry at the altar of St Nicholas
   in the parish church of 27
     ordination of 22-3
     priests of see Turnour, Henry
   inhabitants of 23
   lord of see Percy, Henry
   property in 22
   vicar of 23
Tanfield (Durh.) 84
Tanfield, Robert 1
Tankersley, rector of see Herle, John
Tannesley, John de 79
Tantot, John 80
Tathwell (Lincs.), 24-5, 30
   vicars of see Addestoke, John;
   Asshebury, William de; Qwytcherche,
   David
Tawburn, Thomas 77, 79
Taylour, John 92
   William 78
Tebawte, Nicholas 82
Terrington 52
   rector of see Midilsburgh, John
tenths, grants of, to king 7
Tewer (Tewar, Tewere), Thomas 75, 96
Thomasson, John 19
Thoresby, John, vicar of Skidbrook,
   rector of Gamston 84
   John de, archbishop of York 87
Thorganby 66
Thorlethorp (Thorlathorp), Henry 9
Thornaby 51
Thornehill (Thornhill), John de 13, 35
   William 35
Thorneton see Thornton
Thorney (Notts.) 98
   vicars of see Smyth, Robert; Ward,
   William
Thornhill, lord of see Sayvill, Henry
   rectory of 35
     rectors of see Thornehill, John de;
     Thornehill, William
Thornhill see Thornehill
Thornour, John de 37
Thornton abbey (Lincs.) 62, 68
Thornton (Thorneton), M. John de 13, 17,
   35
   Richard de, rector of a mediety of
   South Otterington 50
   Richard son of Robert de, chantry
   priest at the altar of St John the
   Baptist in St Helen, Stonegate,
   York 44
   Robert 71

Thornton in Pickering Lythe 47, 50
  rector of see Malton, Richard
Thornton le Street, vicar of 108
Thorp, John 73
  Thomas de 23
  Thomas, rector of Somerby near
  Grantham, warden of the chantry at
  Sibthorpe 91
  Thomas de, rector of Fairstead, vicar
  of Blyth 88
  Thomas (recte Normanton) see Normanton,
  Thomas
  William de, vicar of Marske by the
  Sea 50
  William de, vicar of Featherstone 35
Thorpe, prebend of in Howden Minster,
  vicarage of 107
  vicar of see Hemyngburgh, John de
Thorpe Bassett 55, 67
  rector of see Wyndefeld, William
Thorpe in the Glebe (Notts.) 71
Thorpe next Norwich (Norf.) 74
  rectors of see Fuller, Nicholas;
  Revell, Thomas
Thrompton, William de 79
Thurbache, M. William 25, 59, 75, 79
Thurgarton (Notts.), church of 87
  priory at 80, 87, 97-8
      canon of see Elmeton, Walter de
Thurgarton, John de 98
Thurkyll, Thomas of York 12
Thurleby, John de 94
Thurstanton, William de 105
Thweng, Thomas 61
Thwing, church of 62
  rector of 63
  rector of a mediety of see Semer,
  Thomas de
Thyng, Thomas de 60
Tibbay, John 40
  John de, prebendary of South Muskham
  in Southwell Minster 47
Tickhill, chapelwardens of see Felde,
  Richard; Kyngeston, Richard
  fee of 94
  vicar of see Bilton, Thomas de
Tillyng see Tyllyng
Tithby (Notts.) 87
tithes 7, 29, 39, 106
  confirmation of, to religious houses
  34, 51-2, 67, 70-1
Tockerington, prebend of, in York Minster
  3-4
  prebendaries of see Oxton, Robert de;
  Wolvenden, Robert

Tode, Thomas 108
Todwick 40
  rector of see Peyntour, Robert;
  Stanley, William de
Toller, Richard, chantry founded by see
  York, St Martin Micklegate, chantry in
  the chapel of St John the Baptist and
  St Katherine the Virgin
Tollerton (Notts.) 72
  rectory of 85
    rectors of see Basage, John;
    Martill, Hugh
Toneton, Thomas (once William) de 19
Topcliff (Toppcliff, Toppeclyff),
  M. William, notary public 6
  William 4, 81
Torksey (Lincs.) 91
Torre, James 49
Totnes (Devon), lord of see Zouche,
  William la
Totwyk, John de 86
Towton 71
Treeton 36
  rector of see Louther, Thomas de
Trescour, William 53
Treswell (Notts.), rector of a mediety of
  see Fyschlake, Robert
Trottiscliffe (Kent) 86
Trowell, Robert 94, 98
Tuche, John 34
Tunstall, William de 41
Turnour, Henry 22, 27
Twng, William 60
Tydde, Nicholas 3-4, 10
Tyllyng (Tillyng), William 80-1, 85
Tymworth, John 89
Tynet, William 78
Tyryngton, John 66
Ullerston, M. Richard 35
Ulleskelf, prebend of, in York Minster 3
  prebendaries of see Allerthorp,
  Laurence; Scarle, John
Ulverscroft (Leics.), prior of 73
Ulverston, Richard 54
Umfray, William 98
university, licences for non-residence to
  study at 12, 16, 21, 24, 79; see also
  Cambridge university; Oxford university
Uphall, Richard 37
  William, rector of Easington 47
  M. William de, sequestrator and
  commissary general in the archdeaconry
  of Cleveland 47
Upton, Gregory de 76
  br. Roger de 93

Urban VI, pope vi, 55
Usflet, br. John de 16
vacancy, inquisitions into see patronage,
    inquisitions into
Vale, William, of Linby (Notts.) 85
Vavasour (Vavasur, Wavasur, Wavesur),
    Henry 18, 24, 108
    Margaret, wife of 24
Vemelby, Thomas 94-5
vicarages, approval of 33
    ordinations of see ordinations of
    vicarages
Volterra, bishop of see Aliotti, Lewis
Wace, John 41
Wadeslay, John de 50
Wadman, William 34
Wadyngton, John de 89
Waghen, Simon de 42
Wakefeld, br. Richard de, canon of
    Knaresborough, vicar of Foston 44
    Richard de, of Newark (Notts.)
    89-90, 93, 98
Wakefield, chantry chapel of St Mary on
    the bridge, ordination of 28-9
        chaplains of see Spenne, John;
        Whetelay, Henry de
    church of 30
    parishioners of 29
    rector or vicar of 29
    rents from 28
Wakman, John 89
Waldby, Robert, archbishop of York i,
    v, 11, 16
    suffragan bishop of see Oswald
Walden, Roger, archbishop of Canterbury vi,
    54, 72-3
Waldife, Alan 57
Walesby (Notts.) 80, 85
    vicars of see Fryston, John de; Holme,
    John; Ouston, Thomas de; Tyllyng,
    William
Walkeringham (Notts.), church of 88
    vicarage of 71
        vicar of see Clonne, William de
Walkington (Walkyngton), John de, rector
    of Rowley, rector of Sedgebrook 61
    John 59
Walleworth see Walworth
Wallingwells priory (Notts.) 30
    prioress of see Bollesovere, Helen de;
    Durham, Isabella de
    subprioress of see Durham, Isabella de
Walpoole, Roger, of Uffington (?Lincs.) 91
Waltham, M. William de 1, 94
Walworth (Walleworth), M. Thomas 94, 106

Wansford, chantry in the chapel of St
    Nicholas at 58
    priest of see Broun, John
Ward (Warde), Alice 101
    John, knt. 13
    John, vicar of Rudston 60
    Thomas 38
    William 98
Wardell, William 58
Wardrober (Warderober), Thomas 7
Warmfield 28
Warter, church of 65
    priory at 17, 65
Wartyll, Nicholas 100
Wasteness (Wastneys), John 40
    John, esq. 83
Wath, John de 13
Watnall (Notts.) 71
Watton, Thomas de, rector of St Michael,
    Ousebridge, York, rector of Brafferton
    37, 44, 53
    Thomas, rector of Hawksworth 80, 92
Watton priory 55, 61, 67
Wavasur, Wavesur see Vavasour
Wayte, Nicholas 67
Webster, Richard 71
Weighton, prebend of in York Minster 3,
    6, 10
    prebendaries of see Conyngeston,
    Richard de; Gunthorp, William de;
    Hilton, Thomas de; Scarle, John
    vicarage of 8
        vicars of see Bagby, Robert de;
        Malton, Roger de
Wekyngham, br. Nicholas 83
Welbeck abbey (Notts.) 17, 82, 85, 88, 92
Welbury 51
Well, William atte 36
Welles, John 7
Weloghby (Wyloby, Wyloghby, Wylughby),
    Hugh de 71, 83, 96
    Robert de, chantry priest at the altar
    of St Mary in Willoughby on the Wolds
    71, 83
    Robert de, rector of Harlaxton, rector
    of Clifton 74
Welton, M. John de 3, 6-7, 25, 51, 57,
    68, 74, 79, 91, 106
    William de 42
Wentislaw, Simon 59
West Acklam see Acklam, West
West Burton see Burton, West
West Markham see Markham, West
West Retford see Retford, West
West Rounton see Rounton, West

Westby, Henry 26
Westend (Westende), John at 59
    John 60
Westminster 14, 21, 28, 89
    justices at 68
    lodgings of the archbishop of
        York at 1-2, 6-7, 58
        chapel of 74
Westmorland, churches of 17
Weston 26
    vicars of see Humbelton, John;
    Wymbelton, Roger de
Weston, Roger 19, 72
    M. Thomas de 6, 9, 53, 63, 109
Westow, church of 66
    vicarage of 65
        vicar of see Langton,
        William de
Wetewang, Richard 70
Weton, Robert 98
Wetton, John 2
Weyhill (Hants.) 95
    rectors of see Helmesale, Henry;
    Peek, William
Wharram Percy, church of 66
    vicarage of 55, 66
        vicars of see Herle, Alexander;
        Hessay, William; Leek, William
Whatton (Notts.) 88
Wheldrake 47
    rectors of see Holme, John de;
    Ikelyngton, John
Whetelay, Henry de 28
Whihot, Thomas 63
Whiston 25
    rectors of see Ragenhill, Robert;
    Rossedale, Robert
Whiston, Thomas de 35
Whitburn (Durh.) 35
    rectors of see Marunhull, William;
    Popilton, Thomas
Whitby, abbey at 50, 52-3, 67
    church of 52
    parish priest of see Roger
Whithorn, bishop of see Oswald
Whitkirk 24, 33
    vicar of see Hadilsay, Richard
Whitwell (Whtwell), John 37, 65
Wickersley 88
Widmerpool (Notts.) 81, 85
    rectors of see Forthington, Ralph de;
    Kyrk, Robert atte; Lughton, John
Wighill 12
    vicar of see Roby, Richard

Wikireslay (Wykersley), Thomas de 39,
    44, 53, 91-2
Wilford, Henry de 77, 79
Willerby, church of 67
    vicar of 63
William, lord of Sandiacre (Derbys.) 83
William of Wykeham, bishop of Winchester
    91, 95
William son of John son of Roger, of
    South Dalton 54
William, vicar of Bradford 30
Willoughby on the Wolds (Notts.), church
    of 88
    chantry at the altar of St Mary in
    71, 83, 96
        priests of see Alman, Robert;
        Powger, William; Weloghby, Robert;
        William, lord of Sandiacre
Wilton 49
Wilton (Wilts.) 92
Wimborne Minster (Dors.), dean of see
    Coryngham, Roger de
    prebend in see Kentisburn
        prebendaries of see Canonum,
        William; Marunhull, William
Winchester, bishop of see William of
    Wykeham
Windsor Castle (Berks.), royal chapel at
    13, 25-6
    canon of see Spygurnell, William
Winterbourne (Glos.) 40
    rectors of see Botyler, John; Prentys,
    John
Winton 49
Wintringham, church of 51
    pension from 34
Wissenden, M. William de 67
Wistow, prebend in York Minster, vicarage
    of 107
    vicars of see Grene, John; Litster,
    Thomas
Withernsea 30, 33
Wlfeden see Wolvenden
Wodhorn, br. William 104
Wolfeden see Wolvenden
Wollaston, William 92
Wolvenden (Wlfeden, Wolfeden, Wolveden),
    M. Robert, clerk of the archbishop's
    household, prebendary at the altar of
    St Stephen in Beverley Minster,
    prebendary of Tockerington, of South
    Newbald and of Beechill with
    Knaresborough in York Minster,
    prebendary of Norwell Overhall and of

Wolvenden (Wlfeden, Wolfeden, Wolveden) (cont.)
 Oxton and Crophill (Prima Pars) in Southwell Minster 2-6, 10, 68, 91
 Robert, precentor of Lichfield cathedral 2-3, 57, 75, 100, 106
Wombewell, Hugh de, of Darfield 18
 Helen, wife of 18
Womersley 36
 vicar of see Nutteman, John
Woodcoates (Notts.) chapelry 73
 parishioners of 73
Worcester, bishop of see Clifford, Richard
 lodgings of, at Coventry 96
 lodgings of, in London 40
Worksop (Notts.), church of 88
 priory at 71, 88, 93
  canons of see Laghton, John de; Wekyngham, Nicholas
  prior of see Laghton, John de; Upton, Roger de
  subprior and convent of 93
Worsop, Thomas 85
Worstan see Wroghton
Wotton, John, chaplain 103
 John, priest, custodian of the jurisdiction of Gloucestershire 109
Wraneby, John de 20
Wresill, Ralph 55
writ, royal see Levari facias
Writh, Robert 66
Wroghton (Worstan), Thomas 28
Wryde, Richard, of Everingham 15
Wryght, Helen daughter of Ralph 102
 John, chantry priest at Flamborough 59
 John, rector of Holme on Spalding Moor 59
 William 69
Wyclyff, Robert 12
Wygan, M. Adam 13
Wyghall, Richard de 43
Wyght, Thomas 75
Wyke, manor of 14
Wyke, Arnold 31
Wykeham, chantry at 47, 49
  priests of see Cave, John de; Paule, Thomas; Symson, John
 priory at 47
Wykeham, East (Lincs.) 85
 vicars of see Sharp, John; Sutton, Henry de
Wykeham, William of see William of Wykeham

Wykersley see Wikireslay
Wykyngeston, M. John 62
Wylardby, Thomas 12
Wyles, John 16, 26
Wylgyn, John 20
Wyloby, Wyloghby, Wylughby see Weloghby
Wymbelton, Roger de 26
Wymbissh, Nicholas 6
Wynceby, William de 30
Wyndefeld (Wynfeld), William 55, 63, 67
Wyndhill, John de 15
Wynfeld see Wyndefeld
Wynewyk (Wynwyk), M. Richard de 104-5
Wynk, John 27
Wynteryngham, Walter de 62
Wyntlane, Thomas de 86
'Wynton' 49
Wynwyk see Wynewyk
Wysall (Notts.) 88
Wysebech, John 6
Yarm 51
Yedingham, priory at 66
 vicarage of 66
  vicars of see Pokley, John; Writh, Robert
ʒereslay, br. John 55
Yngelby see Ingelby
ʒong (ʒonge), William, chantry priest at the altar of St James in Holy Trinity, Goodramgate, York 40
 William, rector of Grove 72
York i-ii
York, archbishopric of i
 sede vacante administration i, v, 8, 12, 77
 suffragan bishops of 11; see also Arundel, Thomas; Bowet, Henry; Gray, Walter de; Melton, William; Nevill, Alexander; Scrope, Richard le; Thoresby, John de; Waldby, Robert
 vacancy in i, 1, 8, 11, 18, 21-2, 32, 39, 57, 89-90
 archbishop of 7-8, 21-3, 28-9, 32, 39, 45, 52, 77, 82, 89-90
  commissary of 5-6
  palace at York 2, 30, 36, 83
  peculiar jurisdictions of iii; see also Churchdown; Gloucestershire; Hexham and Hexhamshire
  prebend of, at the altar of St Leonard in Beverley Minster; see under Beverley Minster
  prison of 11, 70
York, archdeaconry of iii

York, archdeaconry of (cont.)
  archdeacon of 11-44
    Official of 9, 11-44
  collectors within see Monk Bretton
  priory
  penitentiaries within see Stalmyn,
  William; Thornton, John de
  sequestrators within see Rasyn,
  Richard; Thornton, John de
York, cathedral church of St Peter see
  York Minster
York, chapel of St Mary and the Holy Angels,
  prebends in 2-5. 9-10
    prebendaries of see Burstall, Thomas;
    Cave, Nicholas; Conyngeston, Richard
    de; Deen, John; Gysburn, William;
    Hilton, Thomas; Newerk, John;
    Parker, Thomas; Patteswyk, Walter;
    Popilton, John de; Popilton, John
    (or Thomas) de; Tydde, Nicholas
  sacrist of see Weston, Roger
York, churches of:
  All Saints, North Street, chantry at the
  altar of St Mary 20
    priests of see Brynyston, John;
    Carnaby, Thomas de
  parishioners of (named) 20
  pension from 34
  rectory of 37
    rectors of see Lichefeld, Adam de;
    Whitwell, John
  All Saints, Pavement, chantry founded by
  Thomas de Alwarthorp 30
    priest of see Cressop, William
  chantry of St Mary 19
    priest of see Swerde, William
  chantry of St Thomas 12
    priests of see Basefford, Henry
    de; Rievall, Richard de
  rector of see Lund, John de
  All Saints, Peasholme 12
    rectors of see Bryan, Robert;
    Wylardby, Thomas
  Holy Trinity, Goodramgate, chantry at the
  altar of St Nicholas 41
    priests of Emmeswell, Robert de;
    Wace, John
  chantry of St James 40
    priests of see Holmesfield, John;
    3ong, William
  rectory of 25
    rectors of see Burstall, Thomas;
    Northbrugge, William
  reunification of medieties of 26-7

York, churches of (cont.)
  Holy Trinity, King's Court, rector of
  see Kyrkton, John de
  Holy Trinity, Micklegate 34
  St Crux, Fossgate, chantry of St
  Mary 12
    priests of see Bryan, Robert;
    Wylardby, Thomas
  St Cuthbert, Peasholme 21, 31, 33
    rectors of see Cave, John;
    Clyveland, John; Mowbray, John de;
    Raveneswath, Henry de
  St Denys 21
    rectors of see Suthwell, John de;
    Yreland, William de
  St Edward, rector of see Swynton,
  John de
  St Helen, Fishergate 23, 34
    rectors of see Bukler, Adam;
    Emmeswell, Robert de; Knayton,
    John de
  St Helen on the Walls, John, rector of
  a mediety of 18
  St Helen, Stonegate 18
    chantry at the altar of St John the
    Baptist 44
      priests of see Duggylby, John
      de; Thornton, Richard son of
      Robert de
    chantry at the altar of St Michael
    18-19
      priests of see Balderston,
      Edmund de; Smyth, William
    parochial chaplain of see Melton,
    William de
    rectory of 16
      rector of see Gysburn, William
      de
    vicarage of 35
      vicar of see Sledmer, William
  St James without the Walls 34
  St John Baptist, otherwise St John del
  Pike, rector of see Garton, Thomas
  St Martin, Micklegate, chantry in the
  chapel of St John the Baptist and St
  Katherine the Virgin 31
    priests of see Bird, Peter;
    Clyderowe, Henry
  St Mary Bishophill, Senior, chantry at
  the altar of St Katherine 36
    priest of see Ribstane, William
  rector of see Iwelay, Richard
  St Mary, Castlegate, chantry in the
  chapel of St John the Baptist and

York, churches of (cont.)
St John the Evangelist 27, 31, 37
    priests of see Bird, Peter;
    Clyderowe, Henry; Horslay,
    John; Hoton, John
    rector of see Scardeburgh, Thomas
    de
St Michael, Ousebridge, chantry of
St Mary 13
    priests of see Colne, William
    de; Kydlambe, William
    rectory of 37, 44, 53
    rectors of see Appylgarth,
    Robert; Seteryngton, Richard
    de; Watton, Thomas de
St Peter le Willows, Walmgate 66
    chantry founded by Robert de
    Halton 26
        priest of see Chesterfeld,
        Ralph
    chantry of St Mary 41
        priest of see Halton, Robert
St Peter the Little, rector of see
Aschburn, Robert de
St Sampson, chantry at the altar of
St Mary 41-2
    priests of see Folketon,
    Robert de; Forest, William
    parishioners of (named) 41-2
    rector of see Sherburn, John
St Saviour, chantry of St Anne 34
    priest of see Bergh, William
    chantry at the altar of St Mary 34
        priests of see Bilton, Robert;
        Spede, William
    chantry of St Thomas 33
        priests of see Maltster, John;
        Sparowe, William
    parishioners of (named) 34
    rector of see Wygan, Adam
St Wilfrid 13, 37
    rectors of see Appilton, Robert de;
    Newton, William de; Thornour,
    John de
York, city of, mayor of see Frost, William
    mayor and citizens of 41
York, dean of Christianity of 11, 37, 94;
    see also Shefford, John
York, documents dated at 5, 11, 19, 23,
    26-7, 37, 42, 44, 51-2, 54, 65-6, 68,
    81, 85, 88, 93-4, 100, 107
York, Ecclesiastical Court of
    advocates of see Harwod, John de;
    Newerk, Alan de; Ragenhill, Robert

York, Ecclesiastical Court of (cont.)
    advocates, proctors and notaries of 5
    commissary-general of 2, 42, 106;
    see also Aschburn, Robert de
    Official of 2, 19; see also Newton,
    John de; Suthwell, John de
    proctor of see Staynton, John de
York, hospitals at
    St Leonard ii
        master and brethren of 21
    St Mary, Bootham, master of see
    Donyngton, William de
York Minster iii, 5, 8, 16, 18, 37, 48,
    68, 72, 100-1
    canons of see Allerthorp, Laurence;
    Barnet, John; Barton, Henry de;
    Botlesham, John; Burstall, Thomas;
    Carppe, John; Conyngeston, Richard
    de; Courtney, Richard; Elvet, John;
    Faryndon, Robert; Feriby, Thomas;
    Gaunstede, Simon; Gunthorp, William
    de; Hallom, Robert de; Haxey,
    Thomas; Hexham, John de; Hilton,
    Thomas de; Holme, Richard; Longley,
    Thomas; Noion, William; Oxton,
    Robert de; Ronhall, Richard;
    Scarle, John; Scrope, Geoffrey le;
    Scrope, Stephen le; Waltham,
    William de; Walworth, Thomas;
    Wardrober, Thomas; Weston, Thomas
    de; Wolvenden, Robert
    chantry at the altar of the Holy
    Innocents 9
        priests of see Patryngton,
        William de; Thorlethorp, Henry
    chantry at the altar of St John the
    Evangelist 9
        priests of see Patryngton,
        William de; Thorlethorp, Henry
    chapter of i, 1-10, 11, 14, 21-2,
    26, 29, 34, 39, 41, 57, 59, 89-90,
    95, 104, 106-7
    Chapter house 5, 7-9, 25, 41, 94-5,
    107
    dean of 1, 5-9, 22, 26, 34, 41, 59,
    89-90, 95, 104, 106-7; see also
    Hamelton, William de; Longley,
    Thomas
    dean and canons of, chantry for
    see Lowthorpe, chantry for the dean
    and canons of York
    dean and chapter of 8, 21-2, 25, 28,
    32, 89-90, 92, 94 (see also chapter
    above)

146

York Minster (cont.)
  fabric of 8, 32
    custodian of 8
  lights of 8
  officials of 5
  parsons in see Brygnall, John de;
  Carnaby, Richard; Dernyngton, John;
  Ragenhill, Robert; Rossedale, Robert
  prebends in see Apesthorpe; Barnby;
  Beechill with Knaresborough; Bilton;
  Bole; Cave, South; Driffield;
  Dunnington; Langtoft; Laughten en
  le Morthen; Newbald, North; Newbald,
  South; Osbaldwick; Salton;
  Strensall; Tockerington; Ulleskelf;
  Weighton; Wistow
  Treasurer of see Newton, John de
  tomb of St William 51
  vicars choral of 20, 41
    succentor of see Holme, Nicholas
    warden of 20
York, Ordinal of 46
York, religious houses at
  Holy Trinity priory 21, 23, 31, 33–4,
  37
  St Andrew's priory 33
  St Mary's abbey 13, 18, 33, 37–8, 44,
  51, 53, 64, 82
    abbot of see Pigot, Thomas
    chapter house 18
    property of 17
York, royal justices at 11
York, Use of 28, 45–6
York, vassals of the church of, and clergy
  and people of the city and diocese of 11
York, St William of see St William of
  York
York, Edmund, duke of 28–9
  son of see Rutland, Edward, earl of
  wife of 29
York (Ebor', 3ork), Adam de 50
  M. John de, rector of Sessay 15
  John, vicar of Nafferton, vicar of
  Dunham 64
  Richard 67
Yorkshire, escheator of see Bukton,
  Peter de
Yreland, William de 21
Zouche, William la 82, 84